MW01506133

Life after Teshuvah

MOSAICA PRESS

Rabbi Zecharya Greenwald

Life after Teshuvah

Five, Ten, and Twenty Years Later

Mosaica Press, with its team of acclaimed editors and designers, is attracting some of the most compelling thinkers and teachers in the Jewish community today. Our books are impacting and engaging readers from around the world.

Copyright © 2024 by Mosaica Press

All rights reserved. No part of this book may be used or reproduced or transmitted in any form or by any means, electronic or mechanical, including photocopying, recording, or by any information storage and retrieval system, without written permission from the publisher.

ISBN: 978-1-961602-29-8

Published by Mosaica Press, Inc.
www.mosaicapress.com
info@mosaicapress.com

Dedicated to my beloved father

Rabbi Ronald Greenwald, zt"l

In honor of our dear friend

Rabbi Zecharya Greenwald

and his unwavering commitment to creating
this invaluable resource for the extraordinary among us.

With his *seichel hayashar* and refreshing, candid insight,
Rabbi Greenwald has been *mechanech* thousands of
young women on the cusp of adulthood, preparing them
in his inimitable *derech* for the road of life ahead.
It is with a true sense of appreciation for his incisive
wisdom and courageous integrity that we take part
in making this book a reality.

In honor of all our beloved

Oorah graduates and members

who have made the long journey home.

This book is not for the faint of heart.
It is for those willing to be real with themselves,
unafraid to explore the deep and sensitive recesses of the soul,
and ready to confront head-on challenges that come with
the *teshuvah* journey. May this book be a source of light
and guidance for you for many years to come.

אשה יראת ה׳ היא תתהלל

ספר זה יוצא לאור לע״נ האשה היקרה טובת הלב

מרת אלה בת הר׳ חיים יצחק ע״ה

נכדת הגאון האדיר מעמודי ההוראה בירושלים

מוהר״ר אליהו ראם, זצ״ל

"A God-fearing woman, she is praised."

This book honors the memory
of the dear and kindhearted woman

Ella bas R' Chaim Yitzchok, a"h

Granddaughter of the great Gaon,
from the pillars of *p'sak halachah* in Yerushalayim,
our revered *rav*, Rav Eliyahu Ram, *zt"l*

RABBI AHARON FELDMAN
421 YESHIVA LANE, Apt 3A, BALTIMORE, MD 21208
Tel.: 410-6539433 Fax: 410-6534694
Study: 410-4847200 Ext. 6050
E-mail: RAF@NIRC.EDU

Rosh Hayeshiva
Ner Israel Rabbinical College

ראש הישיבה
ישיבת נר ישראל

Our times have been blessed with the phenomenon of tens of thousands of Jews who grew up non–Torah observant but who became observant later in life. They are inaccurately called "Baalei Teshuvah" for since they were *tinokos shenishbu* from birth they have nothing for which to do teshuva.

When they marry, since many of these have no family or community traditions to follow, they are left without guidance as to how to navigate some of the challenges which might arise in their newly discovered way of life.

For those who do not have a Rav or a teacher to guide them, Rabbi Zecharya Greenwald has written an excellent guide which takes these people by the hand and leads them step by step through the pitfalls involved in establishing a Jewish home, in raising children, in finding schools and shidduchim for them, as well as many other issues.

This book is an invaluable resource and will be welcomed by what has become a significant segment of the Jewish people. Rabbi Greenwald is to be commended for devoting himself to their success.

Rabbi Aharon Feldman

David J. Lieberman, PhD

Life after Teshuvah is a masterful blend of inspiration and practical advice. The path of *baalei teshuvah* is filled with unpredictable obstacles, twists, turns, and profound struggles. Written with wit and wisdom, this book helps readers navigate their paths more soundly and confidently. Equally valuable, *Life after Teshuvah* provides the rest of the world with a rare window into the lives of *baalei teshuvah*, instilling a deep sense of both empathy and awe.

I have had the *zechus* of knowing Rabbi Greenwald for almost two decades and have not only enjoyed our friendship but have also learned tremendously from him. This book beautifully represents his unique blend of wisdom and good old-fashioned common sense. I've gleaned many insights and valuable applications that can be instantly applied. This book is not a theoretical exploration of educational principles—it's a treasure trove of actionable strategies that are real-world ready.

I wish Rabbi Greenwald much success with this book, which will no doubt enjoy a wide and eager readership.

Dr. Lieberman's thirteen books, which have been translated into twenty-eight languages and include two New York Times Best Sellers, have sold millions of copies worldwide.

Table of Contents

Dedication xv

Preface xvii

Acknowledgments xxi

Chapter 1: The Turning Point 1
New Challenges Today / We Are Not Alone / Defining Quantum Change

Chapter 2: Positive Motivation for Change. 9
A Search for Spirituality / Looking Back / Appreciating Where You Are / Knowing Whom to Ask / Holding on to the Truth / The Need to Belong / A Blessing for the Jewish People

Chapter 3: Other Motivations for Change 18
Frustration / Rebellion / Unchallenged Peer Pressure / Making the Mitzvos My Own / Peer Pressure Can Be Used Positively / Growth without Resentment

Chapter 4: Issues and Tissues. 34
Keeping Torah Alive Inside / Renewal / Hiding the Past

Chapter 5: Cycle of Generations 48
*The Builders / Children of the Builders / Where Do **We** Stand? / Society's Influence*

Chapter 6: Overcoming Challenges 54
*The Challenge of Protektzia / What Can Influence Do for Us? / Challenges of the School System / The Matter of Shidduchim / Money Matters—Money **Matters**!*

Chapter 7: Challenges with Our Children and Society 74
The Challenge of Black and White / On "Penguins" and Clothing / Maintaining Individuality

Chapter 8: A Lonely World 91
If It Were Me / Adam—Alone or Individual

Chapter 9: Accessing Support. 95
*Knowing Whom and How to Ask / Seeking Out Former Mentors / Consulting
a "Torah Giant" / When a Rabbi Misrepresents Judaism*

Chapter 10: Building a Support System. 112
*Three Qualities of a Friend / Friendly Advice / How and When to Identify with
Friends / Good People in a Community / Become a Giver / Where to Draw the
Line / See the Good in Others / Be Productive / When We Need to Take / Parents
and Support*

Chapter 11: Who Changed, Anyway? 123
*Rejectionist Damaging / Keeping a Beautiful Relationship / It's Never Too Late /
Respect Is the Key / Respect and Appreciation / Open-Mindedness / Serious
Opposition / Unhealthy Relationships / Abusive Parents*

Chapter 12: Danger! Outreach in Your Family 136
Honoring Parents

Chapter 13: Parents, Continued 142
*Acceptance and Respect…and Denial / When Parents Feel Threatened / Helping
Parents Accept Our Changes / They Are Not Young Anymore / Financial Support*

Chapter 14: Communicating. 156
Communicating in a Service-Oriented Society / Intelligent Communication

Chapter 15: The First Year and Beyond 168
*Roles and Role Models / Distinct Male and Female Roles / Hierarchy of Roles /
Sharing Responsibility*

Chapter 16: Love and Marriage. 178
*Love Means Commitment / Marriage Is a Partnership / Blending Cultural
Differences / Unique Challenges / Some Ground Rules for Marriage / Abuse within
the Family*

Chapter 17: Establishing a Happy Torah Home 192
*With a Smile and a Song / Simchah in Doing Mitzvos / Children Cannot Live in
Two Worlds / Setting Boundaries*

Chapter 18: Large Families: What It Takes 208
Living Up to an Ideal / Preparing Yourself / Time Management / Establishing Priorities / Raising "Good" Children / Raising "Our" Children / Acquiring the Tools / A Mother's Intuition

Chapter 19: Making Your Dream Come True 225
The Shabbos Table / Sibling Rivalry / Each Child Is Unique / A Bed for Every Child / The Child Who Is Different / The Fear of Patterns

Chapter 20: Family Life: A Closer Look. 236
Birth / Moving / Illness / Death / Bringing Simchah into Your Lives

Chapter 21: Your Children and Their Grandparents 245
Taking Control / Building the Relationship / When Grandparents Are Not Observant / Outgrowing Childhood Perceptions / Defining Our Choices

Chapter 22: Bitachon 258
Practical Aspects of Bitachon / Simchah through Sacrifice

Chapter 23: Self-Esteem and Success. 266
It Begins with You / Achievement / Success / The Perfection Syndrome / Sibling Competition / True Success / You Are Alive

Chapter 24: Competition and True Growth .277
Teaching Our Children about Rewards / Mental Health in Our Society / Living with Our Mistakes / Being Comfortable with Themselves / We Believe in You / Not Giving Up / One Step at a Time / Entering New Stages / A Final Thought

Chapter 25: Adapting to a New Life. 295
Decisions in the Formative Years / Decisions at a Later Stage in Life / Decisions: The Process / Disregarding the Opinions of Those Close to You / Decisions within Families

Chapter 26: Choosing a Lifestyle 303
Torah and Earning a Living / Mutual Concern / Some Practical Hints / The Job Market / Maintaining Standards / Career versus Livelihood

Chapter 27: Repairing the Broken Chain 324
Schools and Responsibility / "Yeshivish" / School Location / Dealing with

School Admission / Growing with Our Children / Helping Your Child in School / Dormitories / School and the Self-Esteem Factor / Idealism

Chapter 28: Our Tablet Children 346
*Easy Access / What You Don't Know **Will** Hurt You / Control and Self-Control / Texting / Setting Limits / Addiction / What to Do? / Our iPod Selves*

Chapter 29: Secular Education, Science, and Religion. 364
Informed Decisions / An Education in Science

Chapter 30: In Conclusion: Two Voices 370
Strengthening Our Decisions

Glossary 378

Dedication

This book is dedicated to my beloved father, Rabbi Ronald Greenwald, *zt"l*, who at the age of eighty-two died as one of the youngest people I knew. His love for all people, his youthful enthusiasm for life, his wit, humor, and spirit, coupled with his deep belief in Hashem and His people made him the most beloved person I have ever known to all who have known him.

His life and his accomplishments would fill ten books of this size, and that would include only what we know of his acts of *chessed* and kindness. Although he rarely asked me to do anything of significance, his life and achievements were not only an inspiration to me but a directive, a force, and a demanding imperative, which taught me from a young age that you cannot sit by idly when others are suffering and confused. You cannot ignore the importance of the world around you and its substance. You cannot look at the world through the small eyes of your personal perception and think that you are encompassing the whole picture.

He had a broadness of vision that made him a leader of educational initiatives and social reform within the Jewish community. Simultaneously, he was like a child, learning constantly, listening carefully, and intuitively understanding the hearts of young and old, weak and strong, rich and poor. He had the uncanny ability to connect with every human being with whom he came in contact, from the most powerful and noble leaders of the world to the special child who could hardly articulate her thoughts in words, but whose smile in his presence spoke volumes of love and appreciation.

Rabbi Ronald Greenwald, aka Tatty, will never have the chance to read this book, but his insight, intuition, acceptance, respect, trust, and love for all people have given me the ability to try to follow in his footsteps in understanding and helping others. May all those who read this book and take direction, *chizuk*, or just added appreciation for the wealth and wisdom of our heritage be additional merit in his grand eternal life.

Preface

L ife after Teshuvah was born in response to a very clear need facing the Jewish People. My *rebbi*, Rabbi Shlomo Wolbe, *z"l*, told me in 1981 that the next great challenge to the Jewish nation is going to be dealing with the enormous and most welcome influx of Jews who have returned to Judaism with strong motivation and true fear of Heaven. In the years to come, they will feel the need for guidance both for themselves and their children.

Our generation of religious Jews, Rav Wolbe said, will be facing challenges vastly different from those of generations gone by. With his brilliant foresight, he recognized that many of those extraordinary people who have turned their lives upside down and inside out will face times of confusion and disappointment, disillusionment and frustration, five, ten, and twenty years later. Not only will they be raising children in a world that differs from that in which they grew up, but they will be dealing at times with the occasional fraudulent and counterfeit representatives of the religious world who may make their entire beautiful journey challenging and sometimes questionable.

Their need for guidance has reverberated more and more urgently in my mind over the last thirty-five years as I have been involved with many who have made this spiritual journey. For the past twenty years, I have seen even more of the challenges through teaching so many of the children of those who have made and are making this journey. These idealistic and dedicated parents often find themselves ill-equipped to deal with the challenges inherent in raising their children in a now foreign and sadly, sometimes unfriendly, environment. Many suffer from disillusionment, frustration, unanswered questions, and feelings of lost opportunities. Still others grapple with the pain of loneliness and a sense of alienation or estrangement from their birth families. In addition, there are so many finding difficulties in raising their own children in a world so different than where they came from. When some of these extraordinary individuals who have dedicated so much to learning and developing an entire new way of life are faced with challenges that cause enough confusion to question themselves and their choices, it is painful beyond description. I have seen and spoken to many people who are in this position, which has heightened the imperative for writing this book. I stand with awe before these giants of spirit and action, and with humility, I present my ideas.

Although I am clearly an unworthy *talmid* of Rav Wolbe and everything for which he stood, I remember him sharing with us a famous parable of the Chafetz Chaim.

> The wealthy landowner visited the home of one of his sharecroppers. The simple man prepared a cup of tea for him. After one sip, the guest spat out the tea, disgusted by the sand in the water.
>
> "What is this?" he asked. "How can you drink sandy water? It is revolting."
>
> That night a fire broke out on the property. The wealthy man jumped out of bed and ran out of the house, only to find the poor sharecropper standing next to his hovel, watching the fire devour all his belongings.
>
> "Why are you just standing there, you fool?" yelled the landowner. "Get some water and put out the fire!"
>
> "But, sir," the simple man replied, "you said that I cannot use sandy water."
>
> "For tea you must use only the clearest water," the wealthy man cried, "but when there is a fire burning you must use any water you have to extinguish the flames!"

I feel that I can no longer stand by and watch the burning fire destroy so many lives and homes. Although my Torah is far from the pure water from which the wise and holy may drink, it is all I have to throw on the flames of pain and confusion.

With humility and prayer to Hashem, Who has given me so much more than I deserve, I present my clouded water in the hope that it will help those who have chosen to make tremendous changes in their way of life. May it in some small way prepare them to respond to both the challenges they presently face as well as those that await them.

Important Note

This book is addressed to the many extraordinary people who have made quantum changes in their religious lives, and not to the general readership of *b'nei Torah* who were brought up keeping Torah and mitzvos.

The world of a *baal teshuvah* is filled with conflicts and challenges that are incomparable and unique. Far be it from me to think I can fully comprehend the depth of this experience and the intricacies of thoughts, emotions, fears, and uncertainties that come in its wake. This book is an attempt to provide a positive appreciation of your experiences with alternative approaches to understanding some of their intricacies. If any word or concept in this book seems to trivialize or belittle the profundity of any part of what you have undergone, please understand that it is due to the limitations of the author and his writing skills, but *never* a result of disrespect or lack of appreciation of your experience.

All the stories in this book are representative of true-life stories; however, some are composites of more than one story. All names and places have been changed for the sake of privacy.

I am not a *posek*, halachic expert; there are sensitive areas of halachah discussed in a few places in this work. I have added a footnote in each of these places referencing this disclaimer. In these cases, even though I have consulted very responsible *poskim*—particularly the world-renowned Rabbi Dovid Cohen of Brooklyn, New York, author of over fifty works—as halachah is a delicate and multifaceted concept with many diverse opinions, it is advisable to speak about your particular situation with a person of stature. This book is meant to give direction, advice, and to share ideas, but does not take the place of a rabbinical authority. In addition, it is essential for every Jew to follow the clear message of the Mishnah in *Pirkei Avos* 1:5 regarding the necessity of having a rabbi in your life (see chapter 9).

Rabbi Zecharya Greenwald
Yerushalayim, Kislev 5784

Acknowledgments

The writing of this book has taken place over a period of thirteen years. It began with an invitation by Tvunot, an organization in Yerushalayim run by **Mrs. Rena Orlowick** that helps Anglo *olim* deal with the challenges of Israeli life. They asked me if I would give a series of classes to English speaking *baalei teshuvah* regarding successful integration and acclimatization into the *frum* communities in Eretz Yisrael and America.

My first stop was Neve Yerushalayim, led by **Rabbi Dovid Refson.** There I met with **Rebbetzin Rivka Wolitzky** and **Rebbetzin Rivka Cowan,** the social workers in Neve who have followed up with their alumni for many years. It was they who helped me compile the first of many lists of questions and issues that were common challenges to the wonderful women who had made great changes in their lives. **Mr. and Mrs. Yanky and Esti Yarmish**, the quintessential *machnisei orchim*, hosts of Har Nof, hosted a series of ten lectures in their home, which were the basis of this book.

The feedback from the ten couples who were present at the lectures, and the responses, questions, and meetings that came about as a consequence of the recordings, inspired me to take on my *rebbi*'s call to deal with this important subject in a more thorough and comprehensive manner.

Mrs. Ruth Pepperman transcribed the twelve hours of audio into an initial document.

Mrs. Devorah Kiel, the editor for my column in the *Hamodia* as well as the editor of my first book, *Preparing Your Child for Success* (ArtScroll, 2007), helped me transform the transcript into a workable manuscript.

In addition, she very patiently and consistently worked with me over the years to transform this manuscript into a book in spite of my inconsistent and somewhat intermittent dedication.

Rabbi Eliyahu Miller, editor and publisher, as well as owner of Torah Temima Publishing Company, critically read and wrote notes on the entire transcript with insight and sensitivity. His comments were important enough to delay the publishing of this book by nine months.

Rabbi Dovid Cohen, *posek* emeritus, author of over fifty volumes on a vast array of Torah subjects, took the time to review, discuss, and advise on the halachic issues addressed in this book.

My sincerest gratitude to **Rabbi Eliyahu Mintz** of Oorah, for his unwavering support toward the completion of this book. Rabbi Mintz encouraged and supported the process, encouraging me through the final stages and backing his belief with a preorder for his "alumni" that showed his ultimate confidence in the value of this project. May Hashem help him and the extraordinary staff and volunteers of Oorah to continue their *avodas ha'kodesh* in facilitating the incredible journeys of the remarkable participants of Oorah's many and diverse programs.

Mrs. Miriam Greenwald, aka Mommy, was the main editor. Her wisdom, insight, sensitivity, and professionalism have not only enhanced this book but have been the background and inspiration that has enhanced my entire life.

To my **wife,** your greatest praise is that you will not allow me to write any praise, but it is a known fact that no man in my position can achieve anything without the support and backing of his wife. May Hashem bless us with health, joy, and the *nachas* of our children bringing forth the light of Torah and *chessed* to our family and others.

To our **children,** you are the challenge and the light, the worry and the hope, the test and the purpose, the concern and the *nachas* of our lives. Thank you for understanding, as I sat over the computer for many thousands of hours during "vacation" and late into the night in all the free time of which we have had so little, throughout the thirteen years of this project. May your understanding help you help others someday, as you become motivated givers in Klal Yisrael.

To **Mosaica Press**. Working with Mosaica has been an author's dream. From my first meeting with Rabbi Yaacov Haber and Rabbi Doron Kornbluth, when I came with a manuscript that had been rewritten and edited numerous times, I found them to be respectful, empowering, and considerate of my ideas, needs, and style. Mrs. Sherie Gross, the managing editor, was on top of everything from the go to the finish, professionally and respectfully. Mrs. Henna Eisenman, managing director, followed through on every email, keeping things moving throughout. Mrs. Rayzel Broyde, the art manager, got a bullseye with the cover and with minimal direction. There was a whole team of people on the final editing who were expert, knowledgeable, and surprisingly humble. I would like to make special mention of Robert Sussman who edited the manuscript that I submitted to Mosaica. His insights, questions, and comments were to the point and helpful in clarifying many points. All in all, it has been a wonderful experience.

Special thanks to the hundreds of students, their parents, Shabbos guests—families and individuals—who have visited and come for guidance and direction. Perhaps to you, I stand as a teacher and mentor; but, in truth, I stand as a simple Jew inspired by all of you. I am humbled by your perseverance and dedication and thankful for the sharing of your stories, challenges, tears, and victories that are the fabric of this book.

I have a special debt of gratitude to the following people who reviewed the manuscript through its different stages, many of whom gave very special constructive criticism that brought about the second and third metamorphoses of this book. All of the reviewers are *baalei teshuvah*, their teachers, or both.

In alphabetical order:

Rabbi Aryeh Abowitz, Teacher of Talmud to beginners

Mrs. Tzipora Brezner, Adjunct Professor of Astronomy at RCC, Suffern, New York

Dr. Moshe Finkel, Chiropractor, Jerusalem

Rick Fox, Musician

Mr. Zechariah Freidman, MBA, Administrator of a non-profit organization

Rabbi Beryl Gershenfeld, Rosh Yeshiva of Macnon Shlomo and Machon Yaakov in Jerusalem and Dean of Meor Campus Kiruv organization

Dr. Ronen Hizami, Psychiatrist, New York

Rabbi and Mrs. Jeremy Kagan, Principals of Midreshet Tehilla Seminary, Author: *The Jewish Self: Recovering Spirituality in the Modern World* (Feldheim, 1999) and *The Choice to Be: A Jewish Path to Self and Spirituality* (Feldheim, 2011)

Ariel Kor, PhD, Businessman, Fund Manager, and Psychologist

Mrs. Chana Levitan, MSc, Educator, Speaker, Therapist, Author: *I Only Want to Get Married Once* (Grand Central Publishing, 2013) and *That's Why I Married You!* (Gefen Publishing House, 2016)

David Lieberman, PhD, *New York Times* Bestselling Author: *Never Be Lied to Again*; *Get Anyone to Do Anything*; *Instant Analysis*; *Make Peace with Anyone*; *How to Change Anybody*; and *You Can Read Anyone*

Rabbi Yosef Lynn, Dean of Students, Mashgiach, and a Senior Lecturer at Machon Yaakov. Masters in Applied Positive Psychology and author of *Nurture Their Nature: The Torah's Essential Guidance for Parents and Teachers*, and *Not A Partnership: Why We Keep Getting Marriage Wrong and How We Can Get It Right*

Yehudis Mishell, PhD, Licensed Clinical Psychologist, coauthor of *Beyond Your Ego*

Mr. Philip Mulivor, Writer, Researcher, and Editor, Author of *Proclaiming Liberty* (Brightman Press Publishers, 2011)

Rabbi Dovid Ostroff, Rabbi, Teacher, and *Posek* in Jerusalem

Rabbi Dovid Refson, PhD, Founder and Dean of Neve Yerushalayim Institutions

Mrs. Sarah Rubinfeld, Senior Teacher in EYAHT, Aish HaTorah's College for Women, and other seminaries

Tzvi Scarr, PhD, Biophysics, Researcher, and Writer

Rabbi Yehoshua Styne, Mashgiach and Lecturer, Machon Shlomo

Miriam Turk, LCSW, Former Executive Director of Nefesh International. Outreach Liaison and Recruitment Director, Jewish Community, Touro Graduate School of Social Work

Chapter 1

The Turning Point

We are currently in the midst of a major transformation in Jewish history. In 1974, my *rebbi*, Rav Shlomo Wolbe, may his righteous memory be a blessing, wrote a book called *Bein Sheshes L'Asor* in response to the events that had transpired between 1967 and 1973.[1] With newfound national pride in the victory of the Six Day War, many people began to take a serious look at their Jewish legacy. The shift toward religious observance began with individuals who opened their minds to new concepts and took great strides toward self-discovery and growing interest in their heritage.

These changes, initiated by isolated individuals, soon carried over to entire groups. Jewish institutions flourished everywhere. Yeshivos sprung up to deal with the large influx of Jewish students visiting Israel who wanted a deeper understanding of their birthright. These yeshivos grew, expanded, and eventually began to recruit students.

Rabbi Wolbe's book was a guide to *teshuvah* (literally, "to return"), a compilation of his essays and talks that helped these seekers understand the intelligence of their decision to explore the beauty of their unique history and the ineffable destiny of their nation. Today, as we

---

1   The title of his book is a play on the words of Chazal, our Sages, *"bein kesser l'asor,"* the period of time each year between *kesser* (the crown of Hakadosh Baruch Hu), representing Rosh Hashanah, and *asor—asarah la'chodesh* (the tenth of the month of Tishrei), representing Yom Kippur. Rav Wolbe felt that the Jewish victory in the Six Day War (six=*sheshes*) was a turning point in the great wave of reawakening, a new recognition and feeling of pride among Jews in regard to their affiliation with Judaism. This reawakening continued through the Yom Kippur War (*asor*) of 1973.

1

see, there are many community services and trained rabbis catering to this new population.

We have reached a point where, thankfully, it can be said that there is another overwhelming awakening taking place. Like a sleeping giant who begins to move first his hands and his feet, then shakes his head and finally opens his eyes, entire segments of the Jewish people in different parts of the world are currently returning to a life of Torah.

New Challenges Today

Today's *baalei teshuvah*, returnees, face a constantly changing set of circumstances on a personal level while simultaneously raising their children in environments and value systems that differ radically from those in which they were raised. Although usually integrated into their communities, these intelligent and capable people may confront count-less situations for which they are not prepared. They often do not have the fine-tuned perception or experience to know what is acceptable in this new environment and what is not.

Many questions plague them on a daily basis: How do we know what is right? How should we guide our children? May we get our son a pet dog? Can I allow my children to watch some kinds of movies on our computer? What am I supposed to do with perplexing thoughts and feelings about my own development and changes? Where can I turn when things get rough? What do I do when I fundamentally disagree with values that the Torah society seems to completely accept?

Will anyone take me seriously if I am just a BT (*baal teshuvah*)?

I often refer to Moshe Rabbeinu's father-in-law, Yisro, in the Torah. As a new set of eyes, he was able to help his son-in-law become cognizant of the incongruence of his attempt to guide the Jewish people in an unlimited way.

Yisro was very convinced of the correctness of his criticism, yet he qualified his statement with these words: "If you will do as I say *and Hashem will so command you*."[2]

---

2   *Shemos* 18:23.

Twenty years ago, I had the honor of meeting Avi S., a young man raised in the Orient who returned to a life of Torah and mitzvos in his early twenties. He dedicated a large amount of money to making a difference in his newly discovered world. This young man had a vision: he felt that the yeshiva community could reach out to our brothers and sisters in a whole new way. He brought his idea to Rabbi Yosef Shalom Elyashiv, one of the generation's greatest leaders. The response was cool at best. He was not against the initiative, but dubious as to its chances of success. Avi persevered. Upon seeing the success of the program, the Rav acknowledged the project, which was adopted by the Lev L'Achim organization. The program encourages kollel fellows to knock on doors of homes in nonreligious communities, offering to learn Torah with their occupants once a week. The project continued for over twenty years, bringing the light of Torah to hundreds of Jewish families. A young baal teshuvah with enormous dedication brought about a change in perspective of one of the greatest living rabbis of our times.[3]

It is not the least bit surprising that people who have made life-changing decisions find themselves confused and in need of guidance at various times down the road. They may even question the motivation or reasoning that brought about their initial changes.

Rav Wolbe spoke to me about this phenomenon on many occasions. He made it clear that it is almost impossible *not* to go through this process. Anyone who thinks that it is not normal will just be uselessly browbeating themselves, forgoing the freedom that comes as a result of understanding and acceptance of what they have gone through. Those who make major changes in their lives, no matter the original motivation or how well they have been integrated, must understand that there are going to be times and situations that will arouse questions and doubt. This book was written for those who identify with these struggles.

---

3   This anecdote illustrates the greatness of our leaders, who have the humility to see a new perspective and change their mind accordingly.

We Are Not Alone

We live in a society that encourages us to feel independent. In the final analysis, individuals, couples, and families have to fend for themselves. Nevertheless, when troublesome feelings come to the fore, it is an indication that the time has come to open up and deal with questions and doubts in an honest attempt to find a balanced and healthy position from which to tackle them.

For every thousand people, there are as many situations and challenges. The *teshuvah* process of change was different for every individual. Some came through it easily, while others found it very difficult. The reasons that brought about these changes are myriad, and so are the peripheral factors that helped each person reach the point where they now find themselves. Obviously, a book is not going to be able to take the place of a *rav* and mentor, nor can a book deal specifically with every individual's challenges, yet we will try to address the most common problems facing today's *baalei teshuvah*. It is our hope that the readers, alongside the relationships they have or will develop with teachers and mentors, will be able to use some of the suggested guidelines for their particular circumstances.

Those who can identify with a yeshiva and a *rosh yeshiva*, or a particular group of people who rely on the wisdom of a particular *rebbi* or *rav*, will have the advantage of finding a clearly defined road before them. Although they will have someone to answer their soul-searching questions, hopefully this book will still be a worthwhile read, as it can be a catalyst for further thought and introspection.

While teaching in Yeshivas Ohr Somayach, Rabbi Ephraim Greenbaum,[4] a close friend of mine, went to see the Gerrer Rebbe.

"*Vu bist du?* [Where are you?]" the Rebbe asked.

"I'm in Ohr Somayach...but I'm not a *baal teshuvah*," he answered.

---

4   A *mashgiach* in a very prestigious yeshiva called Be'er HaTorah in Yerushalayim. His grandfather was Rabbi Menachem Kasher, who authored a monumental work on Chumash, *Torah Sheleimah*. At one point, Rav Ephraim headed a *kollel* that continued his grandfather's work and produced a number of subsequent volumes.

The Gerrer Rebbe looked at him. "Why not?" he asked.

My friend's qualifying statement did not please the Rebbe, who clearly felt that *everyone* should be a *baal teshuvah*! Although you might indeed be an accomplished *talmid chacham*, scholar, and successful in the Torah world, there is still something to be learned from those who seem to know so much less than you. We all have to regularly reconsider our actions and position in life, and reconnect to Hashem and His ways in a better way than before.

Today, when we use the designation "*baal teshuvah*," the connotation is clear: people who have come from a nonreligious background and now include themselves in a dedicated religious community, living a more enhanced Torah life. The spectrum, however, is broad.

We will be focusing on the change itself, the transformation from a totally secular life to one of Torah and mitzvos, and that is a matter of quantum change. We will first explore the factors that introduced this quantum change into people's lives, the motivations that inspired or affected them, and then see how they can effectively deal with some of the very normal challenges that they are now confronting five, ten, and twenty years later.

As the principal of a seminary in Yerushalayim that has a student body of wonderful Bais Yaakov girls, mostly from the United States, I can tell you that we often have to deal with a student who represents three diverse generations of change. There are often great disparities between the generations of her grandparents, parents, and that of the girl herself. The changes that have taken place over the years in the Jewish community, as well as in the broader society, represent three different worlds.

My students' parents are raising their children in an America that is vastly different from that of their childhoods. Some were brought up in European-style families or by parents born in America who did not have the opportunity to study in a yeshiva or Bais Yaakov, and others are the first generation to have a yeshiva background. In the latter case, the grandparents may have been totally lost to Judaism, while their children, who found their way back, are now sending the third generation to yeshivos and day schools. Some of the third generation whose parents and grandparents *were* observant, however, are nonetheless being brought up in an environment that is very different from that of the America of forty and fifty years ago.

Fifty years ago, there were five religious girls' high schools in the entire United States, with a total of 100 to 150 graduates per year. Girls growing up today attend over 120 religious high schools with over 8,000 graduates. The religious educational framework has expanded exponentially, giving rise to an enormous number of changes in the religious world alone.

Defining Quantum Change

This book will not be dealing with minor lifestyle changes, with the challenges created when children decide to be more "religious" or careful in observance than their parents, for in such cases the core values instilled by the home remain the same. Even the fact that our parents may have had from one to four children, while we may be raising upward of seven, does not constitute a drastic change. Other superficial differences, such as clothing and wedding styles that have evolved even in the *frum* world, are also not quantum differences.

A quantum change is one that has occurred in the perceived goals in life, in the way family life is organized, the way our children's schools are run, and even the attitude with which they go to school. As what is expected of people in our community changes somewhat from one generation to the next, it is understandable that trying to distinguish right from wrong can be confusing. One who has made quantum changes often does not have the frame of reference with which to make this distinction. It is difficult to live in a new community when you don't always know what is acceptable, borderline, or completely beyond the pale.

You cannot just assume that you will be able to figure out all the answers by observing what others in your circle are doing. When you are a few years into your growth and building a family, you cannot be satisfied merely with imitating your neighbors. In the beginning, perhaps, you watched what page they were on so you knew where you were supposed to be in the siddur. As you develop and reach a more sophisticated level of observance, however, an internal feeling of connection with Hashem and the mitzvos cannot just be imitated. In doing that, you will neither learn how to make life decisions nor understand how to raise your children. At this point, what everybody else is doing should not matter. *There is no such thing as everybody else!* We need the tools and skills to decide what is right for *us*.

Each of you is dealing with a unique situation, with unique experiences. Your children are different from everyone else's. It would be a grave error to just look at someone else, no matter whom, and think, *Well, they are doing this, so it must be OK. I'll do it, too.*

How can we be sure that *they* are doing the right thing? Even if they are intelligent and well informed, perhaps their decisions are based on specific situations that differ from yours. Maybe, they are being hijacked by the *yetzer hara*, evil inclination? Even good people make mistakes. Their decisions have to do with what they understand or feel about their family and their values, and the choices they have to make as a result.

> *When one of my daughters was in seventh grade, she came home to tell me about the "funtabulous" pajama party that "all" of her friends were planning to attend.*
>
> *"All the best girls are going."*
>
> *Aware of the excitement that this kind of activity can generate, I asked which of her friends were participating. She enumerated girls from some of the very fine families in our neighborhood with whom we were friendly. Surprised at some of the names, I decided to call one family to ask if they were indeed comfortable with the plan.*
>
> *The mother answered the phone and candidly told me that they had actually been opposed to the idea, but when they heard that my daughter was going, they had decided to rethink the matter and give permission. It took three minutes to clarify that almost everyone on the list was depending on everyone*

else to make the decision. In the end, the party was canceled. I am not making a blanket statement about pajama parties, but suffice it to say that, in these times, we should be very careful about where and with whom our children are spending their nights.

In the next chapter, we will consider the factors that motivated *baalei teshuvah* to make these major changes in their lives. We hope to provide tools to better equip our readers to meet the many challenges that inevitably crop up even years after they accepted a life of Torah and mitzvos.

Chapter 2

Positive Motivation for Change

W hat were people looking for when they began to search for
something more and better? Many were looking for spirituality and truth. Others felt the need to identify within an ideology that had a history, a lasting track record. And some were attracted to the healthy family relationships they witnessed, the emphasis on spending meaningful time together, home-cooked meals, and wholesome values. That search was often coupled with feeling alienated by the lack of meaning and depth in people around them.

A Search for Spirituality

Many *baalei teshuvah* were looking for more spirituality, more meaning and purpose in their lives. Whether they were somewhat immature eighteen-year-olds or mature thirty-year-olds, the age at which they chose to begin their search is immaterial. It was propelled by the feeling that something was missing, that their lives seemed to have no sensible purpose.

Now, when the search seems a thing of the past, it will be helpful to focus on what was happening when it all began.

Think back to what was going through your mind then.

While initially, life and living took on different meanings amid the awareness of a new sense of spirituality, you were simultaneously meeting groups of people in a new community, which brought fresh challenges.

As you took great strides toward finding meaning and purpose, you soon needed jobs to meet financial and educational responsibilities, possibly together with the exhausting physical challenges of rearing a family.

It suddenly felt as if your world was turned upside down...again. You had found an alternative to the emptiness. It looked beautiful and attractive, yet with it all, you seemed to be on your own, grappling with the challenges of a greater truth. A few years down the road, however, you found yourself in such a different place emotionally that it made your original initiative seem almost irrelevant.

Years later, it is possible for doubts to smolder. *Was I really missing so much before I changed?* you may wonder. *What was so bad about my life then?*

Looking Back

For those who are currently in this very situation, it might be helpful to go back to the beginning. I think that you will see that *nothing has changed in your need for meaning in life*. If you could go back to where you were then, you would undoubtedly make the same decision all over again. If you were suddenly deprived of everything you have now, everything you have gained, even the parts of life that challenge you, you would again feel bereft and empty. This time, however, you would feel the additional lack of meaning and purpose in life because what you now value and take for granted would be missing.

Let us analyze what takes place when people are faced with new challenges.

When life changes in major ways, it is often felt necessary to look back and figure out where we went wrong. Having to face and deal with new realities does not mean that something went wrong. It is important to differentiate between fact and fantasy.

New questions cannot be answered by looking back with regret. You may tend to blame your current stumbling blocks on the changes you have made. Asking, "What did I do wrong, and why is Hashem doing this to me?" while valid, is not productive. Although these questions will be discussed, the answers are not going to resolve the practical problems with which you are now struggling.

At this point, you might be dealing with varying realities of life. You may be married, and the marriage is either good or challenging. Or perhaps you had hoped to be married by now, but the years have gone by and that has not yet happened. Maybe, you are married and some of your children may be developing well, and others falling behind. Your financial situation is excellent, good, fair, or even worsening. Did you choose the wrong place to live? Had you known then what you do now, you might have chosen a different means of livelihood.[1]

These situations cannot be remedied by wishing you could turn the clock back and do things differently. Looking back will not change the realities of your spouse, children, finances, or anything else that is troubling.

Although questioning your earlier search for spiritual meaning is most relevant, there are other issues that seem more pressing at the moment. Second-guessing yourself instead of trying to find the best and most realistic solutions is not productive. In the coming chapters, we will discuss how to go about finding the right guidance, but for a moment, let's look at another fundamental motivation that caused us to change.

Appreciating Where You Are

Some of you chose a life of Torah because of the panoply of splendid values perceived in it. From the outside, the *frum* world looked wonderful and beautiful. There are, of course, many admirable aspects to leading a religious life, including its standards to which thinking people are attracted. The community seems to mesh well, and its members look out for and take care of one another. You see how much *chessed*, kindness, is done. There is Shabbos and the *Yamim Tovim*, festival days. There was something right about these values that attracted you. The lifestyle made sense and seemed to work.

You decided to enrich yourself by participating in this beautiful life. Perhaps the encounter with Shabbos, the mitzvos, and the *chessed* compelled you to take them on and move forward. After a while,

---

1   These are fair considerations, see chapter 3.

however, you gradually discovered the weak links in our society, the foolishness, small-mindedness, and superficialities of some of its members. Becoming more familiar with the community, you were exposed to rigidity in some relationships, and a measure of nonacceptance at times. It was often necessary to come to terms with elements that seemed to go against the very values to which you were so attracted. Disillusionment and disappointment set in, the most debilitating of all the challenges mentioned thus far.

Yet, despite its challenges, and with all its many shortcomings, the beauty seen initially, that of a life led according to the precepts of Torah, remains the same regardless of those who do not live up to its exalted standards. I dare say that if you remove your personal pain from the picture, you can see that it is still the community you admired, that which provides the most wholesome values, the most direction and concern for others. These ideals, which may not be mitzvos but communal standards, raise our expectations to heights that, albeit demanded of us, may be unrealistic for every individual.

I had a close friend who began to keep Torah and mitzvos in ninth grade. He was a highly intelligent young man who was probably the single most influential factor in the development of my own thinking process. In eleventh grade, he left yeshiva because he became extremely disillusioned with the behavior of many of the students. His expectations were so lofty, and his demands on himself so extraordinarily high, that disappointment set in. He went off to university for early admissions to medical school. His parents were traditional Jews, and he went back to their ways. After he had been in a very highly regarded medical school for two years, I received a letter.

> *I see that you cannot compare the middos [character traits] of the group of students with whom I am now studying with those of the boys in yeshiva...trying to compare the people in med school with those religious boys is like trying to compare a corpse with a human being. I don't know what I could have been thinking earlier.*

Today, he lectures widely about social factors affecting health policy. He was always an overachiever. Whatever he does, he wants to do it in the best way. Many years later, in retrospect, I *do* know what he was thinking. The world the Torah portrays is so perfect, the individuals who introduce you to Torah so wonderful...why then is its community so full of limitations and imperfections? If we are taught the halachos of *shemiras ha'lashon*, being careful about the words we use, how can yeshiva boys speak *lashon hara*? Only afterward did he realize that the only community in the world in which telling your friend that a mutual acquaintance just davened *Minchah* very quickly is a sin was the very one he had left.

Now, you are on the inside, questioning your ability to live with imperfect Jews, not to mention coping with frustrating limitations. Be assured that in most cases, your doubts are the result of not knowing how to handle the faults and flaws that make you uncomfortable. The shortcomings and problems in the community bother you. When your child is not accepted into a school because you are still, perhaps, a bit different from other parents, or when some people will not consider your children for *shidduchim*, the pain is immense.

It is advisable, however, to take a step back and compare this community with what you left behind. Remember your friends and peers. Although you may be facing challenges in bringing up your children, think about your original family unit and those in your world today. Are not the values that drew you still valid? Reevaluating your position is not dangerous, and I am not afraid to make the following suggestion.

Go back for a little while, open your eyes, and see how it really is in that other world. I cannot say to you that your life today is more comfortable, more fun, or more pleasurable than before. Hopefully I *can* say that you are living more honestly, closer to the truth, and more altruistically.

The Torah world comprises an environment and a community that has much more inherent goodness than any alternative. We should never fear to go back and question. Be confident of the value of asking these questions. There are people who are wrong, rude, and insensitive.

This is not a result of their Judaism, but of their poor character and, occasionally, poor upbringing. Just imagine what happens when people in the general population have those same poor traits or upbringing.

Knowing Whom to Ask

Hebrew, termed *lashon kodesh*, the holy tongue, is replete with meaning, and each letter has significance. The words *neshamah* (soul) and *chochmah* (wisdom) both contain the letters *mem* and *hei*, which together make the root of the word *mah* (what)—the Hebrew word for questioning. *Chochmah* is *"ko'ach mah,"* the force of the question, which requires me to search more deeply to uncover more and greater understanding.

Questions have an inherent power, and the act of questioning is an essential part of Judaism. Pesach, which commemorates our exodus from Egypt, is the paradigm instructional experience in Jewish life. The Haggadah, read on the Seder nights, guides us through this historic event. It describes four sons and their questions. All the teachings of Torah are said to be a response to them.[2] We describe the type of people they are through their questions.

Good questions define a *chacham*, a wise man. Rhetorical, attitudinal questions define the *rasha*, an evil person, and so on. We learn from our experience during the Seder that we are supposed to ask questions because they can help us to reevaluate and fix things that are wrong.

What is essential is to turn these questions *inward* and ask them of *yourself*. Be sure they are about issues that are really bothersome, and do not let your fears derail you. Bitterness, anger, and resentment have never achieved anything, and no one who approaches life with any of these attitudes has ever advanced. They are negative traits that pull us down, preventing us from growing and developing. By digging down to the source of our negativity, we neutralize it, and turn our questions into tools for change and growth.

---

2   Pesach Haggadah, *"K'neged arbaah banim dibrah Torah."*

Holding On to the Truth

At the beginning of the new road, you might have been bowled over by the truth. When you were confronted with logical and clear arguments, your whole way of thinking was altered. The truth does not change, but we do. Our ability to look at things objectively when we are going through difficulties can definitely be challenged. The immutable truth of the Torah, living with the commandments, and doing the will of Hakadosh Baruch Hu (the Holy One, blessed be He) cannot change. When issues in our lives make us question these verities, there is only one solution: we have to be willing, once again, to separate the core of truth from the issues that conceal or distract us from it.

The Need to Belong

Most people need to feel that they are part of something bigger than themselves. For some who transformed their lives, satisfaction of this need was essential. Belonging to something as large as a community of our own people, Klal Yisrael, is a great feeling for most of us.

But now that you are part of it, why are you, years later, encountering all kinds of personal issues, difficulties, problems, and challenges...alone? No one else seems to be concerned about these things, but you feel disconnected from the life of Torah to which you once felt so close. What happened to the beautiful, supportive group?

What has happened, of course, is that the community has grown and changed as a part of its natural growth, and you may need to learn some skills to respond and/or reconnect to it. The changes are a manifestation of the normal social evolution that occurs in any society or community. They have come about as a result of very natural causes, which we will try to understand.

What often happens when we are slighted or hurt by the behavior of others is that we take the offense personally, which puts us at odds with everyone around us. Then, of course, it snowballs. Everything that happens seems off kilter, seeming to prove that the religious community is not for us. Everything new that bothers us deepens the wound, creating further alienation.

There are ways to break that pattern, to reattach and rebuild that relationship. We hope that the many ideas in this book will help the re-connection to what was deemed so important before all this transpired.

A Blessing for the Jewish People

Before moving on to a discussion of practical methods and techniques, we ought to point out that whatever the motivating factors were that brought this tremendous influx of people from all walks of life to join the Torah community, this movement must be seen as an incredible berachah, a Divine blessing. We cannot interpret Hashem's intentions; His Master Plan is far too transcendent for us to try to second-guess. As an observer, however, there is one thing that stands out.

We are surrounded by a secular, superficial world. As insular as our community attempts to remain, we still need to write contracts, do busi-ness, and interact with professionals like doctors, psychologists, and lawyers. Over the course of a few years, there has been a tremendous incursion of people into even the most insular Yeshiva and Chassidic communities, bringing with their immense professional knowledge and broad experience. In addition, we have artists, performers, and musicians along with designers and inventors, all contributing to the wealth of experience and services that add to our community in so many ways.

This is a blessing for us, as these newcomers contribute greatly to the growth and welfare of the community. Besides the wonderful addition of so many Jewish souls who are doing the will of Hashem, we see the added berachah of people with varied backgrounds who are adding new dimensions of understanding, perception, knowledge, and skills to our nation.

The necessary insularity of our community has caused a certain degree of dissonance to the needs of many of our own children, some of which may go beyond the narrow, restricted path laid out by the community. The influx of Jews untutored in Judaism gave impetus to a widespread response of explanation and elucidation of original texts and com-plex concepts. The deluge of books and lectures not only tutored the untutored but gave a fresh perception to thousands of disillusioned *frum* young men and women who had taken their spiritual heritage for granted, unaware of its beauty and glory.

It is of utmost importance for anyone raising religious children to clarify for them, with pride, the radiant message of Torah. When a community ignores its greatest assets, assuming that its children know the value of those treasures, they risk having their progeny walk away from the very riches that attract the uninitiated.

There have been, and always will be, those who think that asking questions and inquiring into concepts is detrimental. Those who conduct an open dialogue, however, and are in touch with the lives and needs of the masses of students thirsty for information are confident that seeking clarification is a blessing. The brother of the *Maharal* of Prague, writes in his epochal work that there were naysayers who questioned the propriety of the prophets in their presentation of questions![3]

"They say it would have been better not to write those questions so as not to bring doubt into the hearts of our people. However," he continues, "the opposite is true: If not for the doubts and questions mentioned by our prophets, the people of today would think that their questions are unanswerable. They would think that if only the earlier generations had known the challenges we face, they would have given up long ago."

The brilliant and broader elucidations of Torah and mitzvos that came with the arrival of our brothers and sisters who wanted to understand these concepts have enhanced and enriched the keeping of mitzvos and learning of Torah for our entire community.

---

3   Rabbi Chaim Friedberg (brother of the *Maharal*), *Sefer Hachaim* (Machon Sifsei Tzaddikim, Jerusalem, 2001), p. 183.

Chapter 3

Other Motivations
for Change

W hat inspires people to make quantum leaps, introducing earthshaking changes that will affect them for the rest of their lives as well as their future families? While everyone's response will be unique, there are enough similarities to allow us to make some general observations. This chapter will discuss some of the more common motivations for change as well as some basic methods for dealing with their resulting challenges.

Let us address what might be called negative motivations—frustration with an unfulfilling lifestyle, rebellion, and unchallenged peer pressure.

Frustration

Some people were leading lives filled with frustration. When encountering insurmountable problems, some of them arrived at the mistaken conclusion that these problems could be solved by becoming observant. Then, they assumed, Hashem would resolve everything for them.

"If only we make this drastic change in our lives, we'll be doing Hashem a favor and He will do us a favor in return."

Well, why not? If a person is rising to a higher level by becoming *frum*, Hashem is just going to take care of everything. Isn't that the way it works? Based on this assumption, when things are not working out in this scenario, some people may question the validity of observant Judaism as a whole.

Some teachers have promised this type of cosmic relationship to their students. I have even heard lecturers say, "Come to Torah and mitzvos and all your problems will be solved."

This is untrue and phenomenally irresponsible!

Yes, working diligently on our characters and our behavior and keeping more commandments will help us become better people. *"Toras Hashem temimah, meshivas nafesh*—The Torah of Hashem is complete, it revives the self."[1] There is an element of Torah that is *meishiv nefesh*, reviving the heart, settling the soul, and helping a person to find a sense of serenity. To say, however, that all of a person's issues and everything they have to deal with in their life will be resolved as a result of their decision to strengthen their religious commitment fosters an unrealistic expectation. Some people, less mature at an earlier point in their lives, have to again reevaluate: *Am I going to make another decision based on the same mistake and assume that, OK, if I do X, Hashem will do Y for me?*

Although they definitely entertain thought from time to time, most people are not actually wondering if they should drop everything and go back to who they were. Living a committed life is not easy, making it very normal to question whether or not we made the right decisions. It is important, however, to recognize that when we were younger, we might not have faced our real issues. To compound our confusion, we are now facing new, unexpected difficulties.

If we chose Yiddishkeit (Judaism) and turning to Hashem as the solutions to our frustrations and unhappiness, it is reasonable to expect that we will remain frustrated and unhappy if we never dealt with our earlier problems. No one imagines that becoming *frum* is going to relieve symptoms of allergies. While *emunah* can be healing, Torah calming, and a life of meaning and direction fulfilling, deep psychological challenges need to be addressed properly and responsibly

Of course, one can be upset that these issues have not yet been resolved, but rather than zeroing in on them honestly and maturely, some people are ready to throw in the towel and conclude that they made the

---

1 *Tehillim* 19:8.

wrong decision years ago. To the contrary, now that they are motivated and questioning, it is a good time to take stock and look for realistic ways to deal with neglected issues. Perhaps, the time has come to seek the professional help that was needed long ago.

Rebellion

Could the impetus for life changes have been the by-product of a rebellious desire for something different, perhaps a deep-seated revolt against the emptiness of the secular world and the hypocrisies of modern society? It may have simply been a youthful reaction against parents who insisted on unquestioning conformity to plans they had envisioned for their child almost from the time they were born. Either could be a motivation of rebellion.

At some point, a person might have said, "I just don't want to become what you want me to be," and found other ways of doing things—perhaps in the area of religious observance—with which their parents disagreed. Many people were less mature and acted purely for the sake of rebellion, often without thinking things through. They rebelled because they needed to question, to find their own space, in they own way. They were not prepared to accept anyone else telling them what to do.

For most people, this stage of rebellion ends with adulthood, and the reassessment of motives is then relatively easy. In many cases, when rebellion was the only motivation for making changes, there were those who fell out of religion as fast as they fell in.

Some people are perpetual rebels, and I can only wish those who are blessed with this trait to use it well. When they mature, if rebellion is still part of their makeup, the process reverses itself. They've changed, and now they are part of a different community, subject to different pressures, probably holding a whole different worldview, but their rebellious streak has not lessened. If it is in action now, however, it is probably working in reverse.

When they were younger, they fought secular society or their parents and their goals for them, finding their own path. Now, they are in a new environment, but still questioning and swimming against the tide. As a result, they may now find themselves fighting against the very things for which they fought many years ago, questioning all that is imperfect in the religious world. Where is this rebellion going to take them?

Rebellion can also be a blessing. For those who know how to use it well, it can actually function as a force for the good. Rebellion can be the power to think out of the box—the strength needed to remain an individual. It is a person's power to consider and constantly question what they are doing, an opportunity to refine the process of their change and development.

It is now time for such a person to stop rebelling against the world around them and focus the spotlight on themselves. That ability to question can be used to question maturely, facing the challenge to really do what is right, working on themselves until they find the best way possible to achieve their goals.

It is futile to tell someone who has a specific personality trait to ignore it or let go of it. Our traits define who we are—our identity; they are the source of our individual power, and we need to learn to direct them properly.

In *Parashas Ki Sisa* we find a very interesting dialogue between Moshe Rabbeinu and Hakadosh Baruch Hu, Who says, "You are a stubborn nation; in one moment, I will rise up amongst you and destroy you."[2]

The dialogue continues, at the end of which Moshe Rabbeinu pleads, "Please come among us, **because** they are a stubborn nation, **therefore**,[3] forgive them."[4]

Hashem has just finished saying, "I am going to destroy them because they are stubborn." How can Moshe Rabbeinu use that reasoning? Where is the logic in this argument?

As is often the case in life, the very problem is the solution. Moshe Rabbeinu defends the Jewish nation saying, "Ribbono shel Olam [Master of the World], You chose this nation in order to give us the

---

2   *Shemos* 33:5.

3   *Ramban* ibid.

4   Ibid. on *Shemos* 34:9.

Torah and take us into Eretz Yisrael. It is true that they are stubborn, but You have accepted them with this trait. Now that we have become Your nation with Your constant Presence, there will be nothing that can take us away from You. This nation will succeed through all the dispersions, inquisitions, and challenges it will face, utilizing the power of this very trait of obstinacy for which You want to destroy them."

We see that Moshe Rabbeinu's argument was accepted. Hashem forgave the Jewish People.

We can also take this personality trait, applying it to our lives in a way that will strengthen us. Instead of lashing out against all the things we think are wrong, we can use this force constructively, to help initiate changes in ourselves to do things right. We can question and challenge ourselves to continue to develop and do the right thing. There are still many aspects of life in which we are swimming upstream. Many facets of living in the world at large, even within our own communities, require us to evaluate and come to intelligent conclusions that are neither popular nor expected. To thrive in this environment, we all need a bit of rebellion.

Unchallenged Peer Pressure

Another motivation for making the quantum leap to observing the commandments may have been that of peer pressure. Some people may have gone to a school, perhaps a yeshiva or summer program, where everyone was already observant or becoming religious. Obviously, no one was forcing them to make the actual decision to live a Torah life. The resolution to accept Hashem and His Torah as truth cannot be ascribed to peer pressure, but the influence was there, determining much of what those who fit into this grouping gave up and/or took upon themselves.

The younger generation today seems even more easily moved by peer pressure than the previous one, but it definitely exists at all times and at every level. It is present whether a person studies in a school geared especially to *baalei teshuvah* or joins a particular community or congregation. There is peer pressure in the workplace and in the gym. It is a part of life. Perhaps, in yeshiva, some felt pressured by strong-minded students who created the spirit there. Feeling forced to move at a faster pace than that for which they were really prepared can have unexpected repercussions later in life.

Most people who make quantum changes will find themselves at a place they could not even have imagined two or three years earlier. That's fine. If their decisions were strongly influenced by peer pressure and not much else, however, they may now feel resentful or uncomfortable with the person they have become and may deeply question those choices.

If you made such decisions when younger as a result of this pressure, you are probably still being influenced by it. Because you are older now, and dealing with much more significant issues in life, however, it is not enough to keep you comfortable with your doubts. If anything, you may find yourself questioning your peers along with yourself.

I am going to state something now that might seem unrabbinical, but it must be said. Please ponder the following few sentences carefully, as I do not want to be misunderstood.

Perhaps, now *is* the right time to question. It may be time to ask yourself what or who pressured you to make those choices *then*, and why you are making certain important decisions *now*. Were you unduly influenced by peer pressure then, and still living your life under that influence? If so, do you want to continue on that path? Step back, objectively look at yourself, and ask, "Where am I? What am I doing? Should I be doing some things differently? Do I resent what I'm doing now because of the speed with which I took on these obligations?"

> *Larry, the grandson of a Moroccan Jew who settled in the US and lost most of his children to assimilation, was nineteen when he went to Israel. He moved in with his uncle Reb Nosson, his only religious relative, and his righteous wife. Larry had been more than a bit on the wild side throughout high school and came to Israel on a whim. Like so many others, he originally came to visit for a few days. The family accepted him with open arms.*

Living in Petach Tikvah presented him with both challenges and opportunities. It was not common to see boys with long hair and jeans walking the streets there, and it was rare, in those times, to find boys like Larry in the shul where Uncle Nosson davened. He joined a yeshiva with a somewhat intense learning program, where he felt as if he stood out like a weed in a manicured lawn. In two months, Larry was dressing and acting like a full-fledged yeshiva boy. Gone was his long hair, leaving him peyos that would not have embarrassed a young man who had always worn them.

Just two years later, Larry was married and building a family like that of his aunt and uncle. His wife was a sweet, kind-hearted, and somewhat naive young lady, and she lived with his frustrations, outbursts, and constant ill-mannered behavior. It was clearly beyond Larry to live within the confines of his tiny apartment, coupled with the long hours of learning and his meager stipend typical of his Petach Tikvah enclave. It was considered acceptable for him to get a part-time job, which he had done as soon as he felt the pressure of his new friends wearing off. Nobody knew how frustrated and angry he was except his growing family, and of course, his poor wife.

Larry loved people, parties, fun, and freedom. As a single, he had experienced drugs and alcohol as well as other vices. Now a married man with children, he reverted to his old ways. He began to disappear for short and then longer intervals, although his uncle and aunt made it very clear that with five children he could not just get up and leave whenever he felt like it. The short of a very long and painful story is that one day Larry woke up, looked in the mirror, and did not recognize the face he saw. He simply abandoned his family, leaving them to a life of poverty and suffering.

There will be those who say that Larry was no good to begin with. Others will claim that you cannot use such an extreme story to make a point that is relatively simple. I disagree with both. I knew Larry and watched the whole process of change, at first with admiration and then with great anxiety and trepidation. With almost no gradual acclimation, he had allowed peer pressure to push him into a role that he was not capable of sustaining. He had not been granted enough transition time, and there was no dialogue about his personal needs and dreams. It was a makeover whose fallout has affected his large family for many years and will, unfortunately, for many yet to come.

If you are now in such an extreme place that you have reached a point where you cannot comfortably live with yourself and feel as if you are living a lie with no recourse, it is time to take a close look and try to determine what *your* needs are. Do you have a family? How old are your children? What will happen if you take a small step backward and start rebuilding parts of your lifestyle? You have made commitments and raised children with values that are real and important to them. You cannot allow yourself to reach the frustration level of running away. Are there things that you can do to avoid confusing your family, yet will give you some validation and prevent your frustration from coming to a boil?

Obviously, I am not telling you to go out and sin! We are discussing parts of your life as small as shaving beards or shortening *peyos*, slight changes in dress code, and as large as the way you present yourself and where you live. There are more restrictive communities in which you might feel embarrassed to work in your garden, go fishing, ride a bike, or go rollerblading, for example. There are larger cities and smaller ones, stricter schools as well as those that are less limiting. These should all be factors open for discussion if you are feeling the need of renewing your process of change to a more gradual one that will eventually get you to where you are now, rather than the intense peer pressure that brought you there almost overnight.

Making the Mitzvos My Own

The most important aspect of mitzvos is that we own them. Duty is not a contradiction to choice. The *Rambam* makes it very clear that we need to begin the mitzvos with ulterior motives as part of our approach to serving Hashem.[5] It is only at a later part of the process that we can approach things with the love of *lishmah*, total commitment based on the altruistic desire to fulfill Hashem's will. Like anything that we want to own in life, we have to make our individual commitment and investment in order to feel the connection, as opposed to being a visitor or observer.

Finding that you have no motivation to fulfill your duties often comes as a result of having made commitments beyond your comfort level. In the attempt to be good and do what is right, you might have left yourself out of the picture.

Don't be afraid of "doing less," because if your original motivations brought you to stringent positions that are now causing resentment, it means that you began on the wrong foot, and need to "restart" your Yiddishkeit. You restart your computer in order to get it running more accurately and more smoothly. Sometimes, you need to begin in safe mode to be able to adjust things so that you can get to normal mode. You don't turn it off and leave it off.

You need to find a way to attach yourself to the things you are doing, make these actions something in which you can find pleasure, and do them in ways that make you feel connected. It might mean davening less, with more intent, as prescribed by the *Tur*,[6] or singing the davening. It should definitely include finding new interest in your learning. Some people find new areas of Torah they never experienced before, often finding a more interesting *shiur*, class, given by a dynamic or interesting rabbi. Many people whose learning skills are more advanced need to research and study subjects that interest them. You are allowed, and often need, to go back to the basics and find where and how you can find pleasure and appreciation in your learning and mitzvah observance.

---

5   *Rambam, Hilchos Teshuvah* 10:5.
6   *Tur, Orach Chaim* 1.

Peer Pressure Can Be Used Positively

We can use peer pressure as motivation rather than allowing it to force us into uncomfortable situations. It is a powerful tool that can empower us positively when used correctly.

When Rabbi Yochanan ben Zakkai was on his deathbed, his students came to part with him,[7] and they saw him crying.

"Great man and leader," they asked their beloved *rebbi*, "why are you crying [since you lived your life well and correctly]?"

He responded with a parable, saying how frightened he would be to face a king of flesh and blood and hear his judgment. "And now, most certainly, before the King of all kings, Hakadosh Baruch Hu, the Almighty, Whom I cannot bribe and cannot trick, how much more terrified should I be? Whatever Hashem decrees lasts forever…"

After his discourse, his students requested that he bless them. Rabbi Yochanan's response seemed extraordinary to them. "May your fear of God be like your fear of men."

"That is all you wish for us?" asked his astonished students. "This is your parting blessing?"

"Yes," Rabbi Yochanan replied firmly. "Before a person does something wrong, he looks around to see if anyone is looking!"

In other words, it is a normal human response to be concerned about what other people think. Clearly, peer pressure plays a role in our decision making. We cannot allow ourselves, though, to let it push us into doing what we do not feel is right for us. If we want to accomplish something, the urge needs to come from within. We can then use peer pressure to help us achieve our goals.

A few years ago, I had to lose a serious number of pounds because I was in what the doctor referred to as the danger zone. When I started watching what and how I ate, I made it my business to tell everybody I knew about my decision.

"What are you doing?" my wife asked. "Your food intake is nobody's business."

---

7   *Berachos* 28b.

"No, it isn't," I replied, "but telling everyone about it *is* going to help me lose weight. The more people I tell, the more embarrassed I'm going to be if I go back to where I was."

This is an example of positively using peer pressure to help me achieve something *I* want to do, a goal *I* know is right. I can also use it to help me stay as I am, if that is what I want.

Peer pressure that causes you to do something due to fear of negative reactions from friends, however, or because you feel coerced, is clearly unhealthy. If it makes you uncomfortable, causing you to do things with which you cannot happily live, both you and your family will be miserable. If this is the position in which you find yourself, you really need to take a step back, reexamining your past. Peer pressure should not be your current problem.

Perhaps, it was not the sole reason that you made that decision then or now. To really understand yourself, to know what you should do and what you are capable of doing, this question must be addressed honestly.

During Pesach 1980, my father, *zt"l*, returned from an extraordinary adventure in Mozambique, southern Africa, on the border of Swaziland. He had arranged an intricate and, at times, extremely dangerous deal that ultimately resulted in the incredible feat of *pidyon shevuyim*, redeeming a prisoner. He was able to secure the release of a Jewish man from a Swaziland prison. It is a long and exciting story that is not for this book, but upon his return from the airport, I asked my father a question of what was expected of me regarding certain responsibilities I had at the time. He told me his opinion.

"That is not possible," I said.

"Do you know the difference between possible and impossible?" he asked. "The difference is often five more minutes of effort."

After his tremendous achievement, he was not ready to accept that there is such a thing as impossible. With true determination, almost everything is possible. Those are wise words, and they are important to hear sometimes, but we still have to know how to define the difference between possible and impossible when it comes to our own capabilities.

Baruch had been a frequent visitor to our home years ago before he went to yeshiva, and we spent many hours talking about life and Judaism. I saw him seven years after his marriage, when he was studying in kollel and had two children. He seemed sad, but could not define what was bothering him. He looked disheveled, and it was clear that he was not happy with himself. He spoke about an oppressive society, depression, about not feeling good and not being proud. He had not been to kollel for almost a month.

I asked him about his connection with his yeshiva. He replied that he had not felt understood there and had not been in contact with his rebbi since his wedding. He looked as if he were about to cry. I asked him to speak of his time in the yeshiva, and he told me his story.

Baruch, formerly known as Robert, had been a model in the fashion industry prior to his becoming frum. With his charming and charismatic personality, he had been used to having lots of friends, wearing the finest clothing, and was acutely aware of his good looks. At some point, he joined a yeshiva that was pretty low-key. The rosh yeshiva was an unassuming fellow who regarded the material world as about as interesting as last year's snow. Baruch admired this humble, spiritual man and his clear and incisive mind, and grew attached to him. Before long, Baruch was on his way to becoming a real ben Torah. He loved learning, was comfortable with mitzvos, and felt at ease in the many beautiful homes to which he was invited.

The hardest part for him was accepting the dress code. The other fellows at the yeshiva chided his "materialism." They spoke to him late into the night about the farce of current styles, and he finally capitulated and bought a second-hand suit and plain black shoes. For the first week he didn't look in the mirror; after that he convinced himself that if that was what Hashem wanted from him, he'd be just fine. Sixteen weeks after entering yeshiva, Baruch was a full-fledged shlump.

When I heard his tale, I quickly contacted a trustworthy student of mine, and shipped them off to a haberdashery in Yerushalayim with instructions to buy the coolest, most stylish suit he could find. Next, I sent him to the shoe store, and finally, I made him buy a blue hat. A few pairs of cotton slacks and polo shirts, and Baruch would be ready to face his life. He protested, of course, and laughed, and was worried that his neighbors would think badly of him. He also said it wouldn't help his depression. But once I took him in hand, there was no turning back.

The first week he kept looking in the mirror and smiling nervously about falling backward into materialism. A month later, he went out and got a job as the manager of a gym. His wife, who was originally worried about these changes, called me after a few weeks and told me that she felt like she had just remarried a happy, lively person ready to take on the world.

I didn't hear from them again for five years, when we met at the bris of a young neighbor. Lo and behold, Baruch was well-dressed, but all in black and white, black hat and all. I nodded and smiled; Baruch smiled back and then pulled me over.

"Rabbi Greenwald," he said, "I don't understand exactly what happened, but first I was self-conscious all the time with my new clothes. Then I was ecstatic. I felt so good, and most people didn't even seem to notice my change back to materialism. It was as if the fact that I had left kollel and was a working man made it OK to be dressed the way I like. Or," he added with a sly smile, "Maybe, because everyone knows I am a BT, they just figured that I was confused.

"About a year ago, my seven-year-old son was shopping for clothing with my wife and what do you know, he told her he wants clothing just like Abba's. They came home, and my wife and I talked it over. I came to the conclusion that I'm now prepared to do what I was not ready for almost ten years ago. How do I look, rebbi?"

There is a world of difference between what I *want* to do and what I *do not want* to do, and between what I *can* do and what I *cannot* do. When it comes to the issue of peer pressure, this is the key. There are things I do not want to do even though I know they are right. Peer pressure will help me to do them.

There are things that will make me become resentful even if I know that they are right. I must be honest and admit my discomfort. Perhaps, I can try to get used to it because there are some things you can get used to. By trying, I am testing myself. *I am allowing myself to learn my limits.* We should not make decisions before we are prepared to accept everything that comes about as a result of them.

In two very special yeshivos in Israel that deal with young returnees, the *roshei yeshiva* will not allow the boys to put on a black hat for at least two full years. When asked why, they answer, "I would rather you didn't put it on now than have you take it off in a few years."

Growth without Resentment

Rav Wolbe used to tell us an immensely important rule of serving Hashem regarding working on our *middos*. Only through challenge do we grow, and this is not always comfortable. How can we understand the "challenge equals growth" equation when we take into account that "The roads of Torah are pleasant and all of its paths are peace"?[8] The Torah brings, or should bring, pleasantness into a person's life.

After Kayin killed his brother Hevel, Hashem asked him why he looked so downcast.[9]

When a person has done the right thing, it shows on his face.

"When a person does a good deed, it carries him," says the *Ohr Hachaim Hakadosh*.[10] Doing what is right is uplifting. We feel good because serving Hashem makes us both feel and be better.

"Your good deed smiles down on you," Rav Wolbe used to say.

---

8   *Mishlei* 3:17.
9   *Bereishis* 4:6.
10   Ibid., 4:7.

However, if when we become "better," we also become frustrated or resentful, we must be doing something wrong. Becoming better should be a process of fulfillment.

The *Ohr Hachaim* is teaching us a lesson of the highest import. We should be able to sense when we are doing good things.

This does not preclude them from being hard to do. Many things that are good and important are difficult and require great effort, such as completing the study of a tractate in Gemara or acing a term in university. We worked hard, but we felt great satisfaction when we were finished. That good feeling is an important indicator that we were doing something of value.

If we feel resentment when doing Hashem's will, then we are doing something wrong. We might be moving too quickly before being ready for this particular step. We may be trying to do too much at once and cannot yet live up to the standard toward which we are aspiring. Acting in a particular way for the wrong reasons also makes us uncomfortable, at which point something inside of us rebels and begins pushing in the opposite direction, fighting our growth. This is a signal to slow down.

The *mussar* giants describe the rebellion of the *nefesh ha'behamis*, the animal self.[11] When a person wants to change, he has to take into consideration his true state of being. Our "self" includes two opposing elements that pull us in opposite directions. Our soul-self draws us to the heights of achievement and spirituality. Our animal-self pulls us toward distraction and physical pleasure. When we push ourselves beyond our capabilities, trying to be more spiritual than our animal-self is prepared to be, we create a rebellion. The body cries, "Mutiny!" and pushes back very forcefully. Some people crash, some fall apart, and others just get stymied into complacency.

Just as building up physical stamina requires understanding and direction, spiritual growth has similar requirements. We would never try for an Olympic medal without a trainer, pushing our physical limits without

---

11   Rabbi Mendel Zbarez, *Sefer Cheshbon Hanefesh* (Slabodka Student Council of Lithuania), Keiden, Lithuania, ch. 1, pp. 16–19.

guidance. Knowing the dynamics of physical growth, we recognize that we can break down if we push too hard. Spiritual breakdown takes the form of resentment, frustration, and rebellion.

"When I first came to the yeshiva in Mir," recalled Rav Wolbe, "there was an older student who decided that he needed to be *mekarev* me, bring me closer to the truth. Toward that end, he took me out for a walk and talk. After the second walk, I said to myself, 'One more walk like this, and I will become an *apikores* [heretic]!'"

Peer pressure is something we ought to examine carefully. Even now, long afterward, you may find that social pressure is pushing you into situations that cause resentment, confusion, and unhappiness. If so, you need to take a step back and determine whether slowing down is the answer.

Asking ourselves these kinds of questions can open a Pandora's box. It may even mean making changes in your choice of friends or the neighborhood in which you live. It is not a license or excuse for slacking, but a necessity for honest evaluation—preferably with the help of an impartial person whom you respect—of whether you are being truthful with yourself or if you are looking for an easy way out.

For the moment, let us continue to focus on the motivational forces that bring people back to Torah and the challenges that arise from those changes.

No matter what reasons brought you to living with Torah as your guide, an honest evaluation will help you recognize and separate Torah from the limitations of some of the people trying to keep it.

Chapter 4

Issues and Tissues

Most people who have made quantum changes in their lives are thinkers, likely to continue thinking, analyzing, and struggling with issues endemic to their lives. I often tell my students that the difference between a question and an issue is a tissue.

Questions do not need tissues. A question is a logical attempt to understand an idea, concept, or behavior, whereas the very nature of an issue is complex, a conundrum with which one does not know how to deal. Let's leave specific questions for later, and just touch on some of the larger concerns challenging us, such as the following:

- The loss of pleasure and excitement in performing mitzvos
- The difficulties inherent in keeping Torah learning relevant
- Misunderstandings between child and parent

Rav Wolbe used to remind us that every day we say two berachos that are related but different. In the *Birchos HaTorah*,[1] the blessings on the Torah, we say, "Please make the words of Your Torah sweet in our mouths," asking that the Torah remain fresh, alive, and pleasant for us. Later, at the end of the morning blessings, we say, "...let us become used to your Torah...may it become routine for us to obey the commandments."

Which of these two goals do we really want? Are we interested in the pleasant feeling of something new and exciting, or do we wish for the easy complacency that comes with rote?

---

1   Siddur, morning prayers.

Rav Wolbe explains that people who are new to Judaism come to the mitzvos with freshness and zest. They are excited to do them. It is only too easy for FFBs, those *frum* from birth, to view mitzvos with a blasé attitude. They have been doing them ever since they can remember, and often, unfortunately, do not feel any freshness or enthusiasm in their performance. Therefore, Rav Wolbe says, the mitzvos are not challenging.

In contrast, they will all be challenging to the newly observant; in fact, there is so much to remember that it may be somewhat overwhelming. Almost every *baal teshuvah* is familiar with the sense of helplessness in trying to remember and follow all the details of mitzvos. Eventually, however, that person for whom everything was so fresh, exciting, and new, will become adjusted to living a Torah life and all that it entails. Two, three, five, ten, or fifteen years down the line, he is acting like an FFB. There is a strange irony here.

The popular joke says that you know a person is no longer a *baal teshuvah* when he starts talking during davening. That's a sad joke, but there is a kernel of truth in it. (I would say a person is no longer a *baal teshuvah* when he can cry on Tishah B'Av and Yom Kippur.) Those who learn how to daven at the age of eighteen or twenty realize what a valuable opportunity they have just discovered. The act itself is a new experience, and it takes time, effort, and patience to develop a relationship with Hashem. It has more meaning to them than to one who has ceased to appreciate the power of prayer over the years.

Rav Wolbe teaches that this is why every Jew must recite both of these berachos. We need them both. We need the Torah to be fresh and exciting, and at the same time we want the Torah to be familiar enough so that we do not have to start over again each day wondering what to do. Unfortunately, once observing the mitzvos becomes ritualized and automatic, much of the excitement is lost. When this happens, very often the way we look at ourselves and our observance is changed.

Let us go back now to your original decision to make a quantum change in your life. Most people made this change with the help of a great deal of study, classes, and lectures. A certain learning process was initiated to buttress the change, but it was all new. Learning and novelty are the two essential elements of the process. Throughout our lives, we need to maintain them if we wish to keep Torah and mitzvos fresh and alive for us.

Learning tends to take a back seat after rote and routine have taken over, you are building a family, and acquiring new responsibilities. If the learning process in your life drops to a different level, your entire life situation is going to change.

It is not by chance that the request that Torah remain sweet is in the morning blessing. The desire to savor and keep its beauty must become an integral part of our prayers. It is only through *learning* it, however, that we can keep its freshness present in our minds and hearts. We will have to be honest with ourselves to discover whether we still care as much as we should about keeping the Torah alive in our consciousness. If, in fact, we discover that we have lost that element of caring, we will need to rekindle our enthusiasm.

Keeping Torah Alive Inside

Time is a valuable entity of which we never have enough, yet somehow, we manage to find some for things that are extremely important to us. The necessity of keeping the Torah relevant and fresh is just as cogent for people who are still learning in *kollel* after ten years as for the newcomer to Torah.

Most of you began the serious part of your journey with some form of Torah learning. You began the process of change thirsty for knowledge, and you studied in order to learn new things and attempt to catch up with those around you. All of Torah was new and exciting. How has what you learned turned into rote?

There is a difference between learning in yeshiva, where we must study an assigned topic along with the others in our group, and learning because a subject interests us. We must try to integrate this second kind of study into our schedule as a way of addressing our individuality.

Because women do not have a mitzvah to spend huge amounts of time studying, when they do go to a *shiur*, they will usually seek one that interests or inspires them.

Men need to find their satisfaction in Torah. I would suggest that men, no matter how learned or experienced they are, make it a priority to find a part of Torah study that attracts them, that awakens and personally excites them.

You may be learning but feeling like a dry bone. Any action becomes rote when we let our bodies go through the process without using our intellect. Unfortunately, our minds can go on automatic pilot when davening or saying the words of a berachah without thought. We need to re-animate ourselves. It is possible to physically attend a *shiur* but leave our minds and hearts behind; it is therefore urgent to seek the aspects of Torah that speak to our hearts.

Some people are animated by halachah, others by the writings of one of the brilliant latter-day commentaries, another finds inspiration in the words of *mussar* (ethical works), *machshavah*, or Chassidic philosophical treatises. Still others will find that they need to exchange their *Daf Yomi shiur* for a teacher who goes more slowly, quickly, or more in depth. The essential point is to find your place in Torah; it is the only way to stay connected.

Renewal

There is a beautiful and powerful concept in Judaism called *chiddush*, the power of renewal. We say every morning that the Master of the World, in His goodness, renews the entire Creation every single day.[2] There is a constant renewal in and of the world.

Rav Samson Raphael Hirsch wrote a beautiful essay, "Youthful Enthusiasm for Duty,"[3] regarding our ability to achieve renewal in mitzvos. He describes the parallel between the human attitude and that which we see in nature.

For the person who observes a sunrise for the first time, it is the most awesome, beautiful scene he has ever witnessed. When he has seen it a number of times and becomes accustomed to it, it does not signify

---

2   Siddur, *Birchos K'rias Shema.*

3   "Youthful Enthusiasm for Duty" in *Collected Works of Rabbi Samson Raphael Hirsch* (Feldheim), vol. 7, essay 12.

that the sunrise is any the less awesome. His lack of enthusiasm merely indicates that he is allowing the sunrise to occur without opening his eyes, mind, and heart to its wonder. The same holds true in the realm of spirituality: the mitzvah is the same, with all the power it held the first time we did it. What is missing? The two hundredth and two thousandth time we perform it, we do not stop to consider its value; we rush into it without taking advantage of the power of renewal inherent in Creation.

When we say that the Almighty renews the Creation every day on a regular basis, it reminds us that every single morning is entirely new. There is a popular saying that today is the first day of the rest of your life. The Torah says that the Holy One, blessed be He, in His goodness, gives us the opportunity to start over again every single day. It takes work, though. Have you forgotten how difficult it was to start the process of change? Of course, then it was an exciting new challenge.

When things are allowed to become rote, it is we who are responsible. We will suddenly find ourselves realizing, "One second, I don't want to continue like this, just doing and not connecting. Lately during the repetition of the *Amidah*, I've been schmoozing with the fellow next to me instead of participating." Or, "Oh no, Pesach is coming soon!" rather than, "Soon it will be our beautiful Pesach; I can't wait."

It is the same Pesach. What has changed is our attitude, what we are ready to invest. We need to readjust our thought processes.

Sometimes, I scare my students—who are good Bais Yaakov girls— when I tell them they can be living in a rote world devoid of meaning and direction.

There are *frum* people who have never experienced the feeling of renewal or freshness because they never looked for it. We have to work for anything of value or meaning in our lives. Those of us who worked for it once and wish to find it again have to be willing to work for it again.

"For it [the Torah] is not an empty thing from you."[4]

---

4   *Devarim* 32:47.

"And if it is empty," Chazal teach us, "then *from you* it is empty."[5] You are not working hard enough.

It is not necessarily easy to realize that we are empty. After all, it doesn't require as much energy to complain and wallow in sorrow as it does to do what needs to be done. We can reawaken ourselves by strengthening renewal and learning, by recognizing that there is always something we can work toward and achieve.

Those of us who have attempted this know that if we would live for a thousand years and decide to learn something new about every single Yom Tov as it approaches, we would not run out of material. There is so much to learn, so much to know and understand. It may take some effort, but that little something new that we absorb about that Yom Tov will change it for us forever. We will be strengthening both ourselves and those who share the Yom Tov with us. Of course, the same is true for every mitzvah.

Hiding the Past

Many *baalei teshuvah* have encountered social difficulties at one time or another in their lives. When joining the Torah community, they had great expectations of being accepted in a new milieu, and suffer tremendous disappointment when, at times—even rarely—they feel rejected. An almost reflexive reaction to rejection is denial. Just as some people refuse to discuss events that hurt them, acting as if they never happened, people who have made great changes in their lives sometimes try to hide their past experiences from their children and peers. This does not mean sharing one's every transgression or describing the details of *aveiros*. But there is no reason to hide who you were and that there was a time when you did not know and appreciate all that you have now.

Rav Wolbe teaches that people who try to pretend that their previous lives did not exist are cutting away a very important part of themselves. You cannot live in a constant state of denial. It is true that, perhaps, you are not proud of some of the things done in the past, but that is

---

5   *Talmud Yerushalmi, Peah* 3b.

the way you were raised, and it was acceptable then. Living differently now is an extraordinary achievement, but your present life does not automatically make everything you did before evil or terrible. Even if some of those things were unacceptable, they do not make you a bad person. This is part of the beauty of *teshuvah*, the concept of being able to change ourselves, especially when we were formerly ignorant of what is right and wrong. Our sins can become merits.

How can you possibly function as a capable, confident parent if you cannot live with your past and do not share any of it with your children? Children are not unaware, as all parents know. They pick up on a great deal more than we expect them to. You may be uncomfortable with who you are today due to ignoring a very important part of yourself. Those years cannot and should not be erased.

Well, yes, you may want to erase some of the things you did, but *teshuvah* does that! Why should you want to ignore the life experience gained, the happy times and good things, the challenges met, and the lessons learned? Everything you went through is part of what made you who you are today. After having made serious, life-transforming decisions, you now want to bring up your children differently from the way you were raised.

Good! But you don't have to describe everything you did wrong; it isn't necessary to say that you did *anything* wrong. Make peace with your past and don't let it dominate your thinking, which can lead to the great danger of extremism in dealing with your children.

Parents who do not forgive themselves for their past mistakes cannot accept the failings and lapses of their children. They are unable to understand the challenges that their children are facing. This is a treacherous path, with great risk to healthy and balanced *chinuch*, education.

It is false to assume that you will be better accepted in society if you hide your past. If you are comfortable with the person you are now, your friends and acquaintances will be, too. This does not mean announcing everything you ever did wrong. Be sensible! Much of your personal history is not even relevant today, and there is no need to deny or be afraid of it.

Think about approaching a job interview at IBM after working at Sony, where you got fired because you really messed up. Of course, you need to be careful about what you say. If IBM asks you about your previous position and you mention every place where you've worked, except Sony, they're going to find out that you worked there, and they are going to find out why you were fired.

There is a more intelligent way to deal with that situation.

"I worked with Ericson and did fairly well. At Apex, I did really well. When I worked at Sony, to tell you the truth, I messed up, but I learned from my mistake and am prepared to take this job because I am ready to do much better."

Any professional will respect a person who speaks the truth, shows a willingness to learn from his mistakes, and is now ready to make better decisions and commitments. Now, once you get the job and work up to foreman or manager, you're not going to walk in and announce, "Hi, I am the guy that messed up in…!" Obviously, you don't need to wear every mistake you ever made on your sleeve. On the other hand, hiding things causes suspicion and distrust, and makes open communication difficult.

There has to be a level of comfort with your past so that you can converse with your children about your youth. You want to talk to your children about the challenges and excitement of growing up, both the good and bad times, because that is part of being who you are. We all had difficult moral decisions to make, as well as pressures from peers that might have broken us.

Social acceptance comes with people being comfortable with who they are, knowing their place in the scheme of things, and not trying to be someone else. Don't even try to live up to your perception of someone else's expectations. Even if you haven't yet reached your ideal, other people will be comfortable in your presence, respecting you because you accept yourself.

Achieving self-acceptance is extremely difficult for people who have made quantum changes in their lives. It is even more difficult when raising children. Trying to conceal your whole past from them will only create a barrier and cause great discomfort all around.

Why do you think you cannot share the wisdom you gained from your decisions? I know parents who have never discussed anything that happened in their lives before the age of twenty-two with their children. Don't think your children don't have thoughts and opinions about that hidden time in their parent's lives. They are going to find out the broader picture anyway, and the less you tell them, the more curious they will become about what you are concealing. It is extremely important to come to terms not only with the changes in your life, but to use *certain* former experiences as lessons to help your children appreciate the life that you are currently living together.

> *Yaakov Kargon (Jake), a resident of Bnei Brak, came from the Deep South. When he married Rochelle, the daughter of Dutch baalei teshuvah living in Ashdod, his father was unwell and, in Yaakov's words, "wasn't about to take a ride on any old plane, not in this life." Yaakov eventually became Rav Yaakov, and had five children. They knew that they had grandparents in the US who were unwell, but nothing else. There were no pictures ("My parents are not into pictures," Yaakov explained), no stories, no history, and no family traditions. That was all fine until a number of years ago when Grandma Kargon passed away, and four days later Grandpa Kargon followed her. Rav Yaakov had to travel to the States to the first funeral but could not sit shivah in the house in which he'd grown up. There were no religious Jews within sixty miles and there was no shul within at least ninety. He was back at home in thirty-six hours.*
>
> *Sitting shivah in Bnei Brak, where he is an accepted member of his community, began as a travesty. Feeling that he had nothing to say, he feigned depression and remorse for having been away from his parents for so long, which was partially true. He spoke very little until he was visited by a very great man, one who had been instrumental in his initiation into Yiddishkeit, and with whom he had long lost contact.*

A flood of memories washed over Yaakov as he recalled the discussions they'd had about his home. His dad had been a warm, soft-hearted farmer, his mom a housewife who could handle a shotgun. Neither had been too happy about Jake's newfound religious zealousness. Kashrus was not an option, in his mom's opinion, "cause nobody gonna be messin' with my kitchen." Shabbos was otherworldly in concept, and about as realistic as an underwater campfire to them. He remembered the questions he'd asked about his brother Bob marrying a non-Jewish girl, his own girlfriend, Cindy, and thoughts about whether or not she should convert. The list of his discussions with this rabbi went on and on in his head.

"Reb Yaakov, do your children know what a warm and good-hearted person your father was?" the rav asked with sensitivity and compassion. "I remember you telling me that when the farmhouse down the road burned down, your dad, without even thinking twice, brought the whole family to your place and took care of them for three months until they rebuilt their home. If I recall, although they offered, he did not allow them to pay him a red cent!"

Yaakov looked at his rav incredulously. "You remember that story out of all the hundreds of things I told you?"

"Of course," responded the rav. "Do you think you are who you are without any help from Above? Your father has credits and merits; he was a tinok she'nishbah,[6] a baby who was brought up knowing nothing about Yiddishkeit, but with a caring heart that a Yid could be proud of. And if I remember correctly," he continued, "your mother was a woman of integrity who had values and stuck to them. Unfortunately, she was not privileged to know the values of Torah, but didn't you tell me that

---

6   Literally, "a child who was abducted," a Talmudic term for someone who grew up with no knowledge of Torah and mitzvos. He cannot be considered a sinner because he is simply following the way in which he was brought up.

she once said she would die before doing something she thought was wrong?"

Yaakov was shocked to the core, and as his rav got up to leave, he burst out crying.

My parents were not evil people, he thought, they were special. They were different from anyone I have met since I left home, and nobody I've known in the past ten years would even know how to approach talking to them, but they were good people.

"Thank you, rebbi, you helped me more than you can imagine."

The rest of the shivah for his mother and the subsequent days sitting for his father were occupied with finding the legacy of goodness that his parents had and sharing it with everyone who came in.

At one point, Yaakov heard a neighbor ask his younger son, "Your grandfather sounds like he was a very special man, was he a rav?"

The boy smiled and shrugged. "Maybe, I'm not sure."

Yaakov's father was obviously not a rav, but there was enough goodness in his simple heart to pass on lessons to his grandchildren.

Are your children really ashamed of you, or are you superimposing your feelings onto them? If they seem to be embarrassed about something, it's either a reflection of your personal discomfort, or a natural intergenerational pathology. Almost all children feel humiliated at times because their parents don't know what's "in," and it has nothing to do with being *frum*. When your child concludes that you have made a mistake in front of one of their peers, and reacts as if it's the end of the world, take it for what it is: a typically childish perception. All parents have to deal with this kind of embarrassment.

If your children are embarrassed by the fact that you are from a different background than that of their friends' parents, however, it can well be a result of your personal sense of inadequacy. They can tell that you are not comfortable with yourself when you act socially awkward, are overly protective, or try to compensate for your past lack of observance by being the most stringent parents around.

The other extreme involves parents who decide to make sure that *everyone* knows exactly where they came from. It is as if they walk into the room announcing, "I am not an FFB!" They are proud of the fact that they have it right despite their upbringing and that they've discovered the truth and want the world to know it. "Look at me, I am for real!"

Some people come to a foreign country and the first thing they do is try to adapt. They work on walking the walk and talking the talk. They walk into a store in Jerusalem and say "*Shalom*," because it is important for them to integrate. There are others who walk around clad in green pants and an orange shirt, carry a camera, speak loudly, and wonder why everybody is speaking to them in English. They have made a statement: *Hey, everybody, I am a tourist.*

They forget that they are raising their children among people who do not appreciate statements. We are an understated community that traditionally appreciates *tz'nius*, modesty, in all things. I am not referring to orange socks now; I am referring to an unostentatious lifestyle. The *frum* community has always respected understatement.

Unfortunately, today this has taken on a new form. There are those in the community who live quite ostentatiously within the new norms that have developed. You are allowed to be loud and showy, just not different!

Nevertheless, those who make statements are often placing themselves at odds with the community, which will clearly make their children uncomfortable. Children are embarrassed when their parents look, sound, and do things differently from everyone else. This may well result in a feeling of alienation and possible rebellion.

We need not be embarrassed about our backgrounds, as Hashem has created each of us as a unique being with a special purpose in this world. We can feel good about who we are, not because of doing this, that, or the other. We do not need excuses or pronouncements, and we certainly do not need to go against the stream to show our differences.

It is important to remember at this point that we are all—every single person in the world—"a work in progress." No one expects us to know everything, as no one can answer all the questions that arise in life. What we are expected to do is be honest about what we know and what we don't, try to analyze the true root of the challenges we face, and not be afraid to ask questions. We should feel neither inadequate nor overconfident, but honest and aware, ready to deal with whatever comes our way.

> *Joseph was having difficulty with his twelve-year-old son Dovid's integration into the local cheder. The boy was challenging the school's authority and constantly complaining about the rules. Dovid, with whom he had always had a close relationship, refused to let him come to the school to discuss the issues, and of late, Joseph felt that his son was distancing himself from his home environment.*
>
> *I was asked to try to help the parents deal with the situation.*
>
> *When they came to my office, I found myself facing a friendly, cool fellow from Chicago who came in wearing torn jeans, an orange polo shirt, and Crocs. A quick background discussion made it clear that he spoke no Hebrew, pronounced the few words he knew with a heavy new-to-the-language accent, and was grappling with going to daven in shul because his reading was so poor.*
>
> *Puzzled by their description of their decision to move to Jerusalem, I allowed my confusion to be apparent. "Well," said Joseph, "you must understand that we wanted what is best for our children's Jewish development, and a number of friends back home told us that the highest standards and finest education are in Jerusalem."*
>
> *With whatever sensitivity and care I could muster, I had to explain that making this move would only be good for the children if the parents come along on the journey. Joseph was trying to*

retain his cool American identity—the only one in which he felt confident—among people who, although friendly, made him feel woefully inadequate. His personality and lack of language skills made him stand out like an elephant in a cornfield in the quiet, respectful community to which he had moved.

I explained that when you send your son to a school with rules and a dress code, you cannot be presenting a different agenda at home. You need to be, in your children's eyes at least, trying to integrate.

Joseph's lack of integration was sending a message to Dovid that he did not have to keep to the school's rules about dress. On the other hand, Dovid was so embarrassed by his father's eccentric presentation that he did not want anyone to know of their relationship. This explained his unwillingness to have Joseph visit the school, and his distancing from the family.

After an hour's discussion, it was clear that Joseph was not yet ready to forgo his preferred style to conform with the community, even for the sake of enabling his son's integration. His son ended up leaving the school and did not find an alternative placement.

It was even sadder, two years down the line, to meet Dovid in the streets with a mixed group of teenagers who were terrorizing the community, disrupting the Shabbos atmosphere with their anger and hatred.

I strongly believe that this scenario could have been avoided. In making decisions, we must consider the fact that our children are a part of our lives and cannot be expected to just take whatever we hand to them.

Chapter 5

Cycle of Generations

I t will be useful to take a look at our present generation from a historical perspective by sharing what both Chazal and more contemporary Torah giants, with their clear picture of history, have taught us.

Rav Meir Simchah of Dvinsk, author of the Torah classic *Meshech Chochmah*,[1] gave a somewhat sad, albeit very clear, depiction of the mechanics of history. Written in 1900, it is a succinct picture of the cyclical saga of Klal Yisrael, its extreme lows, and tremendous highs. The great sage maintained that a cycle has three components: rejuvenation, assimilation, and destruction. He described a strong, vibrant community, which blossoms as a generation of rejuvenation for a hundred years or so, followed by a generation of disillusionment, whose mitzvos become rote actions that are just an imitation of those in the beginning of the cycle. The next generation continues to deteriorate into an abyss of assimilation and ultimate destruction, until the cycle restarts and a new stage of rejuvenation occurs.

With these words, the *Meshech Chochmah* predicted with horrifying accuracy what was to follow only four decades later. He foresaw the imminent Holocaust. Warning that it would occur as a result of the assimilation manifested by Jews who called Germany the "motherland," he vividly described the horrible destruction that would follow. He also predicted that the destruction would be followed by a new generation of builders, who would, in time, revive Klal Yisrael.

---

1   Rabbi Meir Simchah Hakohen of Dvinsk, *Meshech Chochmah, Parashas Bechukosai* (Feldheim, 2006), pp. 364–65.

The Builders

When Klal Yisrael falls, it can only be rebuilt with the tremendous power of spiritual rejuvenation. Whether we suffer physical decimation as in Europe, voluntary integration as in America, or forced assimilation as in Russia, the only power that can possibly bring about a reawakening of the indestructible soul of Klal Yisrael is our own remarkable spiritual strength. To draw forth the astounding sacred forces inherent in our people and realize our incredible potential for selflessness, requires the emergence of a few extraordinary people to initiate and lead the process.

Concerned and idealistic, they often devote their entire lives to re-building a strong spiritual edifice. Their enthusiasm inspires others to join in the process, which may require two or even three generations to complete.

Then a new generation arises: their children are born into a world that already has a framework. Everything is already in place for them, as the far-seeing builders have provided for everything needed.

Children of the Builders

As each generation blossoms and develops, we see a period of geo-metrical expansion as many climb on the bandwagon. Many of those caught up in the rising tide do not necessarily understand the essence of the movement or its true depth, nor do they recognize what must be passed on to the next generation or how that can be accomplished.

Translating this into contemporary terms, in the *frum* world we see a generation of people who are committed to Judaism, who are study-ing in the yeshivos provided by their forebears. There will always be some builders, but the preponderance of the generation is going to take things for granted. Its members ask less of themselves because little is required of them. They are already "walking the walk and talking the talk." Everything is ready and waiting on a silver platter. They expect more of their communities because they never knew a time when they were lacking anything.

If I were born into a society where there were no schools, I would hopefully recognize the lack and try to figure out how to build them.

Once I have all the schools I need, however, I see their imperfections. This generation that has everything can afford to sit back and criticize what has already been built. Whether or not this is a legitimate attitude is not the point. Such criticism may be intended to add to and develop what has already been built, but more often it is done for the subconscious purpose of removing responsibility from the one offering it.

Where Do WE Stand?

Many have already returned to observance. Over the past forty years, tens of thousands of Jews have rejoined the Klal Yisrael of the *mesorah*. You have opened your eyes, seen the beauty and the *emes*, truth, and want to be a part of what Torah offers. Unfortunately, once within the community that represents *emes*, we find a lot of falsehood. Many who are already observant have no inkling of the beauty of their heritage because they take it for granted.

You joined it because you saw something special; but they've had it all their lives. Unless their parents were unusually creative and aware individuals, they were not necessarily successful at passing on the enthusiasm and understanding that they received from the previous generation.

The newcomers were, and still are, worried about giving their children much more than they had both spiritually and materially, and those who have everything are growing up expecting all that and more. Theirs is a generation of young, observant parents who are very aware of what is going on in the world around them. They know what the world has to offer, so their expectations are vastly different from those of their parents, who followed the builders. Many people raised in the large Torah communities in the bigger cities today are more interested in how many new varieties of kosher Oriental food they can find, in serving sushi at their affairs to impress the guests, and in keeping up with the new technologies, rather than in the goals of the generation that preceded them.

This is the painful reality of many of those who made great life decisions ten and twenty years ago. Many of you changed your lives because you knew the builders; the Yiddishkeit to which you were introduced emanated from those extraordinary achievers. Perhaps you met them at a function, or at a seminar or class. They went wherever they were needed, and even if they landed in a place where there wasn't even one kosher pizza shop, a minyan, or a mikveh for miles around, they found their way and planted many seeds. They were invariably capable and intelligent people who could have been earning more money, acquiring prestige, and enjoying comfort by doing other things, yet they committed themselves to building.

It is understandable that when you met such individuals and glimpsed a little bit of that *emes*, you wanted to be part of it, and were later disappointed when you found out that not everyone is a builder. You are now in the third generation to be born after a devastating war and the massive assimilation that came in its wake. This is a generation whose grandfathers were among the first builders.

You find yourself surrounded by a community that includes many who are taking much of their environment for granted, whose expectations have more to do with fashion and luxuries than with finding meaning in their mitzvos and connection in their davening. Even small cities have stores filled with the latest styles, restaurants, and grocery stores that cater to the most diverse tastes; the generation is mesmerized by the materialism of the dominant society. This focus has taken the place of inspiration, creation, self-development, and giving to the community. Some of the second and many of the third generation have lost contact with those things that inspired you in your search for meaning.

Most people in our community today are *not* builders. The current generation has high expectations in all areas of life, including many that embrace various assimilated values such as preoccupation with the entertainment industry, overindulgence in cars, gadgets, and elegant homes, and—what is unfortunately very difficult to acknowledge—the serious breakdown of moral boundaries.

Assimilation extends its tentacles far beyond the religious aspects of life, encompassing cultural aspirations as well. We are defined by the set of values to which we cling, yet it is very difficult to divorce ourselves totally from those around us. We read widely, and we bring into our homes many outside influences that affect not only our outlook on life, but the way in which we and our children live.

Society's Influence

I remember speaking to Rav Wolbe shortly after my marriage.

"I never really thanked the Rebbi for something very basic that the Rebbi gave me. When I first came to Eretz Yisrael, I was in a way a goy, a gentile. Through the *chinuch* I received in the Rebbi's yeshiva, I feel more connected as a Jew."

Of course, I was raised in a religious home and kept Torah and mitzvos, but my way of thinking was very much a product of the wider world in which I grew up, as I was exposed to it on every single level. Well-read and curious, I realized that there was an enormous world outside of my controlled and limited one, and I was interested in understanding it.

Only after hearing and understanding the Torah perspective on so many areas of life did I become aware of *how few* of my thought processes had anything to do with the Torah's perception of things but were coming instead from the secular society around me. My *rebbi* introduced me to the Yid within me. He taught me that I am a Jew with innate spiritual capacity and, as such, have some awesome responsibilities. With those responsibilities, of course, came parallel opportunities to live up to them.

Rav Wolbe's answering smile to my expression of gratitude was enough for me to know that he agreed with my evaluation of my previous mindset. Or, perhaps, he smiled because he thought I still had a lot to find out; I am not quite sure.

It is clear to me that the broader society in which we are raising our *frum* children is bombarding them on all sides with the evils of computers, internet, portable devices, smartphones, and much else, in a way that's difficult to avoid. This makes the challenge of educating our children today an awesome task. The fact that many in our community are connected to externals—and have forgotten or are unaware of the beauty and essence of the lives they are living—does not change that truth or splendor by one iota. It is important to bear this in mind!

When the initial decision to change your life was made, you were living in a society where no one else was aware of the *emes*. The exciting part of being where you are now, despite all these challenges, is that you have a chance to educate *your* children properly, to be a builder on whatever level you can. You have the ability to affect and change your life as well as those of your friends and neighbors.

If you identify with what I am saying, you can consider this a call to you, my brothers and sisters who have made life-altering decisions, to rise now to the challenge and become builders! You, who saw the power of *emes*, now have the opportunity to reconnect to it years later and carry the fire that was once lit in your hearts to others.

And to those of you who feel that this call is unrealistic and demands more than is possible, I offer two options:

1. Recognize the amazing journey you have made, which places you at the forefront of mankind.

2. Connect yourself with builders, making sure that you are there to help and support them in any way you can.

Chapter 6
Overcoming Challenges

The following are some of the common challenges faced by *baalei teshuvah* after having made quantum changes in their lives. Although several might be more pronounced or acute in some communities, we will deal with those that are universal. Examining them from a realistic perspective is imperative if you wish your life to run smoothly, so we will identify and attempt to understand the problems. In this chapter we will analyze the challenge of "pull," or influence (otherwise known as *protektzia*), the challenge of elitism, and the nonacceptance of the "other" in our school and *shidduch* systems. It is sad to say, but unfortunately true, that in some of our institutions in the bigger cities a *baal teshuvah* could still be considered an "outsider" or "other."

The Challenge of Protektzia

Professor Moshe Mandelbaum was the Governor of the Bank of Israel from 1982 to 1986. I met him while acting as an agent for my father and enjoyed our conversations. While discussing the challenges of doing business in Israel, he turned to me and said candidly, "You know what I like about doing business in Israel? If you know the right people, you don't need *protektzia!*"

Because the Jewish People lived for hundreds of years in the European ghetto culture, there exists among us a *shtiebel* (small shul) mentality. It might be a byproduct of a people that was fighting for its survival, where you had to be "connected" in order to get things done, or perhaps it's this way in the whole world. It is not a secret that political goals in America and Europe are not exactly attained by straightforward means at all times. It is often not what you know, but who you know that counts. In every country the world over, all men are *not* treated equally.

In the political arena, that is only to be expected, but one would hope that this practice does not extend to a world that teaches us to deal in *emes*. In our educational and community arenas, which are so reflective of the high standards of their builders, we would have hoped that this mentality would not prevail. Yet, as even very good people move up into the "higher echelons" of society, they are presented with a difficult challenge. Not everyone can avoid using the influence he now has when power plays a main role in every part of society. It is disturbing and painful that *protektzia* is most needed and least practiced by those of us who do not wield it.

In all honesty, *protektzia* is not disturbing to most of us because of the lack of integrity, but because that is the way the world works—and feeling that we are not receiving what is due to us is painful. We resent the fact that those who receive special treatment really seem to have the advantage, and none of us wants to be at a disadvantage.

What Can Influence Do for Us?

Although it is true that *protektzia* can achieve a lot, it does not necessarily result in the acceptance you really want. Nor does it mean that what you get is good for you.

Let us imagine for a minute that we are simple Jews without influence. Let us be *maaminim b'nei maaminim*, believers and descendants of believers, with deep trust in Hashem. We see that one who is well-connected receives certain benefits that we do not, but would they be beneficial to *us*? Would they ensure the achievement of our goals, or confirm whether we've "made it" or not?

It is true, for example, that well-connected people have their children accepted in the better schools, but it does not necessarily follow that those children will do better than others. As one who for many years has dealt with children who are not doing well in school, I would like to share something important with you.

Among those who have the hardest time in school (and sometimes outside school as well) are the children of the best-connected people. Although they are admitted into the most exclusive schools and obtain the best jobs, parental influence cannot guarantee that these children will do well. "Pull" assures them of neither happiness nor success. Acceptance into certain "top" schools may not even be suitable for those who might thrive in a less demanding structure.

When we are at the bottom of the barrel looking out at the world, and we see children not as capable or smart as ours, or someone far less qualified than we, landing a coveted position, we have to wonder. We know that we could probably do the job better, but the other person is connected. One-upmanship that can be achieved through unfair means, however, is not necessarily a rung on the ladder to success. Success, whether in school or life, is achieved through the efforts we put in, the challenges we rise to meet, and the obstacles we overcome despite their difficulties. Those who go forward with simplicity and integrity, doing what they know to be right, generally have more success with their children than those with fancy connections.

Most trouble in life comes from envy, which can work both ways. Those with influence who are envious of the great kids their uncon-nected neighbors have, or the ordinary guy who wishes he had the connections of his wealthier neighbor, are the ones with real problems. Trouble comes when we are not satisfied with what we have; it does not come from a lack of connections. *Protektzia* can be a double-edged sword. It gives people access to places and material things that they may not need or really want, will not satisfy them, and most often, will not even be good for them.

I know of many cases where children were accepted into good schools as a result of their parents' connections instead of their own efforts and achievements, and did poorly later in life. As they never had to strive to attain an important goal, they never learned what it means to work hard to achieve something. In the end, most of their achievements were not truly theirs because they did not reach them on their own. Even those who did not fail dismally in school (unfortunately, many of them did), and many of those who managed to get through that yeshiva with passing marks, will have a hard time getting through real life.

When these same coddled kids are facing marriage, raising children, and all the challenges that life holds after yeshiva, they may well find that they have not acquired the tools they need. Until now, their way was paved for them, but that kind of assistance does not last forever. They wake up one day and suddenly find that they are on their own. They have a wife to consider, they have children for whom they are responsible, they have *parnassah*, earning a livelihood, to deal with, and they do not have the tools to cope because they have never been challenged to grow.

When we look around, therefore, and see the people who make things happen and think that their children are better off than ours, we must look to the One Above, thanking Him that our children are attending schools not only where they belong, but where they can and will work hard to achieve. When we are happy with their progress, speak highly of the schools and their ability to help their students do well, and appreciate our children instead of criticizing them, they learn to accept their positions in life and rejoice in them.

Challenges of the School System

Let me first say that I am not out to knock our religious school system. Any criticism I may voice is intended to be purely constructive. Being very much an integral part of that system myself, I hope that my words will be understood as pointers to improvement and positive changes, and not to denigration.

I am also a parent, and as educated consumers we need to know what to look for when dealing with the system. We encounter many problems in the religious world as a whole and its school system in particular, as an element of the entire structure. There's no denying that our problems range from not having enough space for children to play at recess to the unavoidably large size of classes; from the often-serious lack of professionalism in young teachers to the manner in which problematic issues are dealt with; from the way rules are made to the structure of the system itself.

In this matter, too, I believe that some historical background will provide our comments with a more realistic and firmer grounding. The following true story is a good beginning.

> *In 1953, a young man who was learning in Yeshiva Torah Vodaath received a phone call before Pesach from the principal of one of the three frum girls' high schools in New York. (Yes, there were only three religious girls' high schools in New York then, with fewer than three hundred students all told.)*
>
> *"We just lost our tenth-grade math teacher for the fifth time," the principal said, "and we cannot find anyone to replace him. It is a rowdy class. You've been a head counselor and have charisma. We need you to teach two periods a day."*
>
> *"I am an unmarried bachur," the young man responded.*
>
> *"I know," the principal said.*
>
> *"I am nineteen years old!"*
>
> *"Yes, I know," the principal replied calmly.*
>
> *"How can I possibly agree to take the job?"*
>
> *"Well, we will pay you ten dollars a week plus carfare."*
>
> *The young man was working as a caterer's assistant several nights a week, as his parents were impoverished immigrants and he preferred to do without things he needed rather than ask them for money. The salary from the school would be very helpful. He decided to try it for two weeks and earn enough that he would not have to work at night for a while and would be able to sit and learn. It sounded good.*
>
> *"Oh, no!" said the principal. "You have to make a commitment right now to teach until the end of the year. This cannot be a trial. You take on the full job or you don't get it."*
>
> *It was an offer the young man could not refuse.*

Just imagine a nineteen-year-old boy from Torah Vodaath being called down by one of the many Bais Yaakov schools in New York today! The school would be closed (if not burned down); there would be posters plastered all over the neighborhood and beyond, and the principal, of course, would be history. A demonstration in Meah Shearim would look small in comparison. All of New York would be on fire.

Fifty-five years ago in New York, there were simply no knowledgeable religious schoolteachers available. Although it does not seem like so long ago, the religious educational scene for girls was almost entirely blank. There were no trained teachers, no girls graduating from seminary. It is difficult to comprehend today when we take it for granted that between two thousand and three thousand young women graduate seminaries every year.

RJJ (Yeshiva Rav Yaakov Yosef), on Manhattan's East Side, was one of the largest yeshiva day schools in existence at the time. My cousin learned under *rebbeim* there who were not Shabbos observers. These men taught Gemara because there was no one else available. The yeshiva in Lakewood was not producing two thousand students a year as it does now. If you needed someone to teach Gemara, you had to find someone who had once learned it. In most cases the only men available who were capable of teaching it were survivors of the death camps, many no longer *shomrei Shabbos*. They had left the camps angry and embittered, having lost their faith along with everything else, but they knew how to learn. With notable exceptions, it was mainly these men who taught in the Brooklyn and Manhattan yeshivas in those days.

When we examine a school system that now has, *baruch Hashem*, tens of thousands of students, we have to take this rapid growth into consideration before we can criticize.

When we first opened up Darchei Shalom in Eretz Yisrael in 1989,[1] we did a statistical study with the help of the Jerusalem municipality. We looked into the four-year-olds who were registered in kindergarten

---

1   A yeshiva high school for intelligent boys who needed more than the generally accepted forms of mental stimulation and intellectual motivation to facilitate their success in a school environment. The curriculum included afternoon workshops in computers, electronics, carpentry, photography, gardening, and the like.

and would be going into pre-1A for the upcoming year, 1990, and the numbers of children who would be graduating from eighth grade in the same year. I shared this information with a friend who is a physicist and mathematician.

He looked at the numbers incredulously and said, "This is what happened in Egypt, the kind of geometric population growth described in the Torah as miraculous and beyond the norm. You are talking about above and beyond a 10 percent growth per year, which is almost impossible."

"I did not make this up," I answered defensively. "These are the statistics from the municipal records." The statistics showed more than *three times* the number of children going into pre-1A than those who were finishing eighth grade that year.

We must be aware of all this when we look at our yeshiva and Bais Yaakov educational system today and realize that we are looking at a miraculous regeneration. We are witnessing a phenomenon that has no explanation except the Heavenly assistance that was granted to the builders we mentioned earlier. With tremendous selfless devotion, vision, energy, and creativity, they achieved the impossible. In the spiritual deserts that existed on every continent, new schools and institutions have blossomed thanks to those who dedicated their lives to building Yiddishkeit. Recognizing this will help mitigate our criticism and help us understand and appreciate why things are still far from perfect.

We, in our generation, are the children and grandchildren either of those pioneers or of those who stood by and watched them build (hopefully, not of those who stood by and criticized while the others gave their lives for this ideal!). Our generation is accustomed to having numerous day schools (and even more numerous pizza shops) in every city where there is a large Jewish population. We have high expectations.

"The schools are terrible," we say. "Look at how many problems there are." Yes, it's true that there are problems. That is only to be expected when, as we have shown, geometrical expansion occurs in the space of only fifty years. During that time, an almost total absence of Jewish schools mushroomed into a huge system with hundreds of components. Of course, there will be problems.

Just one of the current issues we have to deal with is the employment of teachers/*rebbeim* who have not been sufficiently or properly trained to handle the countless and varied needs of this enormous spectrum of students. Although various stages of training are taking place in most seminaries and in a few yeshivos, we are still far from where we need to be. We must not ignore the blessing of these small beginnings, but neither can we sit back and accept the status quo. Anything we can do to further the training and skills of our teachers and principals should be initiated.

Another enormous obstacle to improving our children's education is the financial burden of opening school after school with no governmental support. We are deeply indebted to the scores of generous Jews who contribute with unbelievable goodwill and commitment year after year to help the escalating needs of our community. How can we expect experienced teachers and educators to remain in *chinuch* if the average salary in a yeshiva day school is half of that in a public school? Why should we expect the most talented, charismatic, and capable people in our community to consider such a career if we, the community, do not make it our priority?

If we remain mere spectators, expecting things to improve unaided, our schools will not reach their potential. We need to recognize our responsibility for our children's education and become builders ourselves. It may seem like a small thing, but if we will all pay tuition without griping, and go a bit out of our way to encourage our underpaid principals and teachers, it will be a beginning. Our teachers are for the most part extraordinarily idealistic, dedicated, and responsible individuals who remain in their jobs despite their ability to choose much higher-paying professions. There are, of course, others who are none of the above but cannot find any other employment.

Along with the establishment of parallel schools in a community comes a need for more teachers, more funding, and the unfortunate negative phenomenon of competition. While the Mishnah lauded the competition of parallel schools,[2] at that time it merely made teachers work harder to teach more effectively so that Torah would be better understood. Today, such rivalry often sidetracks parents and principals, who lose sight of the true focus and goals of our educational system.

Some of our schools have even lost the spirit of the love of Torah, the enjoyment of life, and concern for mitzvos, which are essential components of teaching Torah. They place their entire emphasis on academic excellence and students who conform to one mold. This seems to have become the driving force of many schools, along with the tendency to see the "good" child as the one who conforms.

In this struggle to be the "best," we have lost some of the warmth and humanity that should always be a part of our educational experience. We sometimes forget just whom we are educating and the most effective ways to educate them. Instead of becoming better teachers, learning how best to deal with differing levels of scholarship, we have created better filters to make sure that we accept only "top" students.

With gratitude to Hashem, however, I believe that we are seeing a re-awakening of this important concern in our classrooms. Many schools are learning to help students who have difficulty keeping up, and there are more people working in mainstream schools who are sensitive to this issue. More schools are accepting the need for a school psychologist, a resource room, and a social worker.

P'tach, for example, an adjunct in-school resource organization that helps a child with learning and/or emotional disabilities to function within the school, is becoming more and more accepted. These are changes for the good that are a result of the fact that the *frum* community as a whole wants to do what is right. That still leaves us with the apparently insurmountable impediment of geometric growth.

This factor forces us to deal with real challenges. We parents have a choice: to complain and be upset at the school system's imperfections, or understand where it is being held back and think about how we can be of assistance.

2　*Bava Basra* 22a.

One way in which we can be helpful is to try to compensate when necessary. While the schools are trying to devise better methods of responding to the new issues that confront them, parents can encourage rather than criticize. We can choose schools wisely for our children when there is a selection available. When there are no choices, we can be proactive and seek outside help as required, seeking out the professionals and dedicated people in education to help build whatever support systems are needed within, or in addition to, the school framework.

The Matter of Shidduchim

Another topic of great challenge both to us and our children is the matter of *shidduchim*. How and why does matchmaking work? Can we actually turn this chapter of our lives into a beneficial tool, rather than view it as a difficult and frustrating period in our lives?

The Torah way of introducing couples is not in consonance with the ways of the rest of the world. It is interesting to note, however, that there is a movement today in both Jewish and gentile nonreligious circles mimicking the *shidduch* process. Instead of waiting for couples to meet serendipitously, organizations and some very successful business groups are attempting to create forums with facilitators to assist men and women to meet suitable partners. This attempt to gather and process information about a potential mate is actually an astonishing growth industry in cyberspace. Its focus is to make reasonable matches instead of singles just wandering the world, hoping to bump into that special somebody.

Our way is light years ahead of this cyber fad. The *shidduch* procedure is a process that we must learn to understand thoroughly if we want to see our children through it, especially if we haven't gone through it ourselves.

———————

Having married off twelve children so far, with the immense help of Hakadosh Baruch Hu, I can say unequivocally that the whole *shidduch* process is beyond my comprehension. Among the *shidduchim* suggested to us were some families who were interested in meeting our children and some who preferred not to. There were families in which we were interested, and others that we preferred to avoid. We sought a different type of family or candidate for each child, as each person needs a different type of life partner. It is only through *tefillah*, prayer, that we can hope for Hashem's help in this improbable and inscrutable process.

In addition to *tefillah*, we have the obligation to attempt to understand both what is good for each child and for us as a family, with a very clear and focused emphasis on what will be best for our children.

The first step, therefore, is to discuss the subject seriously with them. Allow them to clarify and define the elements they deem most nonnegotiable. Are you on the same page? Do you understand and respect that which is important to them?

Many of us forget that we made very big decisions when we were about nineteen or twenty years old. Some of those choices were good ones, and at times we made mistakes. Although it seems a virtue to take care of our children to make sure they do not take any missteps, taking this too far would inherently be the greatest error. We must be sensitive to the values and decisions that our children are making at the same age we made ours.

These discussions should be followed by searching, networking, and asking many questions to ascertain that the proposed *shidduch* will fit the desired description. We must be honest with each other in defining our needs, and we must also be confident in our convictions to follow through when appropriate.

If the other party rejects the *shidduch* after all the phone calls and verification because of their concerns about their future grandchildren's great-grandfather or great-uncle, you may feel hurt and rejected. In reality, what they are doing is defining what it is that *they* feel they need. Instead of regarding their behavior as offensive and feeling insulted, try to understand that you were saved from an incompatible match. Their negative attitude is giving you vital information about that family. What they said and the way in which they reacted are real indications of character.

I have heard people ask, "Why were we rejected? I do everything I can. We are raising a *Torahdik* family. It is true that my parents and grandparents are not like the children I am raising, but just look at my wonderful kids. Are there really people who will turn them down because of my background or my parents' degree of observance?"

My answer to this question is *yes!* Thank your lucky stars that they said no before the engagement. Be thankful that your children will *not* be part of a family that will not respect their personal integrity and achievements. Such an attitude ignores your children's efforts and successes and focuses instead on aspects of their lives over which they have no control. You wouldn't want your child to be part of a family that looks at things superficially, not considering an individual's merits and shortcomings. Every *shidduch* bears myriad elements of Hashem's Divine providence, an important part of the selection process that matches our loved ones to the partners with whom they will build their homes.

I am aware that this reality is a bit difficult to swallow.

We had a wonderful student in our seminary a number of years ago who was blind. She successfully completed elementary and high school, and when all her friends applied to seminary, she did too. It was a privilege and a pleasure to accept her into our school, and she sailed through her studies beautifully. At the end of the year, she came into my office to discuss the challenge that lay in her path. She sat down in front of my desk and asked, "Who is going to marry me?"

"Most boys will not be interested," I answered frankly. "Probably ninety-nine percent will not even consider the *shidduch*. But you are not marrying ninety-nine percent of the candidates. You only want, with Hashem's help, to get married once, to one person. All you need is one prospective husband, so that fact alone will spare you a large part of the agony of the elimination process that many of your friends will have to go through.

"It stands to reason," I continued, "that if a girl is short, pretty, and of mediocre ability, she can consider just about anybody. If she is extremely tall, she already has a limitation; if she is extremely bright, she is also limited. You will have a very small selection, but there will assuredly be someone who, for some reason, will not be bothered by your limitation. I have no explanation for this, but you will meet a young man of remarkable character who is going to be able to see you for the extraordinary person that you are. He will be the one you will marry."

Sure enough, a year went by and then two years and three. One friend was engaged and then another and another. Every once in a while, she would contact me, and I would repeat, "You know that many of your friends are still not married, and they've met so many young men that they are already sick of the process. They do not even want to go out on any more *shidduch* dates, and that is **their** *nisayon*, challenge. You did not have to go through that; your *nisayon* is different."

Today, *baruch Hashem*, she is happily married to a fine, sighted young man, who learned in an excellent yeshiva and has wonderful *middos*. We have had the pleasure of their delightful company at our Shabbos table on numerous occasions, and rejoiced upon hearing that they were blessed with a healthy child.

There is, of course, no guarantee that every girl or boy will find a mate within any definite period of time. Some will have to endure greater challenges than others, and there are some, unfortunately, who will have to make their peace with not having their hopes and dreams fulfilled.

Although it entails great *emunah* and *bitachon*, you should not fight your situation. You need not hide your past, nor should you try to beat the system. You are who you are, and Hashem will bring you the *shidduch* you need and deserve. Trust in Him and daven profusely, because ultimately, He is the One Who brings us our other half at the time that is right. It is not difficult to understand why Rav Wolbe quoted these words of the Chazon Ish:[3] "The greatest effort in *shidduchim* is davening."

No one really understands how and why we come to our decisions in the matter of *shidduchim*, why we choose this one and not the other. Many people say, "If I had known that he/she was older/younger, taller/

---

3   Rav Avraham Yeshayah Karelitz, a primarily Litvishe Torah scholar and leader in Eretz Yisrael during the first half of the twentieth century, and author of monumental works of halachah called *Chazon Ish*, which then became his identifying name.

shorter before we met, I would not have even considered the *shidduch*, but once we met and clicked, the point was moot and now it makes no difference." And it truly does not matter, because that was the *shidduch* that was intended. He or she was exactly the person the other one needed.

I received a phone call from a father who asked me a very specific question about a former student. For some inexplicable reason I did not catch the family name and thought he was talking about a girl who had studied in my school four or five years previously. I gave a beautiful report of the girl and her background. When he asked the one question that he had thought might be an issue, it was very clear to me that he was mistaken in regard to this particular girl. I told him that he could be completely calm about it, there was no problem. The couple had already met a number of times and it was very clear that they were close to closing. I did not hear the man's name either, but I was very comfortable with our conversation.

The next day the man's wife called me and said, "You know, my husband went over his conversation with you, and he mentioned two things that do not make sense. Are you sure you were talking about [and she gave me the girl's name again], because you mentioned that you have kept a close connection to this young lady over the past few years and this girl who we are discussing was in your school last year."

This time I heard the last name clearly and hastened to confess my mistake. "Oh my," I said. "I am so sorry. Such a thing has never happened to me before!"

"That's all right. We are really quite close to finishing, and we have only some minor concerns, so let me ask you just two or three questions."

Thankfully, I was able to answer her in an honest and positive manner. When the conversation had concluded, I realized that she had not asked me the one specific question that had

*concerned her husband. I would have been able to give her an
acceptable answer, but not with the same confidence as with
the other questions.*

Why, after realizing that I had made a mistake, she did not repeat
her husband's question, is just as puzzling as why I hadn't heard right
the first time. A week or two later, I understood. The couple became
engaged, and so obviously Hashem had planned the whole mix-up. The
question was really minor in terms of affecting their decision to marry,
but it certainly might have put off their continuing to date before things
became clear. *Baruch Hashem*, this couple is doing well.

What caused this strange chain of events? Perhaps Hakadosh Baruch
Hu caused it because He knew that if I had answered this question the
day before, they would have broken off the *shidduch*, and a beautiful
family might not be around today. I had no way of correcting my initial
information, as I did not know the name or number of the people who
had called.

There are thousands of similar stories occurring in the world of *shidduchim* every day, which should indicate pretty clearly that we should
not feel rejected if a *shidduch* is refused by the other party. We need this
elimination process to give us an idea of the values and identity of the
other side. It is all part of *hashgachah pratis*, His Divine plan, an integral
component of the system. *Hashgachah pratis* goes hand in hand with
hishtadlus, our own efforts to do the right thing.

"Last night I received a letter asking me my opinion of Moshe *Ploni* in
regard to a *shidduch*," an individual once said to the *Chasam Sofer*. Now
I know that everyone in our community dislikes him and thinks that he
is terrible, but he happens to be my best friend and I think he is a wonderful fellow. How should I respond to the man who wrote me the letter?"

"If Hashem caused that fellow to call upon the one person in the whole
town who is his best friend," the sage replied, "then He wants you to
tell him how *you* feel about this person. He could have done research by

speaking to anyone else and probably received a different answer, but he reached out to *you* so that you should tell him the truth as you know it."

Even when we think that we are aware of all there is to know about a proposed *shidduch*, we can never *really* know. It is nevertheless our responsibility to do our best to seek information. We must check into as many aspects of the suggested person as we can, knowing that the best *hishtadlus*, as the Chazon Ish said, remains *tefillah*!

Money Matters—Money MATTERS!

Finances are another challenging aspect of the *shidduch* system. Many young men today have expectations that are far from reasonable. Some *roshei yeshiva* take the position that it is necessary to support a young man for a certain number of years, and this burden seems to fall mostly on the father-in-law-to-be. Parents who were raised in other milieus often find it difficult to integrate this kind of thinking.

In the secular world, the feeling is that once children finish college and/or marry, they should be financially independent. While education is important enough to those parents that they will support their children through college, they do so with a specific goal in mind: a degree that will ensure financial independence. The rationale is: no degree, no future. If education equals financial gain, then studying without the outcome that provides for one's family does not cut it.

This is even more confusing for many people who have no serious learning experience or have not had at least some intense contact with *talmidei chachamim*, Torah scholars. It does not mean that they do not respect Torah, but there will understandably be a lower appreciation of the value of Torah learning.

To understand the merit of young people learning Torah after their marriage, consider that our generation faces awesome spiritual challenges that require tremendous fortitude and commitment. Educators and rabbis from all strata of the Orthodox world, including those who thirty years ago thought little of the *kollel* system, are establishing *kollelim* for their married students. Clearly, our young people need those extra years of learning to establish themselves in their marriages and lives. Those with greater aspirations require even more years of study to grow and develop into the next generation of teachers and leaders. While we all know that not everyone will undertake roles in education and community leadership, it is almost universally understood within the Chareidi community that many couples will at least begin their marriage in the framework of learning Torah.

When you are involved in this aspect of *shidduchim*, it is necessary to sit down with your children and try to come to an understanding of their hopes, dreams and expectations. They may think that you can do more financially than you can, or they may not realize what you are willing to do for them. You may be on the same page; you may be on very different pages. Do not take anything for granted.

Without discussing this issue with them, you really don't know where you stand. Try to discover if they comprehend what is meaningful to them and why. See if there is a way to make things work. Many of my friends have found that their children had really thought things through and had a clear picture of their preferences and what they were willing to do to achieve them. Others were surprised at how unclear and confused their adult children were about marriage and what sort of life they really wanted.

The world around us changes, and it is urgent that we be flexible. We are at the beginning of a transitional period in terms of *shidduchim*, but this transition will likely take many years to unfold. The *shidduch* process today sometimes resembles a marketplace. There are "prices" and expectations. In America they are translated into years of support; in Eretz Yisrael, apartments; in both, it is a ridiculously unsustainable situation. Ideally, I would like to make a call for change, a cry for everyone to agree to just stop the madness. However, while it is quite obvious to me that this book and its readers will not spearhead this change, we most certainly may take advantage of the slowly changing environment.

If you have the means to buy into the system and you feel that you are getting value for your investment, you most certainly have the right to do so. However, if you are like most people today, there is little chance that you can afford the astronomical expectations so often presented. Do not be afraid to face your limitations while offering all that you can to help, because you love your children and will do anything possible for them—with the emphasis on "possible." We will extend ourselves for our children, but we must do so responsibly.

In this respect, we may be feeling helpless once again as we watch those who have better financial means being sought as *shidduch* partners. Once again, we need to draw from the faith and trust that brought us to this place in our lives and add to those sometimes elusive resources some common sense as well. There are thousands of poor couples getting married in our communities every year. Their parents are realistic as to their abilities and limitations and have raised their children to be aware of this. These boys went to the same yeshivos as the others, heard the same *rosh yeshiva* lay down the rules of the world, but they married within their reach. The Gemara says explicitly, when "looking for a wife, step down a grade,"[4] so that you can meet her expectations and needs.

There are, of course, exceptions to this rule, such as wealthy couples who are looking for the next Torah leader, or people whose love and respect for Torah is so great that they are willing to give everything they have in order to have their daughter marry a genuine *talmid chacham*. In such cases it is understood that the young man is not going to be the one providing his wife with the physical conveniences of life, but rather the spiritual amenities. When people are more devoted to a concern for the World to Come than to the comforts of this world, and their daughter shares those values, then there is room for an exception.

When we complain about unreasonable expectations, let's stop and consider if we *want* those boys to marry our daughters. Young men who are deeply devoted to learning do not need so much; they are happy in the *beis midrash*, study hall. Boys who demand a high level of support might be demanding in more ways than you'd like to consider. There are boys who expect nothing, yet merit everything we have to give. There

---

4   *Yevamos* 63a.

are others who expect everything, and although we do not have it—and at times wonder if they deserve it—we feel we must give in.

Today a balance can be struck by knowing that, indeed, there are more of us who do not have extraordinary means than those who have. This allows us to speak up and ask for the mensch, the moral young man who does not want his in-laws and parents to go into debt to support him. I believe that when most people are in the same boat, the young man who feels entitled is not the giving, loving spouse we are looking for anyway. If I, as a parent or in-law, can afford to do more than the minimum for my children, I can choose to do so. I may even decide to take on reasonable loans to help my children achieve that which they strongly feel they need.

The key word is "prerogative." We have the right to decide what we can and cannot do, as well as what we want and do not want to do. There are people who look for families with money; that's their prerogative. We want to help our children; we do not want to harm ourselves or our families. Be generous, be supportive, but live responsibly within your means.

———————

Reaching the stage of seeking *shidduchim* for our children is a good time to take stock of what we are looking for in life—what we really want and why we want it. We must try to see the true motivating factors in our desire to be accepted in a specific type of society. Are we looking for a particular type of family because we think it will make us feel more accepted? If that kind of thinking is guiding us, I have to say that it is very desirable to retain simplicity throughout the process. Our attitude should be that our offspring will find those worthy of them because the Ribbono shel Olam takes care of our children.

We should be looking for the one who is going to appreciate our children for who they are. We will run into trouble if we are looking to achieve status, or something elusive that we do not necessarily need but want. Do not become blinded by the dazzle of what seems like really "making it" when a family we regard as "in" accepts us. Maybe there is something that is not above board. Look beneath the surface and ask just as many, if not more, questions than you would about any ordinary family. The *shidduch* process of asking and checking forces us to define what we really seek, and we must go through a careful process of elimination no matter who the future in-laws will be. In the end we want a match that is good for our child. For that we need, as I have stressed, *emunah* and *bitachon*.

———————

I would like to cap this discussion with a short anecdote.

"I married off ten children," a friend of mine once told me, "and it is clear to me that Hashem did not help me with a single one of the *shidduchim*."

I looked at him as if he had just fallen from the moon.

He shook his head forcefully and repeated, "I am telling you, He did not *help* me with a single *shidduch*…He did them all completely on His own!"

Chapter 7

Challenges with Our Children and Society

The necessity of maintaining open, honest communication with our children cannot be overemphasized. The basic mechanics of successful communication will be addressed in chapter 15, but at this point we will focus on it in relation to two common difficulties that affect those who have made major changes in their lives.

The first occurs when parents try to hide their past. Your son or daughter's résumé should be informative, not concealing. While there are some people who will be less inclined to date *baalei teshuvah*, there are those who have respect and admiration for people who have undergone such a serious process of introspection and change. Either way, you have nothing to hide. You are only interested in finding a spouse for your child who will embrace that child, including the child's entire story. This does not mean that you need to write in block letters "parents: *baalei teshuvah*" but when meeting *shadchanim* and sharing information with others, it is prudent to share background information.

The second crops up when parents do not understand what their children who are of dating age are experiencing because of the vast dissimilarity between their personal courting and dating experience and that of their children.

This is not something to sweep under the rug. Many young people feel lost and afraid during the *shidduch* process, which is daunting enough without these added difficulties. They find their parents clueless about what they, the children, want and what is considered normal in the community in which they have been raised. They consequently feel that they are not getting the proper direction.

Open communication between you and your children will allow you to lay their fears to rest. Find a *rav* or *rebbi* whose guidance you both accept so that they can feel confident that you are looking for the kind of boy or girl your child seeks.

The need to investigate is often not understood by people who courted their way to marriage. The *shidduch* process assumes at its core that the parents will do all the necessary investigations and clarifications as to how compatible this young man will be for their daughter. Because every *shidduch* is somewhat of a shot in the dark, and the dating process is focused to measure that compatibility, the questions are meant to filter the possibilities and come to the best option. For your children, lack of investigation is basically a "blind date," and blind dating is not a focused meeting with the intent of finding a marriage partner.

When investigating a *shidduch* candidate, ask specific but open-ended questions that will require the responder to address any concerns about the character traits and values most important to you and your child.

"How does the person react when upset?" "Does s/he lose her/his temper easily?" "Please describe the person." Do you hear the source saying that he or she is generous, caring or patient, etc.? If not, ask directly, "Is he kind and considerate?" His intelligence might be important to you and learning might be paramount, but as your daughter's parent, it is important to hear that he is responsible and will take care of her needs. Do not be afraid to seek the answers your child needs to hear.

Many of my colleagues in *chinuch* today are in close touch with their students during this process without the knowledge of the parents, who have not had the good sense or sufficient awareness to understand their children regarding this challenging process. Young men and women should not feel that they must get outside help gathering information about a suggested *shidduch* because their parents simply don't know what to do.

On the other hand, many educators get frequent calls from parents who are involved in *shidduchim* for the first time and are asking for direction.

Parents should use every tool available to acquire information, and the boy's *rebbi* or the girl's teacher is often the right address to ask for help in gathering more information. When parents work together with their children, confidence and trust are established, and the probability of having a continuing good relationship in the future is increased manifold.

If you are not communicating well enough to know what your children are thinking, or you do know what they are thinking but cannot maintain a dialogue with them, seek a mediator from the community, their school, or a relative whose opinion they respect. We do not control everything anyway. Knowing when to allow someone else to be involved and when to ask for advice is extremely important, not only in the *shidduch* process but in life in general.

> *When Victor began his journey toward religious life in Hungary, he never dreamed that the day would come when Brachah, his second of seven children, would be one of the most respected girls in her Bais Yaakov. He was a dedicated, hardworking man, an overachiever with a serious commitment to integrity. When his daughter came home from seminary speaking about her desire to marry a boy who would become a talmid chacham and a link in the chain of the transmission of the Torah, he looked at her in disbelief.*
>
> *"Over my dead body will you marry an idle parasite!"*
>
> *Brachah tearfully tried to explain her position, to no avail. Victor, now called Chaim, had worked hard all his life and could not understand why he should be expected to help support his son-in-law in learning when he had always assumed that his daughter would want someone like himself. The two were so far apart that every discussion ended in anger and frustration.*
>
> *By the time I became involved, Brachah had told her parents that she did not expect any support after the wedding. She would find someone who would not ask for support, but at least she wanted her parents to help her find the kind of inspired,*

dedicated, responsible boy that she sought. Her father was adamant that he would not allow her to marry "another one of those unmotivated young men who was just learning because it was in style and besides, the whole system was ridiculous, etc. His daughters would marry professionals who would contribute to society..."

While she was my student, Brachah and I had had a couple of productive and comfortable conversations. When I suggested that she ask her father if we could discuss the situation together, she did so happily, and Chaim complied.

Our discussion began with the difficulty of raising children in a world so different from our own. Chaim, an Eastern European baal teshuvah who had never learned in a yeshiva, is nevertheless a dedicated observant Jew who goes to a shiur every day at 5:30 a.m. and studies from three sefarim, volumes of Torah, daily.

Brachah was born and raised in Monsey, New York, went to the best schools, and has a slew of friends who are all headed in the same direction. She had never once discussed anything of meaning or purpose with her father, who is so...different. Chaim, who worked to build and support a family for Torah and Hashem, has no rav and no direction other than his common sense and integrity. Brachah was filled with desire and ambition to take the next generation to higher inspiration and closeness to Hashem. Chaim looked at his daughter as superficial and spoiled; Brachah saw her father as ignorant and unable to understand. They were both mistaken.

I explained to Chaim that many young people in our generation are indeed superficial, but that his daughter was not one of them. Her presentation seemed that way to him, but only because he did not understand what she was fighting against in her social crowd, where the use of labels and superficial descriptions were rampant. Her aspirations to find a husband who truly wished to be a link in Torah education for the next generation were sincere. He would have to be one of those very special young men with real and meaningful dedication. How could he become the talmid chacham he needed to be in order to teach other young men, if he himself would not learn for a number of years?

I told Brachah that her father was a holy Jew who had done much more for her Yiddishkeit than anything she had done for herself. It was important for her to understand that her father's dedication to her education was what had given her whatever appreciation she had developed, and that his sensitivities were due to lack of experience. When he would meet the quality ben Torah she sought, all would be fine.

From that mediation were born two couples, Brachah and her younger sister, who have the enthusiastic support of a very appreciative Jew who loves and respects his sons-in-law. These two young men, who each spent serious time in *kollel* with the help of their dedicated spouses and a proud father-in-law, now work hard to support their families, each in his own way.

When you are faced with the differences that will invariably arise between your worldview or your perception of the Torah world and your child's regarding *shidduchim*, it is imperative that you invest in understanding your child's world. This can happen in either direction. Some children will choose to fully engage in the school you chose for them and decide that they want a "higher standard" than you raised them with. Others might feel that you went extreme, and they are looking for something less intense. Either way, there is a connection between your life decisions and the decisions of your children. When wanting to help our children find their spouse, we need to make sure we are taking their hopes and dreams as the lead. If there are elements that are important to you, they have to blend with that which is important to them. I have seen unbelievable blends of people that perfectly fit the dreams of parents and children alike.

The Challenge of Black and White

The next challenge we will talk about is the world of black and white, and we are not only referring to clothing. At first glance, the *frum* world appears to comprise radically different components, as people seem to gravitate toward absolutes in their behavior, choices, and judgments. With a bit more scrutiny, though, as when consulting with a graphic artist, it becomes obvious that even black and white are relative: there are about two hundred shades of gray!

While not everything is as black or white as it appears, our community seems to be drawn to extremes on certain issues that are the most visual, although not necessarily the most significant, ideals in life. There are other essential values as well, such as priorities in education, which are often decided on the basis of superficial absolutes like clothing and reputation or status.

When you have made great changes in your life, you may find some of those absolutes untenable. You have already carefully evaluated your goals, and it wasn't easy.

Although you accepted a working system, there may be some aspects of it that are still not perfectly clear right now, mainly because the structure itself is not totally integrated. There are facets of the community that have taken on a disproportionate place in your value system, like the aforementioned dress code. In addition, because of your metamorphosing development, you are often still dealing in gray areas that require leaps of faith.

> *Sandy, for most of her teen and early adult years, would have a couple of bottles of beer on Saturday nights. After three years into the process of accepting the mitzvos, she could still not see herself giving up the brew, but convinced herself that she did not need it anymore when she wanted to marry a religious man. Five years later, she found herself joining the men for a beer after the Friday night meal. Her husband didn't mind too much, but she worried that in a few more years her child would not understand why she was doing this.*

Sometimes, we too retain elements of our pasts that our children will find difficult to integrate into their lives. These could be the pursuit of major sports activities like skiing and team rowing, or certain arts like acting, moviemaking, or enjoying divergent types of music.

Let's say you went to college, studied a profession, and were on the wrestling team. A few years later you took the leap, enrolled in a yeshiva, and began to study Torah. You most likely integrated a number of elements of your past into your new way of life. Competitive sports are still very much a part of who you are; you now learn, work, take care of your family, and work out at a gym every day. Your child, on the other hand, is being brought up in a community where some of those elements seem not to exist. Your world is multifaceted, while his seems to be solely black and white.

As children need clarity and definition, we teach them basics in a simplified form. Simplicity, however, often falsifies reality because it paints a picture of the world in absolutes.

As a result, to a certain extent, it can seem that we are lying to our children. When they are three years old, we tell them that the road is dangerous. That is a lie. The road itself is not dangerous, but we want to ensure the awareness that the road is an absolute "no" for them at the age of three.

When children are four or five, we tell them that cars are dangerous; that, too, is false. Automobiles in themselves are not dangerous, but we want them to consider them as such, especially if they are being driven. At the age of six, they already understand that *moving* cars are dangerous and they cannot go anywhere near a road with traffic. That, too, is a lie because moving cars are not dangerous in themselves. The danger depends on the direction and speed of their movement, and whether or not there is ample time for them to cross the street safely.

Not until children are nine or ten are they capable of integrating the values of time, space, and velocity to judge when it is OK to cross the road. Only then can they understand the true danger. Until this point, we were not attempting to deceive them, but we were giving simple, understandable, and possibly life-saving information.

Manny, originally from the town of Mesquite, known as the rodeo capital of Texas, enjoys wearing his ten-gallon hat and riding boots. He is now living an observant life and is trying to raise his children in a frum community in Israel.

Faced with many diverse challenges, Manny has had to negotiate his way through the demands and expectations of his community while holding on to some values that are still very dear to him. He wants his children to love horses. He wants them to be in good shape physically, and would really like to live on a farm, but has not found the right location for his frum American family.

At the same time, his present community has to cope with a plethora of negative influences issuing from the surrounding society that can breach the healthy and wholesome atmosphere in which he and his wife are striving to raise their children. The community has therefore taken steps to draw some clear, simple, and absolute lines of defense. Those lines include a certain style of dress, subjects of speech and, most difficult for Manny, controlled use of recreational time.

Manny has already comfortably incorporated various elements of his former life into his mitzvah observance and dedication to Torah. He cannot understand why his son, who is going to the day school in the community, is embarrassed by his father's clothing and will not go to shul with him in the morning.

When Manny complains about the rules of acceptable recreation and argues with the school principal about the foolishness of some of the rules or about the importance of children having outside interests, he is giving his children a mixed message. Were he to take his children riding during the summer, vacation times, and even occasionally on Friday afternoons, exercise with them at home and buy some pet rabbits, hamsters, or gerbils, he could accomplish most of his goals without causing confusion and tension. Because there are no halachic issues involved, it is not even necessary to discuss those decisions in advance with the school.

If you formerly had a hobby, an interest, or even just a favorite pastime that was very much a part of your life, you should not ignore it now. It is vital to acknowledge this part of you that still exists deep down inside. However, if that particular activity was an *aveirah*, impermissible to you now, it leaves a void that you must find a creative way to fill.

Angela had been adept at figure skating from the age of three. By twenty she was in top form, and well-known in her hometown of Mississauga, Ontario. Her first trip to Israel with Birthright stirred something Jewish inside her, and it was not long before she came back a second and third time.

As Judaism began to play a stronger role in her life, skating seemed to fall into second place, and she dropped out of all competitions and exhibitions. Before anyone could say, "Angela is becoming religious," she was a full-time student in a yeshiva seminary for women in Jerusalem, where she never told a soul that she was a figure skater. She spoke of her degree in accounting and of her love for the outdoors, but never a word about her talent. Whenever she went home, she would skate with love and enjoyment for hours on end, but never in Israel.

When the time came for Angela, now known as Malka, to marry, we had the pleasure of her presence at our Shabbos table. After the meal she asked if we could speak privately for a few minutes. She told me that her husband-to-be knew she had loved skating when she was younger, but she had never really told him how important it was in her life. Now she was afraid that when she married, she would be burying a part of herself that she would never be able to relinquish entirely.

I told her that she must tell her chassan about her love for the sport, and that a rabbi she trusts said that when they choose a place to live, they must make sure that there is a professional skating rink within ten to fifteen miles of their home. This way she would be able to skate when she needed to, and perhaps, even give skating lessons.

Today, Angela, her husband, and their growing family live in a very large frum community in the Northeast. She no longer does accounting, but works five to seven hours a day training mostly non-Jewish girls to figure skate.

Live your life quietly and do not make announcements about your hobbies. Raise your children with joy, and make sure that your home is a happy place. Do the things you love with your children, but with a moderation that does not make them stand out from the crowd, and they will do well in their environment.

When children are young, strict guidelines create a supervised, safe, and non-confusing setting for their growth. As they grow older, it is our job to help them make ever more sophisticated judgments as to what is true and what is not. We do this only when they are capable of integrating these judgments into their lives without thinking that everything is a game. By gradually and carefully introducing our children to more sophisticated concepts of truth and falsehood with respect to the dangers of the street, level by level, we can teach them to adjust to the multiple elements of life.

When you taught your children about safety in the street, you understood that the truth had to be simplified, distorting it a bit for safety's sake. When it comes to school rules and your community's preferred standards of dress, recreation, and speech, however, you might feel the need to rebelliously stand up for the "truth."

By rebelling, we confuse our children with mixed messages. They go to schools where they hear clearly defined, simple guidelines. How can we expect them to understand our complex, sophisticated outlook, which differentiates between different levels of halachah and varying degrees of sensitivity, and indicates that we consider some standards more central than others?

We may not give our children mixed messages. We introduce them to sophisticated thinking slowly as they mature, and then only if they are able to integrate it into their lives without rebelling. Take note, however, that if they see *us* rebelling, they are likely to do the same. If we understand the need for uncomplicated messages and accept the reasons that a community will insist on conformance to certain absolutes, our children will thrive. We can compensate and bring other elements into our children's lives as long as we do not create conflict.

There are times when school rules extend beyond the school and into the home, which can lead to significant frustration. For example, while you may have no compunctions about telling three-year-olds that the road is a dangerous place, you may get riled up about your children being told not to take private music lessons from a certain teacher. Perhaps you have an emotional response when told that going to ball games or some other enjoyable public event is prohibited. While you do not have to comply, you do have to be respectful and understanding of the school's policy and position.

If we are going to react emotionally to restrictions with which we may disagree, we will never succeed in introducing new concepts that are unfamiliar into our child's life without causing confusion and rebellion. It is all too often *our* rebelling that causes our child to rebel.

On "Penguins" and Clothing

We need to recognize the methods our community has adopted to convey and encourage certain principles before we can think of creative ways to help our children acquire additional helpful tools. This may require both maturity and a higher level of tolerance on our part than we have at present. When we talk about schools, communities, and our choices of them, as we shall do later, we will need to deal with these very basic concepts.

The simplicity of absolutes in regard to clothing and similar questions is an obvious falsehood. It does, however, provide a framework in which to live, an identity in which to grow, and a system with which we and our children can identify. When parents do not accept that system, when we dress independently, or make judgments on the system's standards of right and wrong, we create confusion. We must be very careful in condemning the system's absolutes because our children, who are receiving this mixed message, can easily conclude that their school does not teach the truth.

Young people often ask why there is a problem with a yeshiva boy wearing blue shirts. Is there really a halachah, law, about wearing only white shirts?

No, there is no halachah about wearing white shirts, and there is no prohibition against wearing blue shirts. As a matter of fact, as far as halachah goes, one can wear pink shirts with yellow polka dots and orange stripes. Why then, are those who dress differently from the crowd looked down upon? This disturbs many young people, who cannot understand why they are being judged by what they wear.

My answer is always the same.

"We all make statements. My dress code is not only a testimony to my taste and preferences, but a proclamation. I am identifying myself by the way I dress."

About thirty years ago, an article appeared in a magazine called *Shema Yisroel*, published by Yeshiva Ohr Somayach, which featured a dialogue between a young new-to-yeshiva student and his rabbi.

"You guys are so formal and snobbish with your clothes; all you wear is long black coats, black hats, black shoes, and a white shirt. I have a very casual attitude about clothes. I don't care so much about what I wear; it's you who care so much about clothes."

"Just imagine," the rabbi answered, "if tomorrow morning you woke up and found a pair of alligator shoes and a tweed suit next to your bed and had nothing else to wear. You'd put on a barrel and run to the nearest store because you wouldn't be caught dead wearing a tweed suit. And those fancy shoes! You are not casual about your clothing. You dress that way because it is how you wish to be perceived; you are making a statement."

When everybody in a group dresses a certain way and one person dresses differently, there is no sin involved, nor is there anything inherently wrong with this. Is that person making a statement? Of course, he is. Is it a bad statement? No, but he is claiming to be different. He gets up in the morning, puts on something that no one else in his class wears, and is upset when somebody says he is different.

"I am not different," he says defensively. "I am just like everybody else. Why are they judging me?"

Well, he has made a statement. Society respects people's statements. Perhaps, he is only trying to express his individuality; there is certainly nothing *wrong* with that. Choosing self-expression through externals, however, will often result in unwarranted assumptions.

Clothes are just an example. There are many aspects of our lifestyle that make similar statements.

While I was in *kollel* after my marriage, I owned a small, secondhand red-and-white motorbike, which was very convenient and inexpensive to operate. A big basket stuck on the back was convenient for shopping. I bought it for fifty dollars, and it cost about three dollars a week to keep in gas. On my *kollel* check that was just perfect.

Suddenly, however, in 1988, I was a *rosh yeshiva*.

"You will have to buy a car. You cannot ride that bike," said the members of the board who had asked me to take over the position.

"But the best lesson I could teach the boys is to be thrifty," I objected, "not to spend beyond their means. I can't afford a car."

"That may be true," they replied, "but you cannot ride the motorbike."

I went to my *rebbi* and asked him what to do. "I'll have to borrow money to buy a car, as I need some method of transportation; the bike just makes the most sense."

Rav Wolbe considered my question. "You are right, but in our generation, you cannot always do that which seems to make the most sense. In our generation, perception is so superficial that a motorbike will make you look like someone who is not worthy of your position, and you cannot do that. You would be the only *rosh yeshiva* in America and in Eretz Yisrael riding a motorbike."

In those years, owning a car in Yerushalayim was a statement of status for which I had no interest. I sold the bike for fifty dollars, borrowed a lot more money, and bought a car. The first time I came to pick up Rav Wolbe with it, he smiled. "Oh, now you have a four-wheeled horse," he joked. It was his way of saying, "Don't let it go to your head; you are still just a wagon driver."

We must understand that our superficial society is a result of over-simplification. When we make decisions to do things that differ from the accepted norms, to be nonconformist and expose our families to different activities, dress them differently, and so on, we must realize that these choices—while not in any way influencing the *community* to change (i.e., become less one-dimensional)—can very possibly harm our children. Our choices cannot disturb the balance between their acceptance of what they are learning in school and what they see at home. We need to be very careful not to make them feel out of place because they don't do what the people they admire do, or because they, like you, begin to find fault with the community and as a result lose their respect for authority.

The conflict we cause with mixed messages can well place our children at risk. If we are not capable of conforming, there are two options to avoid this. We can work toward changing some things in our community, or we can move to a different one. We cannot, however, live somewhere and make choices that will be perceived as statements that go against the values of those around us and then be upset because we are being looked at askance. Nor should we be surprised when our children give up on the chief values for which we joined this community as a result of our not giving up on the less vital ones. Our decisions teach our children exactly how much or how little we respect the community in which we are living.

———————————

One of my friends, a dedicated *talmid chacham*, loved working in his garden. He once told me that one of the more difficult transitions he faced in becoming a *mashgiach* in a prestigious yeshiva was that he could no longer work in his garden. Is there anything wrong with working in the garden? Is there any halachah against it? Of course not! This was in Eretz Yisrael; if anything, it is a mitzvah to work the land here. In fact, it is written that we will receive great reward for settling (planting) the land.[1]

In the type of community where gardeners are gardeners and *roshei yeshiva* are *roshei yeshiva*, however, there is a clear delineation between the two, and you cannot expect those around you to understand your broad-mindedness. The general public is neither knowledgeable nor broad-minded. It is up to you to find a way to integrate what is central in your life without becoming a stye in the eye of your community.

We have already discussed the dangers of living our lives according to peer pressure, and I want to make it quite clear that this is not what I am referring to.

If you are raising your children with an emphasis on values with which you are not yet comfortable, it should be due to an intelligent decision based on the options available. Just as I tell my young child that the road is dangerous, I should not have an issue with teaching him what is acceptable in the community because I understand the values it exemplifies. The negative peer pressure we discussed earlier occurs when we assume behaviors without thinking about them, merely as a result of societal demands.

I am making a judgment call, weighing the pros and cons, when I approve of doing something with which I initially may have categorically disagreed. What is more essential?

I do not agree that wearing certain clothes makes me a better or lesser person, but I am even less comfortable with my child thinking that I disagree with the way of life I have chosen. When I decide to buy a felt hat that I feel costs far too much for my son who is entering yeshiva, I may have to cede a principle that in my opinion is important, that of not buying overpriced clothing. I understand, however, that it is better for my child to be accepted among the boys, and not make him stand out.

---

1   "Mitzvos of the Ramban Not Mentioned by Him" in *Minchas Chinuch* (Machon Yerushalayim 2009), vol. 3, p. 444, mitzvah 4.

These decisions are the correct thing for me to do. I am giving up my comfort level because I know that being accepted, both to the school and socially, is healthier for my child. It is not peer pressure, but clear logic that tells me it is smarter to buy the hat than not to. It is not merely, "If everyone else is doing it, perhaps there's a reason that I should do it as well."

I am fully aware of the fact that I do not want to but that I *have* to—because I want my child to feel comfortable in the community in which I have decided to live, whether or not I agree with all its idiosyncrasies. There is an enormous difference in motivation here.

Maintaining Individuality

Individuality has to take on a more internal form when we try to live a Torah life. Its greatest measure will be expressed in the *way* in which we do the same thing that everybody else does while maintaining our inner integrity—not by the clothing we wear or other superficial diversions from the norm.

Three hundred people are davening *Minchah* in shul. All are wearing similar clothing, standing with their feet together, using the same siddur, each of them saying the same words, yet each and every one is an individual standing before *his* Creator. Each is asking for *his* needs with all *his* heart and *his* concentration, on *his* level of understanding, and submitting *himself* to the mercy of Hashem. I need to be in touch with all of those parts of myself to claim individuality: heart, mind, thoughts, needs, and ego.

The wider society in which we grew up has a diametrically opposed perception. Individuality in its view is determined by doing "my own thing," be it hair color and styling, mode of dress, or the things in which I do or do not engage. Most of the factors that identify and define the individual in our surrounding society are external.

When three hundred people are dressed similarly and performing the same actions, they need to develop a much deeper sense of self. The individuality we pursue internally should not be challenged because I arrive at a wedding and someone else is wearing the same dress, suit, or tie. It is quite pathetic when apparel is the defining element that establishes an individual's uniqueness. It is also sad when we define ourselves as religious Jews by our clothing alone. The Torah provides us with a multitude of tasks and responsibilities that empower us to develop every aspect of our personality. The mitzvos do not allow us to generalize ourselves with pitiful labels that limit our inclusion in Hashem's world of *chessed* and *emes*, kindness and truth.

We cannot say, "I am an introvert, I cannot do *chessed*," or, "I am an extrovert, prayer does not work for me." We each need to challenge ourselves in all the different aspects of human development to fulfill the entire Torah. This develops us into individuals, bringing each of us to realize his potential, which in turn, creates individuality. When three hundred people are doing the "same thing," it is never the same thing. Each person is doing his best with the natural and nurtured aspects of his persona. His experiences will never be the same as someone else's. His thoughts, intentions, and feelings, his detailed approach and his joy, are all playing a role in making his actions his own.

Chapter 8

A Lonely World

As individuals engaged in an unending process of growth that requires a tremendous amount of personal strength and fortitude, let us see what we can learn from one of the great men of history, Noach.

I emphasize this story because very often, when dealing with complicated issues in our home, marriage, finances, and bringing up our children, we often feel that we are doing it all on our own. This feeling of isolation induces a feeling of helplessness, a sense of uselessness, and sometimes tempts us to just give up.

Noach's example teaches us that we are never alone, and certainly not helpless. Hashem does not leave man without resources to deal with his situation. If we cannot find an equitable solution to a problem, we have not looked carefully enough for the tools already in our possession.

True, things are not the way they were when you started out on this path, but, by looking around, you can find a great deal of support. Noach was a man who was forced to confront tremendous hardships during his lifetime. Mankind exists as a result of his fortitude, and his legacy is worthy of study. From his struggles, we can learn more about looking inward to find the courage we need to tackle the all-encompassing challenges we may have already overcome or still face in our lives.

Curiously, the Torah tells us almost nothing about Noach; he is an enigma.

"Noach was a righteous and complete man in his generation; Noach walked with Hashem."[1]

Midrashim add to this sketchy information that he was a tremendous *baal chessed*, a giving person, which we deduce from being told that he fed all the animals faithfully during the long months they lived together in the ark. Nothing, however, is said of his personal or spiritual stature. We are all *b'nei Noach*, Noach's children, yet we find no crucial distinction to explain why he was chosen to be our common ancestor. We obviously have to search more deeply.

Noach was born 1,056 years after Creation, 126 years after Adam's demise. What distinguishes the two is that Adam is the father of all mankind simply by virtue of having been the first individual created, while Noach was required to achieve something extraordinary.

I pondered this question for many years. At one point, something struck me, and I conjured up the following imaginary scenario.

If It Were Me

In the highly remote likelihood that Hashem would say to me, "Listen, Greenwald, the world is soon going to be destroyed. Everything and everyone will vanish, but you alone have been chosen to survive," what would be my initial response, my secondary response, and final one? First, I would think, *Does Hashem really mean everyone? What about my wife, children, mother, father, brothers, sisters, uncles, cousins, friends, relatives, neighbors, and so on?* Then I would wonder what would remain in existence. Nothing. I would have to start from scratch. I think that my final response to this assignment would be, "Don't do me any favors; take me along with everyone else! Why should I alone survive?"

Noach did not respond with questions or despair. To clearly understand his greatness, we must remember that when he was informed that the Flood was on its way, he did not yet have any children. As far as he knew, there would be nobody after him.

---

1   *Bereishis* 6:9.

Imagine! Believing that everything would be destroyed, he, nonetheless, brought children into the world, choosing to go right on normally living his life. On hearing about the Flood, his only question was, "What should I do about it?"

Hashem told him, "Build an ark. Begin by planting cedar trees from which to harvest the timber."

We can now begin to understand why Noach essentially replaced Adam as the father of all humanity.

Adam—Alone or Individual

"Why was Adam, the first human being, created alone?" the Mishnah asks.[2] Everything else in the world was created in herds, flocks, schools, prides, etc. Why was man the only creature created as a single individual?

"So that every person can say," the Mishnah answers, "that 'the whole world was created for me.'"

Adam could not have thought that something was missing in the world he found, because as everything was formed before him, it was obvious that all was there for his sake. Adam was created by himself because he was meant to understand that he had everything he needed.

Just as Adam realized that all his needs had already been provided by Hashem, so too, must every human being understand that anything and everything he or she may need to succeed in life is available. That is the meaning of "*bishvili nivra ha'olam*—the world was created for me." We must apply this idea to our own outlook: *My environment has been set up by Hashem to give me everything I need for whatever it is that I am meant to accomplish.*

Not recognizing this brought Adam and Chavah to the fatal sin. Believing that they needed the one thing they did not have was a terrible mistake. The first *aveirah*, sin, in the world was brought about by people looking at something they could not have and thinking they needed it. Hashem had told them that everything was theirs to utilize

---

2   *Sanhedrin* 37a: "Every man must say, 'The world was created for me.'"

except for the fruits of the Trees of Life and of Knowledge. At that point in their development, it was antithetical to their best interests.

Our challenge as human beings is to acquire the same perspective that Adam was supposed to have had. What we need is right here, but we have to look for it.

Noach had family, friends, neighbors, a community, and a society. When Hashem told him that the world as he knew it would no longer exist, he had two options.

Since he would no longer have what he considered vital for his existence, he could have questioned why he should continue to live.

"Hashem, take me, too!"

His second choice was to believe that he would survive without all the things he thought he needed and have confidence that he would be granted everything necessary at the right time.

Noach had learned from Adam's mistake and chose the second option. He understood the concept of "*bishvili nivra ha'olam*" so profoundly that he could "restart" the whole world all over again with no regrets. That tremendous clarity of responsibility was what made him worthy of that gargantuan task. Noach was the first person who not only embodied that lesson, but completely internalized and lived it to the fullest extent.

When informed of the impending destruction, he accepted it.

"What is my job now?" he asked. "I know that the world of the future will include whatever I will need. Just tell me what You want me to do."

Hashem told him to make an ark and he did so, continuing to live his life as he was meant to do.

Chapter 9

Accessing Support

Your tools may not be the same as those that you had five or fifteen years ago, or whenever it was that you began the process of change. You may have acquired new and different ones, or your original tools may still be within your grasp.

Very few of us are totally alone in the world. Support systems do exist in our communities and lives, but we need to know how to identify, approach, and utilize each of them to the fullest. Although you may feel alone, you are not. It is a matter of access.

My father used to tell a story about Yankel, who one night sees a man on his hands and knees searching for something under a streetlight on a Brooklyn street.

"What are you looking for?" Yankel asks.

"I dropped my lens," the man replies.

Yankel gets down on all fours and begins looking. Another man joins him. Before you know it, there are ten people down on the sidewalk, searching for the lens.

"Where exactly were you when you noticed you lost it?" one fellow finally asks,

"About two blocks from here."

They all look at the guy as if he's crazy. "Then why are we looking here?"

"Here there's a streetlight," he replies, "and there it is too dark to find anything."

Sometimes, we look for a solution superficially, far from where the problem originated. We do not really think about the underlying questions: Where did I get stuck? What kind of help do I really need, and where can I find it?

"The *bayshan* [he who is embarrassed] does not learn,"[1] says the Mishnah.

What makes someone a *bayshan*? The common denominator in all cases of embarrassment is that something we want to keep hidden is revealed. It's the way you would feel if a page from your diary were tacked to the bulletin board in the dining room at school, or if everyone found out about something you had done wrong.

We tend to feel embarrassed when we are still learning, and we fear to ask questions that point out our ignorance because we think we should have learned the answers ten or fifteen years ago.

"He who is embarrassed cannot learn" means that one cannot learn without asking questions and admitting the need to know.

We are defined by the questions we ask, as Chazal tell us in the *Haggadah shel Pesach* in reference to the four sons: "For this reason Hashem did this for *me* in Egypt." Why does the son who does not know how to ask receive the same answer as the wicked son? He is just a little child.

The *Maharal* explains that the Haggadah is clearly not dealing with younger or older children, but rather with four adults.[2] This explains why the son who does not know how to ask receives the same answer that we give to the *rasha*, the wicked son. He is not a young child who does not know, but a complacent adult. He does not know because he does not care. A person who does not ask questions is virtually on his way to becoming a *rasha*.

The simpleton asks a simple question; the smart person an intelligent one. The wicked son asks a rhetorical question because he does not want an answer. The fourth son does not know enough to ask a question at all. Do you know where you end up when you do not ask questions?

---

1   *Pirkei Avos* 2:5.
2   *Maharal* on the *Haggadah*, p. 71, *Sifrei Maharal*; Rabbi Yehudah Livai (Yehadus Publishers, B'nei Brak 1980).

The answer is taught to us by the Haggadah: You tell the fourth son, "Hashem did this for me, not for you!" Yes, he receives the same answer as the wicked son. Perhaps, this will shake him up a bit, and he will ask why you are saying this to him. Now, we've got him to at least ask a question. It is we who need to instigate the thought process so that he might begin to question.

This is a difficult situation for us. When we have a question, when something is bothering us, we may have to learn just whom and how to ask, but refraining from asking is not an option.

Knowing Whom and How to Ask

If your child seems to have asthma, you don't say, "Well, I don't know how to deal with this, so I'll just go to sleep."

Perhaps you'll call a few friends to find a recommendation for a good doctor with a good track record in dealing with asthma in a reasonable, normal way; one who does not turn minor issues into a major calamity. You would certainly not assume that if you don't know, nobody does; nor would you ask your neighbor what he does for his child's asthma and try to buy the same medication. You don't do that with health issues.

When you have a question regarding your spiritual health, whether it is in regard to halachah, Jewish outlook, education, marriage, or *parnassah*, you also need to seek expert advice.

When we feel overwhelmed and need someone to help carry our load, a support system is usually there for the asking, but we have to take the responsibility to look for it.

There are many special people around, such as local rabbis who are involved in the community, who take responsibility, and are active and eager to help people. Even more accessible might be the mentors you have either built or should build into your life, and friends who are further along the journey. When you are ready to ask a question, don't hesitate; never be embarrassed to admit that you don't have an answer.

You wouldn't go to a podiatrist to treat asthma. Rabbis, like everyone else, have somewhat defined areas of experience. Once you have clarity as to what your questions are, you can gather information until you are certain you have found someone who can deal with your situation. There are always people who have something unkind to say about a rabbi, and others who have not much nice to say about anyone; but don't be put off by those who ignore your needs. Network with people you trust, as well as those who are either similar to you or are in somewhat of the same circumstances until you find a knowledgeable and understanding mentor.

A community rabbi is a very busy person, but those who accomplish a great deal are always busy. My very dear friend, Rabbi Yaakov Visel, is the founder of Yad Eliezer,[3] one of the extraordinary charitable organizations in Jerusalem. He taught me a key rule in life: If you want to get something done, ask a busy person. Does that mean he will not want to help? No, the reason he is so busy is precisely because he *wants* to help.

There is a proper way to approach a busy person. A community *rav* who takes responsibility for the people he serves has intentionally placed himself in that position. Because his time is limited, however, we do not want to waste it. If your questions have been carefully formulated before meeting with him, he will be better able to assist you.

A well-prepared question is what our Sages call "*sh'eilas chacham chatzi teshuvah*—a wise man's question is half the answer."[4] This means that I have already carefully regarded different aspects of the problem and I am not coming at him all tied up in my emotions. I have a basis to think one way, and/or I have equal grounds to think otherwise, or I have three options that I can present to the *rav* for his advice along with my reasons for considering each one.

Often, when you take the time to do that, you will find that you've arrived at the solution yourself. Sometimes, when your questions are carefully couched after having thought through the issues, you will be able to present them in two or three minutes rather than half an hour. Try to formulate your questions beforehand instead of taking up the

---

3   Presently run by his son, Rabbi Dov Visel.
4   *D'var Avraham* 1:67 in the name of Rav Yosef Karo.

rav's time while his phone is ringing and other people are waiting to speak with him.

The next time you show up with a question, he will welcome you. If you are not emotionally capable of thinking a particular issue through carefully and coming up with a clear and well-thought-out question, you ought to talk it over with a friend until it is clarified in your thoughts. If that doesn't work, preface your question with your state of mind, "Rabbi, I usually try to come to you with a clear question, but my emotional involvement in this situation is blurring things, so please bear with me because I need help getting through the fuzz."

I've always wondered how the President of the United States or of any country for that matter, makes decisions regarding thousands of issues. How can he possibly make intelligent decisions most, or at least some of the time? The answer is that he has a staff of experts who prepare the material beforehand and come to him with acutely focused questions. A clearly posed question takes far less time to answer. If the president (or the rabbi) requires more information, he can request it. An insightful person deals with information intelligently, and in our case, it doesn't matter if the question is a practical one in kashrus or a question of *hashkafah*. The *rav* has no need to hear where and when the chicken was bought to answer a question of mixed meat and dairy.

Questions in *chinuch*, however, may require more background information. If so, the *rav* may say he cannot answer the question on the phone, or that it requires a face-to-face meeting. Just present the problem and let *him* indicate the need to make an appointment to discuss it.

When you call and say, "I need an hour of your time," he doesn't know if you actually need an hour or if your question can be resolved in five minutes. By setting aside that hour, he could be taking away time from others who need his assistance. If he hesitates, don't assume that he isn't interested in helping you. He is interested, but his time is limited. If he knows the hour is necessary, he will look for the time and find it, or he might not even have an hour for one question. Knowing that a *rav* has a lot of responsibilities and is a busy person will help you understand his response.

If a *rav* pushes you off for a day or two, accept it. If, however, your dilemma is extremely urgent, you can say, "I know that the Rav's time is extremely tight, but I think I may be dealing with an emergency situation. If there is a closer spot, please notify me."

When a *rav* hears a person speaking like that, he hears an intelligent person being reasonable about a problem. If he finds an opening, he will call you or may even decide to somehow fit you in the same day. You have to learn how to talk to busy people, because they take their time seriously.

You must keep in mind that a *rav*, like any other human being, is limited in time, money, and other resources. You find it totally acceptable to pay a lawyer, accountant, or psychologist exorbitant fees for their time and advice. Most of the rabbis you are contacting will never request, and may even turn down, any attempt to remunerate them for their time and advice. Despite this, we often unreasonably expect that they should be there for us whenever needed.

Seeking Out Former Mentors

Another possible resource is that of a former mentor.

Who was the person who impressed you at the beginning? Who were the ones you first trusted and relied on to help with those big decisions in your life? Very often, either as a result of moving from place to place, sometimes even to a different country, or just due to life's normal passages—marriage, child-rearing, earning a living—you lost touch with this significant connection. Perhaps you are embarrassed to renew contact with this person once you've dropped it for a number of years. Why would that be?

One reason is that you might be afraid that returning to them after all this time with questions will be a disappointment, fearing they will be dissatisfied with where you are holding today. I can tell you from years of experience in this area that most mentors will not be disappointed in the least.

Anyone who works with those who are growing, developing, and changing their lives knows that it is a continuous process that takes many years. They are aware that life is such a constantly changing, fluctuating procession of events that even issues that were apparently resolved can reappear and cause doubt. It is a certainty that the people who were involved with you at the beginning of the road, in your first yeshiva or seminary, the *rabbanim* from whom you first heard *shiurim*, are people who will always care about you. They will *always* be proud of you and happy when you come back to them.

As dedicated teachers and mentors, they will certainly have thought about you over the years and would be happy for you to be in touch and let them know how you're doing. They know they were the first to effect a change in your life. They sat with you and talked far into the night, discussing, arguing, and helping you to reach new appreciations and aspirations. They gave something of themselves to you; there is a part of them within you, and when contact is renewed, they often feel great satisfaction, real *nachas*.

Don't let your fear of not meeting your mentors' expectations keep you from seeking their help once again. The only expectations they will have of you is that you continue to be an honest, searching person, which is what led you to them in the first place. That is all they were interested in then, and that is all they hope for now, even twenty years later. The fact that you want to reach out and are still thinking enough to ask a question means you are still honest and searching, and as such, you are still their student. You don't have to be afraid to call up after ten years of silence. You may have to brace yourselves for a comment like, "Ahhh! You are still alive!" All that means is, "I missed you." It means, "I would have liked to have had a connection with you throughout all these years, but I did not and that is OK. Go ahead, now you can talk."

It is rare for a mentor to rebuff a former student. Should this occur, try to judge favorably. Consider that the person may not be currently able to continue giving you support for any number of reasons that have nothing to do with you. If that is the case, then you need to look at other options.

There is a great rabbi in Yerushalayim whose disciple I can only aspire to be. He is not only a genius in Torah but is also very kind when I am with him, greeting me warmly and drawing me close. There was a period of time when I was very busy with yeshiva affairs and didn't have time to visit and talk to him about the many things I should have. After a lapse of six months, I went to see him on Purim, when I was slightly under the influence of "the mitzvah." He pulled me toward him and rebuked me in front of the whole crowd.

"Am I a *Purim Rav*? Am I your *Purim Rav*?"

I cherished that reprimand for many years. He was so confident in our close relationship and in my respect for him that he knew I would understand that it had been given with love.

When your *rav* gives you *mussar*, moral instruction, it is because he trusts your relationship enough to know he can reprimand your behavior without you feeling insulted. If you *do* feel insulted, it is essentially *your* problem. Your *rav* wants to know that he can say something constructive to you without hurting you, because that is a measure of your closeness to him. There are a number of books that speak about the different language patterns of men and women. Let us learn the language of a *rav*.

When a *rav* asks, "Where have you been for the last ten years?" it is not an insult, but a compliment. If he says, "I'm glad to know that you are alive," it is not sarcasm, but a little piece of him that hurts because he cared about you all this time. Should he say, "I cannot speak to you right now," you should hear, "I am really happy to hear from you, but I cannot speak right now so please do call again." It doesn't mean, "You are not important to me." He is busy and you respect him, but you have to learn the language.

Perhaps you are a little bit in awe of him. The best approach is to ask when it is convenient for you to meet. Even if he says, "I don't know," it doesn't mean, "I'm not interested." It is probable that he is in the middle of something that is taking his entire concentration at this moment. You have to learn the language.

Busy people often have a markedly different lingo. I know a man who is extraordinarily busy. When you call him on the phone, he is always too busy to talk; he tells you to send a letter or a fax. If you fax is more than eight lines long, forget it. He does not have time to read it. When he says, "Send me a fax," it means, "Write your request in four sentences." If he needs more information, he will ask for it. A four-sentence question merits an answer within a few hours. A two-page essay will sit on his desk for a month or until he has time to read it, and that sometimes does not happen. When and if he does read it, he has to figure out which part of your story is relevant and what you really want from him. When you approach any busy person, take this into consideration. Make it short and sweet—whether in person or on the phone. If your relationship allows for longer meetings and discussion, treasure your opportunities.

You have to make yourself available to your *rav*. I remember that Rav Wolbe was an extraordinarily patient man and very kind to his *talmidim*. He would usually see me within twenty-four hours after I requested a meeting; on rare occasions, forty-eight. He once told me at the end of *bein hazmanim*, three days before the beginning of the learning term, that there were a hundred people who wanted to see him and they all needed to see him "right *now*," because they had a question that had to do with the beginning of the school year. Where were those hundred people during the previous three weeks? Chaim was on vacation and Shmuel was out of the city, and so forth. Then Chaim calls three days before the *z'man* and expects the *rav* to kindly accommodate the request.

"Okay, come to see me at two o'clock in the afternoon."

"But, Rebbi, I have a *chavrusa* at two o'clock; could we do it at four?"

But the *rav* also has a life! You just called your *rebbi*, or your mentor, because you need his help. When he gives you an appointment, don't give him a hard time. Make yourself available because *you* are the one who needs *him*. If you really cannot take the time offered because you will lose your job, preface your response by saying, "I would come any time the Rav wants, but I will lose my job if I come between two and four. Is there any other time available?"

Give him the space. When he gives you a time slot, go the extra mile. He wants to help you. For some strange reason, I have encountered many intelligent people who do not think of these little courtesies. I heard this problem from my *rebbi* twenty-something years ago, and I see it happening now all the time.

When a *rav* has to go through his appointment book to find a time that matches a petitioner's request, he may start to wonder, *Why am I working so hard to make this appointment if it isn't important enough to him to try to accommodate my schedule?* It is a sensitive point of which we have to be aware.

When I call an important Torah figure or my local *rav* to ask a question, I say, "Whenever you can see me is when I will come. The only exceptions are the weekday hours between two and four, which is when I teach. If I come then, I could be causing eighty students to lose the time in which they should be learning."

Whatever it takes to meet with him, take advantage of his offer.

I know that there are many people who have called a *rav* and been asked to call back in an hour, or in two or three days, but they don't call back. *That's it,* they decide, *he is not interested.* That is not true. He *is* interested. He just can't talk to the caller at the moment. When he tells you to call back in an hour, it is because in an hour he has an open slot of time. He may not have it in an hour and a half. This happens so often.

Rabbanim have told me, "I tell someone to call me back in an hour because I know I'll have a break then. He calls back an hour and a half, or an hour and forty-five minutes or two hours later, and I probably won't be free then. You want to be there for them, but they don't even listen to what you say."

Learn to hear what your mentor is really saying. If he says, "Bother me, get on my case, call me again and again," don't hesitate.

"What? I have to be a *nudge*? That's one of the things we learned we're not supposed to be. What does it mean when a *rav* says *nudge* me?"

Semi-retired, Rabbi Yaakov Visel was one of the busiest people in the world. He founded the world-renowned organization, Yad Eliezer, which funnels ten to twenty million dollars a year to needy people in

Jerusalem. He was a *rebbi* who, in addition to his regular job teaching in a yeshiva high school, gave *shiurim* in jails to hardened criminals, some of whom made their way back to Hashem. He is still involved in perhaps sixteen worthwhile organizations. When you call him, he holds you on the line and makes a call on another line to try to solve your problem *at that moment.* If he cannot get through on the other line, he says, "Call me back, call me again."

What he is really saying is that when you have me on the phone, I'm dealing with you; the minute you hang up, I am dealing with twenty-five other things. He really *wants* you to call him again. Therefore, when your *rav* says "*Nudge* me," he is saying, "I am so overwhelmed and so busy with all I have to do that I know the only way I'll be able to deal with your problem is while you are speaking to me on the phone. When you hang up, the phone is going to ring again, I'll have six urgent letters to answer, and another person is going to knock on my door. I want to be here for you, I want to help you deal with it, but you'd better remind me by calling again."

Not every *rav* is going to articulate all of that, of course.

On the other hand, some people from whom we seek help do *not* want to be pushed. If these busy people say, "I'll get back to you," it usually means that *they* have made a note, mental or written, and they will get back to you when they are ready or have more time. These people do not want to be prodded. You can, however, legitimately ask them, "Is there a time by which I should call back if I don't hear from you?" because they may for some reason not get through to you. If they tell you when to call, by all means do so.

One more tip about consulting mentors.

If you called someone who gave you advice and it worked, call him back and say, "Thank you. I did what you said, and it helped." The next time you call, yours will be a welcome voice.

The Steipler used to bemoan, "People come to me with troubles, suffering. One is dying, another is sick, a third one has no children. No one ever comes back to say, '*Baruch Hashem* we had a *refuah*; my wife went through a difficult labor and all is well. They "disappear."'"

The *rav* gives advice, davens, pours his heart out to Hashem on your behalf, and then sits in limbo not knowing if he was successful. Was the advice well received and on the mark? Is the person doing well now? Don't disappear! If you can't go, send a friend to let the *rav*/mentor/ *rebbi* know you had a *refuah sheleimah*, a mazel tov. *Rabbanim* are also people.

Acknowledge their efforts. Remember that not only do you take energy from them, you *return* energy to them when you give them *nachas*. This may seem to be a little thing on the world stage of events, but it makes a very big difference in building a support system.

———————

I know that when a student of mine from whom I haven't heard in fifteen years calls, just hearing his voice is a pleasure. Even if he's not calling with a question, even if he just calls to say, "Rebbi, we had another child," it's *nachas* for me.

Another reason I suggest returning to your original mentors is that because you and they have already established a certain chemistry, the lines of communication are probably still open. You need to talk to someone who understands your language and whose language you understand, whether it is literally English, Hebrew, Yiddish, French, Chinese, or the metaphorical language you both speak—someone with whom you can identify.

You don't have to identify with a financial wizard to whom you turn for advice. If you have a technological question, you go to an expert whether or not he "speaks your language," or is a nice guy. The financial adviser will hopefully invest well and collect his percentage. The "techie" will fix your computer, and that's enough for you. You don't particularly care about his *middos* or if he knows how you feel about your Yiddishkeit. But when you have a question about something that has to do with you or your family, you need an individual who can really understand where you are coming from.

I met Cynthia on a flight from Tel Aviv to New York, and her story is the kind of nightmare that comes with asking serious questions to the wrong people. During her first months of introduction to Jewish law and culture, she asked one of her favorite rabbis an important question.

She was going home for a family wedding, after which she would return to Israel to continue her studies. Gary was as warm, loving, and doting a stepfather as any girl could have asked for. Cynthia was wondering about what Jewish law has to say about kissing and hugging the person who had raised her since birth. She was shocked and hurt when the rabbi said, "It is absolutely forbidden for you to touch him or have him touch you." At the same time, she was committed to becoming religious and did not want to "mess up" on this auspicious occasion.

When she got off the plane and Gary ran to greet her, she put out her hands and said, "Dad, I can't!" That was the beginning of the fallout. At the wedding, she was angry that Gary did not respect her attempt to be religious, so she didn't stand between him and her mother for fear that he would put his hand around her waist. So, while cousins, old friends, and acquaintances pecked her unexpectedly on the cheek or took her hand or shoulders in their hands, Gary felt estranged and insulted. The ensuing mudslinging was so hurtful, offensive, and caused so much distress that Cynthia's journey was unfortunately brought to an end.

While I will not discuss the halachic reliability of this particular rabbi,[5] I will unequivocally call him to task on the total insensitivity of his dealings with Cynthia in regard to where she was holding in her personal stage of growth, and where she was headed. Although there are differentiating views in halachah, a rabbi must know that a newly initiated and not fully committed young woman must be dealt with very carefully. I am equally appalled by a rabbi who, clueless as to

---

5   See "Important Note" in the Preface.

the process of *teshuvah*, determines halachic questions for people in complicated and intricate situations that require a full understanding of the ramifications and consequences of those decisions. As in all aspects of halachah, a *rav* needs real training ("*shimush*" in the halachic vernacular) in this particular field. I have heard great men say things that would surprise people of lesser stature, but those who deal with *baalei teshuvah* not only understand but build their approach on the broad shoulders of those giants. Rav Moshe Feinstein's responsa, for instance, allows a parent who raised a child from infancy to kiss her, and the decision by the *Tzitz Eliezer* saying that if she stands near him and he kisses her without her initiating the contact, she doesn't not have to shy away.

A very sad incident occurred a few years ago when a well-known *rav* was brought to a community to speak about *chinuch*. He gave a fire-and-brimstone speech about *chinuch*, after which many people in the community walked away completely confused. They had no idea what he was talking about. No one had thought to explain to the *rav* beforehand that 85 percent of his audience either had a non-Jewish spouse or was not himself Jewish or *shomer Shabbos*. The *rav* spoke heatedly about not bringing secular newspapers into the house and decried the evils of television, sports, and the like. It was a great truth...for the right crowd.

Your rabbi needs to know to whom he is talking. You have to tell the *rav* about your background so he can relate to your questions. If he has no experience in the area in which you need advice, or if you cannot speak to him openly and honestly, he is not a suitable halachic authority for you.

A final suggestion: Please do not seek assistance irresponsibly. Don't go to a great man if you are not really interested in hearing his advice. Don't waste his time with a nonessential question just to be able to say that you heard the advice of a *tzaddik* with a direct line to Heaven.

When I need an answer, I go to my regular *rav*. Only if your question is one that no one else in the world can answer except a great man, one that requires his vast knowledge and tremendously broad perspective in certain areas, then by all means seek an audience with him.

Some people used to go to Rav Chaim Kanievsky to ask petty questions. He was a *tzaddik* with angelic patience and brimming over with loving-kindness, so he answered every question posed to him.

Imagine going to the top neurosurgeon in Columbia Presbyterian Hospital and saying, "Sir, I have a headache."

"Very well," says the specialist. "Please give a thousand dollars to the receptionist, and I will examine you for twenty minutes and decide if you need surgery."

You come in, he gives you twenty minutes and two aspirins, and you leave. If you have an extra thousand dollars to throw away you could do that, but one doesn't go to a top neurosurgeon for a headache. You didn't have to go to Rav Chaim Kanievsky to ask him a question that fifteen rabbis in your community could answer.

I have seen books (bestsellers, by the way) that list some of the foolish questions people have asked Rav Chaim Kanievsky. This clearly demonstrates his virtue but says little for the insensitive people who take advantage of it. We go to a great man when the question is one of life and death, or after we have spoken first to three ordinary rabbis who have told us that this question requires the *p'sak*, ruling, of an *adam gadol*, Torah giant.

Consulting a "Torah Giant"

When several other *rabbanim* send you to consult individuals who are more learned and experienced than they, you are on the way to needing help from the top neurosurgeon. In the past, I have gone to my *rebbi*, Rav Wolbe, with my questions, and there were times when he said, "Go to Rav Shach. He is the only one who can answer this question." I knew then that I had no other option. When your rabbi suggests going to a Torah giant because of the intricacy of the question, ask him if he can ask for you or go with you.

When a Rabbi Misrepresents Judaism

This is a very sensitive issue, and I will try to deal with it in a truthful and frank manner. As we often overlook the necessity to recognize the limitations of human nature, high expectations are the antecedent for the greatest disappointments.

One of the most challenging things for a *baal teshuvah* to experience is when a rabbi is inappropriate in his dealings with morality or finances. It is confusing and hurtful when a rabbi behaves in a way that makes us lose respect for him. The worst part is that it can also make us lose respect for what he represents.

There is a famous adage: "Judaism is perfect; Jews are not."

Rabbis represent, teach, and are meant to exemplify the ideals of the Torah. The Torah is *emes*, truth, and the integrity of a rabbi should be manifest in everything he does and says. Of course, this is a tall order for any human being.

The Gemara has an extensive discussion regarding a rabbi who, due to indiscretions, is shunned, a level lower than *cherem*, excommunication.[6] The discussion relates to the concept that teaches us to learn Torah from a man who is like an angel in our eyes and not to learn from one whom we see as lacking. This is brought in halachah as well.[7]

The notion at the core of this ruling is that the Torah was given to Moshe Rabbeinu at Sinai. The *mesorah*, tradition, which continues until today is the source of our confidence in the Torah's veracity. When a person learns Torah, he must be confident in its integrity. If he loses respect for the person teaching him, he misperceives the real Giver of the Torah. This is the chief message that I can share with you.

The Torah itself teaches us not to learn it from someone whom you do not respect greatly as its true representative. The Gemara deals with what to do with this man after the first and possibly repeated offenses, how he is treated, and when he may be forgiven. The Gemara

---

6   *Moed Katan* 17a.
7   *Tur* and *Shulchan Aruch, Yoreh Deah* 246.

and Rishonim, early commentators,[8] discuss when one may or may not continue to learn from a man who has really strayed. The essential idea is that not every indiscretion warrants shunning or excommunication, and there are times when one must give his rabbi the benefit of the doubt. Taking on a teacher and mentor requires a great level of respect, in the absence of which one should seek instruction elsewhere.

In addition to a *rav* or former mentor, there may be people in your community you can involve, friends and neighbors whom you can ask for advice, but identify your resources realistically.

We are all challenged when someone in whom we had placed our trust errs, yet should this occur, it does not invalidate everything learned from this person. It does not even nullify the moral integrity of the many actions we observed and respected. While this unfortunate behavior will undermine my faith in this person's integrity from then on, it should not disallow my past experience from remaining the foundation building blocks of my present and future. Except in rare and extreme situations, they represent a truth and awareness that is valid even if this individual will no longer be my mentor.

---

8   *Chagigah* 15b.

Chapter 10

Building a Support System

Friends you made during the *teshuvah* process will often be the best source of support as you move forward in life. *Teshuvah* is not just a process, it is an all-encompassing, life-altering, mind-and-heart-challenging process. People who shared that process with us, or who were with us during this very crucial time will often become very special friends. In addition, they will often replace old friendships that are no longer practical.

However, it is important at times to think twice about your relationships. Do they uplift you, or do you feel dragged down by them? "Friends" who depress you, or usually leave you feeling a bit worse than before, are not the ones from whom to seek advice. They may always be there for you, but they cannot help with your difficulties. They may identify with you so deeply that you can't move on, as they do not have the tools to help you see another side of the issue. Their validation of your feelings may initially make you feel better, but in the long run will not be helpful with any issues and questions that you may have.

Three Qualities of a Friend

Rabbeinu Yonah, in his commentary on the Mishnah in *Avos*, "Acquire a friend,"[1] specifies three reasons why a person needs a good one.

---

1   *Pirkei Avos* 1:5.

A. *Friendship and Learning*

The first reason, he says, is to share the intellectual learning process that we all experience throughout our lives.

Although one learns from a mentor who imparts wisdom, the knowledge is received in the form of raw material. It is with friends—with whom we experience the discussion of the information—that this knowledge is developed. "I have learned much from my teachers," the Gemara says,[2] "and even more from my friends." The dialogue with my peers helps me clarify the information at a level where it becomes stored as my personal information.

B. *Friendship and Spiritual Growth*

Rabbeinu Yonah's second reason is that a friend is needed for growth in performing mitzvos, to progress spiritually. He makes a very interesting comment, which is essential for us to know and to transmit to our children as well.

We often tell our children that if a friend is less than they are in some ways, it isn't a worthwhile friendship. The problem with that rule is that if this is true, they should not have *you* for a friend because you are not better than they are. This expectation is both illogical and irresponsible.

What Rabbeinu Yonah is saying is that even though your friend may be on a lower level spiritually, or not as punctilious in mitzvos, it does not make a difference if you are really friends. A true friend only wants what is good for you because he wants you to be fulfilled and successful in life.

I would never want my friend to do something wrong, even if I do it. If I go to certain places that may not be on the highest spiritual plane and my friend does not, I will never say to him, "Come with me." If I invite him to come along, it means I no longer care about him.

What should I say when a friend who has never done some of my activities wants to join me in them?

---

2   *Taanis* 7a.

"No way! It's bad enough that I am in this, but you should not get involved."

Real friends never want to drag you down. They want you to be a successful, growing person. One who does not respect your values or want to see you moving forward is not a friend.

C. Friendship and Trust

Rabbeinu Yonah finally teaches us that a friend is someone you can trust. The ability to confidently share a secret, discuss issues, and receive advice is a crucial element of trustworthy friendship. If your relationship is missing any one of these elements, it is on a lower level.

Those three things comprise the litmus test of friendship: one with whom you can learn things to become a better person, whom you can trust with a secret, and from whom you can get good ideas and advice.

Friendly Advice

Talking things through with a friend often helps us to resolve our issues. You may be embarrassed to talk about your problems because you think of them as very personal, and you may believe you are the only one in the community who is undergoing such challenges. Once you open up and speak with a trustworthy friend or two, you will undoubtedly discover that almost everyone on the block is dealing with very similar questions.

Friends in your stage of life most probably have questions about the future, their children, *hashkafah*, and more. Perhaps you have more questions in one area while they have in another, but both of you need answers. Talking to friends whom you can trust and who care about the things you need help with is a good idea.

You will find that sharing relieves you of part of the load. Although it may seem to you as if there are no solutions, someone else may see an obvious answer. Perhaps he faced a similar situation, or has already spoken to a *rav* about the same question. It is even possible that this was never an issue for him because he has a different perspective that just resolves the whole problem. Conferring with friends can be a very potent element in your support system.

How and When to Identify with Friends

Your friend may not be dealing with your difficulties, and you do not have to identify with him to the point of turning his problem into yours, but being aware that you have each other for support is vital.

We often lose touch with good friends. Circumstances may have changed, we are distracted by many daily cares, or we might have moved to a different community. We still share many aspects of our lives. Distance shouldn't be a barrier.

Just think about how businesses operate today. Many companies now function well without a central office. You can and should use the telephone, email, and any other appropriate medium available to you to perpetuate friendship. Take the little time that's required to keep in touch with people who were once significant to you. You can still hold on to them, and they can be key to your support system. There is no excuse not to reach out and take advantage of their friendship.

Sometimes, the most significant help you can receive from speaking to a friend is the realization that you really need to ask somebody more experienced than either of you for advice. After you've discussed the problem once or twice and seen that you have not gained any clarity, you know that you will have to go elsewhere. That, too, is a level of help, because you have finally accepted your need for further direction.

Good People in a Community

The next level in a support system will come from the extraordinary people who exist in every community. In every new circumstance in life, we have two choices. We can attempt to speculate on the best way to deal with it, or we can accept guidance from people who have experience and insight into such situations.

Many *baalei teshuvah* have found great wisdom and guidance by connecting with a family that not only has more experience than they but has been successful in navigating life's challenges. It is a wise investment of time and effort.

What makes them "extraordinary" people is that they give of themselves. They are people who, when you knock on their doors at 8:30 in the evening, are capable of accepting you graciously and are ready to invite you in and deal with whatever it is that you need.

Most people who are absorbed in their own questions, problems, and worries do not have the ability to be so giving. When you find those who can really help, make sure you take into consideration that everyone has limitations. Take care not to become someone who is so totally self-absorbed that you do not see the one helping you. No one can be a one hundred percent giver—and no one should ever be a one hundred percent taker.

Become a Giver

It is important to become involved in your community. This does not mean that you run the biggest *chessed* organization, constantly leaving your family and doing everything else in the world except taking care of your main responsibilities.

Being involved in the community means that you make sure to not always be a taker, but look for ways to contribute. Each person gives according to what he or she can do. When someone is making a *simchah*, we can bake a cake. A neighbor had a baby, can we make an occasional supper? This may seem difficult because it can be hard enough to prepare supper every night for our own family, but as we're doing it anyway, we can go the extra mile.

I know a family that most people assume has everything under control, so it is rare that others offer to help them. The parents told me how pleased and surprised they were when one evening, after the birth of a child, a neighbor decided to make supper for them. It was clear that she spent a lot of time making a gourmet meal, but the children would not even look at it. The father smiled and said thank you to the neighbor, closed the door, and all the children groaned, "Oh no! Not spinach quiche!" It pays to take an extra two minutes and find out what the children like.

Prepare something easy, basic, but make *something*. By becoming givers, we will become involved in our communities.

When your children's schools host an event, party, or *siyum*, who are the parents who somehow find the time to come twenty minutes early and help set up? It seems that there are always people who manage to do these things. We admire the refreshments. "Beautiful! This is really so nice."

Without being judgmental, we need to ask ourselves where we want to be in this equation. Is it really so difficult to be the one who makes the pie rather than the one who takes it for granted? Do we want to be the parents the principal tries to avoid, or the ones he runs to greet because he knows we are willing to give him some time or effort when he needs it?

In all community affairs, the good people in the community join together to do things. When we ask how we can be of help, even in small ways, we become givers. Remember, however, that *chessed* begins at home, and there is a limit to how much each person can do. Sacrificing our families to help others is not an option.

Where to Draw the Line

Once we become known as givers, there will often be people who try to take advantage of us, whom we feel are demanding too much. It is essential to know when to say no. One of the best indications of where to draw the line is to become aware of how we feel when helping someone.

Positive acts engender good feelings. If someone is pushing us beyond our limits, however, we begin to feel resentful. Try not to reach that point. The Torah teaches us that feeling regret for a bad deed or a sin is part of *teshuvah*, repentance, as regret washes away our wrongdoing. The frightening power of regret, though, is that feeling that way in regard to having done a mitzvah causes its reward to be lost.[3]

If we feel tense when certain people call for help, we must learn to say, "I'm sorry, but I can't discuss/get involved with this right now."

Not setting limits can cause us to lose our capacity for giving. While we would like to be able to handle everyone's requests with a happy, open heart, we have to be honest with ourselves and know what we can reasonably do.

---

3   *Kiddushin* 40b: *"Toheh al ha'rishonos."*

As one of the givers in your community, known as a caring person, you gain access to others in that category who will become an accepted part of the infrastructure of your support system. They know many other people, and can open doors heretofore closed to you. You may thus become part of the community that knows how to get things done.

See the Good in Others

An extraordinary young student of mine came to me some time ago saying, "Rabbi Greenwald, I read this book, *How to Win Friends and Influence People*, by Dale Carnegie. Ever since I read it, I have not been able to look anybody in the face. I learned how false and manipulative people can be, and I find it difficult to trust anybody."

"You know," I answered, "you are such an understanding, sensitive person that you realized something that many people who read the book do not grasp. While the book provides good tools to achieve the goals set out in the title, it is too easy to use those tools on the basis of deceitful flattery. Flattery is forbidden by the Torah.[4] As Chazal say, 'Flatterers bring wrath to the world...their prayers are not heard...they fall into Hell,'[5] and 'Flatterers do not get to see the countenance of Hashem in the World to Come.'"[6]

I explained to my student that what he had read between the lines of the book was the ulterior motive inherent in this behavior: being nice in order to get something.

"Dale Carnegie is a good read, but that is not the *emes* on which we base our lives. The Torah asks us to see the good in someone and acknowledge it not for our own sakes, but because we want to help him appreciate himself. A compliment is giving; flattery is taking. It is fine to read Dale Carnegie, but you have to keep in mind that our ultimate goal is to have the *ayin tovah*, the good eye, of our father Avraham,[7] to see the good in, and want only the good for, the people around us."

---

4   *Sifri, Bamidbar* 35:33.
5   *Sotah* 41b.
6   *Sefer Chareidim*, in the name of Rabbi Shimon ibn Gabirol, Spain (1021–1058).
7   *Pirkei Avos* 5:19.

Be Productive

Let us take this a step further. Pushing ourselves to become involved in the needs of others will help us to become better people. Giving helps us to feel good, and healthy too.

Those of my students who live in smaller communities away from the main centers of Jewish population are often concerned with regard to finding a *shidduch* after graduation. Is it better for them to live at home, settled and happy in a familiar environment, or to board with strangers and risk being unhappy? Should they remain in their small town or city where they might have a problem finding a job, or move to a place where there would be more prospects for both work and *shidduchim*?

My answer is invariably that the place where you can be most productive is where you should live, as that will allow you to feel good about yourself. Your best bet at becoming good marriage material is being in an environment where you function well, even if there are fewer prospects there.

If you are considering living where you are uncomfortable because there may be many prospective *shidduchim* there, you must realize that misery is the antithesis of a productive life. Frustrated, unhappy people do not draw others to them. Putting on a smiling face for a date does not come close to being happy and productive.

Productive people become more involved with others, adding to their own support system.

When We Need to Take

One of the difficulties in life is that there are times when we need others, when we have no choice and must take. There are even halachos that deal with the best way to trick people who are reluctant to receive into taking something they need from others.[8] Nobody wants to feel indebted. It is difficult to owe people, and especially embarrassing when we cannot foresee the ability to repay them.

---

8   *Shulchan Aruch, Yoreh Deah* 253:9.

The secret of surviving and growing from such an experience lies in acknowledging that which we received, being thankful and showing our appreciation. In this way we build yet another relationship. By not taking help for granted, we are living with some level of reciprocity. Thanks, in a sense, is giving back. Appreciation is a limited but sufficient method of giving back when we are not capable of doing more.

Parents and Support

Last, but certainly not least, on this list of people for possible support are our parents. When we don't seem to see eye to eye with them, needing their help can be a bit tricky. Speaking to parents who are on a different page can be delicate, and we wonder how we can deal openly with them. How can we approach them about issues and problems that are foreign to them?

How, for example, can you talk about a spouse they did not want you to marry, or about your children's schooling if they don't think your children are getting a proper education in the first place? To add to the confusion, many people conclude that because their parents do not agree with anything they are doing, they will never understand.

In his secular childhood, Sean had a great relationship with his father, Dave. They loved fishing every Sunday and playing handball together every other Wednesday evening. They spoke about school, friends, and especially sports. Sean was a state champion in handball, as had been his father. They had both been captains of their team at the same college—twenty-five years apart. They knew the name of every player in the US, his style and record.

With his father's blessings, he visited Israel on a Birthright tour, met an incredible family who invited him to a Shabbos meal during his extended stay, and something moved inside him. When he took a year's leave of absence from school to go to yeshiva, he left the team. His father's dreams of his becoming an Olympic champion were smashed, and chaos was the only

way to describe the sentiment at home. Dave, who was usually
so loving and friendly, ranted and raved for a week. He con-
tinued his angry response by not speaking to anyone who was
nice to Sean for the next three months. Sean understandably
withdrew, sadly losing out on a beautiful relationship.

Sean made two grave mistakes in not discussing the process of his decision with his family. He should have entered into a dialogue with them and explained his perspective. He didn't do that because he reasoned that his dad would never agree to it. He was correct regarding his father's unchanging opinion, but he was wrong for not presenting his own. Second, by withdrawing, he let go of something that was both central to his life and precious. He will have wonderful friends, perhaps extraordinary mentors, but he will never have another father.

When I met Sean at my Shabbos table in 2002, it had been two years since he had spoken to his Dad. His pain was real, yet his determination to "do what is right" helped him keep his resolve and not give in. After his third visit to our home, having thought about a comment I had made, he came by one evening to talk about the situation.

We discussed his not having brought his father into his initial decision. It was clear that doing so would have been uncomfortable, and perhaps even painful, but in retrospect, nowhere near as distressing as the present relationship. They would have disagreed, argued, and maybe even said some harsh words, but there would have been a basis for further dialogue. There would have been a time to come back and say, "Dad, you were right about point A, but I want you to know how happy I am about so many other things. What do you think about my next step?"

Seven years have passed. Sean, now called Simcha by everyone
except his family, is working in his father's business. They play
handball once a week, and study as learning partners every day.
Last summer, Grandpa took Simcha and his four-year-old son,
Yaakov Dovid, for a three-day camping and fishing trip during
which they ate the kosher fish they caught. On returning home,

Sean's father agreed with his wife that the time had come to make their kitchen kosher.

It would be a grave mistake to think that you cannot respect your parents just because they do not agree with you on many things. It is unnecessary, and usually wrong, to cut them out of your lives.

There are obviously subjects that you are not going to discuss with your parents. You won't ask them for advice regarding the *cheder* or day school for your child if they know nothing about religious education, but you can talk to them about many things in which they do have life experience.

Life experience is *chochmah*, wisdom.[9] There are many opportunities to explain some of your dilemmas and hear what they have to say. After all, they love and care about you, and are by far the most interested in your continued development. (The issue of families that are antagonistic, angry, and looking for retribution for the changes you made will be discussed in chapter 11.)

There are many aspects of your life that most certainly can be discussed with your parents. Suitable topics can include your daily activities, hobbies and special interests, their grandchildren, possible job offers, dealing with kids who throw tantrums, and which car to buy. These discussions build a relationship, bringing them into your life, helping them to realize that there can be mutual respect despite ideological and theological differences.

You must not think that you are alone. Healthy parents (as many of us know, now that we are in that position) are loving, giving, and forgiving, and truly desire what is best for their children. The fact that there are issues on which you disagree does not detract from their interest in remaining or becoming part of your support system.

---

9   *Maharal, Nesivos Shalom, Nesiv Hashalom*, ch. 3.

Chapter 11

Who Changed, Anyway?

"The Family in Which We Grew Up" is a very intricate and challenging topic with many different aspects. Included in it are emotional and, very often, complicated issues involving relationships, finances, family dynamics, politics, and the ways in which they affect our lives.

There are *baalei teshuvah* who came home from Israel and created a horrible state of affairs at home. Parents had to deal with changes and expectations that were truly out of bounds in their eyes.

Perhaps one did not receive elementary direction from his mentors, or perhaps they failed to internalize what had been taught. It cannot fall to the parents to overcome the challenges their child has created in choosing a different lifestyle.

Whatever the background, inappropriate behavior toward our parents and family is unacceptable.

It is interesting that we are convinced that our parents need to accept us as we are, expecting them to totally embrace any of the decisions that we make in our lives. When we do things that differ from the way they raised us, we assume it is their role to be accepting of our new circumstances. The truth is, and with honest introspection it should be clear, that it is we who must continue to accept our parents and family because they are the same as they always were.

Rejectionist Damaging

As you are the one who has changed, you have to recognize that you cannot show lack of respect to your family. Their automatic, default perception of your new way of life is that they, their values, and everything they have taught you are being rejected. Although you never thought of it that way, it is nonetheless the subliminal message that was received.

From your point of view, you discovered new concepts that were at first interesting, then important, and eventually essential, comprising what you now know is *emes*. As everything about it was mind-blowing and exhilarating, your decision followed naturally.

In the simplest terms, however, the only thing your parents could possibly understand is that they and their values have been rebuffed. Despite your protests, the act of strengthening your religious beliefs beyond any of their teachings and actions signifies rejection of their value system. Their attitudes will reflect what they suppose yours to be.

It is vital, therefore, to make sure that your parents and family know how you truly feel. One of your chief goals is to make sure that everyone, especially your parents, knows that they are still loved and respected.

Keeping a Beautiful Relationship

> There is a very special couple I'd like to tell you about. The wife became frum when she was still in college, and before she knew it, she was dating no less than an aspiring young rabbi. Her parents were not too excited about the shidduch, but they were kind, understanding people, and they tried to be accepting of the match.
>
> The day after the wedding, the husband turned to his new wife. "OK," he said, "let's go."
>
> "Where are we going?" she asked.
>
> "To visit your parents."
>
> "Today?" She was surprised. "We just saw them at the wedding, and we'll be with them at sheva berachos tonight. Is it really so necessary to go there right now?"
>
> "I want to tell you something," he replied. "Your parents were a thousand percent sure when they walked you down the aisle

last night that it was the last time that they were going to see you. By marrying a rabbi, you were rejecting their way of life, and they thought you would be happy to be out of their house because you will be living differently now. Somewhere inside them, there is a fear, a sense that they've lost you. I think we have to give them a very strong and immediate message that this is not true."

"Ridiculous!" she answered. "How could they possibly think that?"

Although skeptical, she agreed to go. Later that morning, they knocked on her parents' door. The look on their faces, when they opened it, immediately told her that her husband had been right. It was clear that the young couple were the last people in the world her parents had been expecting to see.

I can tell you from having known this family for many years that they had an unusually close, beautiful relationship for forty-some years, until the parents passed away. This relationship, I believe, was greatly enhanced by that first day's kindness, a monumental moment that said better than any words: We still love you, care about you, and are happy to see you. We have not put you out of our lives.

The couple never attempted to tell their elders what to do. As far as I know, the parents never once came for Shabbos to the children's home, nor did they end up having a strictly kosher home themselves.

They were, however, a most loving, caring family that supported everything their children decided to do at various points in their lives. They were always there for them as well as for their grandchildren, and it all hinged on the fact that they felt understood and respected.

Parents automatically feel rejected unless clearly given a different kind of message. I give this advice to students who are going back to live near their parents in the States after having lived a couple of years in Eretz Yisrael.

It makes no difference whether it is a young man or woman who became religious in yeshiva or seminary, or an observant student who is inspired to greater heights. The process is the same on different levels. The one thing that parents fear more than anything else is losing the child they have raised. They cannot accept the different lifestyle because they assume that if their children have new values, they have lost them.

The time to prevent that feeling of rejection is before it sets in. If you missed that first opportunity, begin from the moment you realize that this is what has happened. Keep in constant touch, visit when possible, send pictures, emails, and make phone calls, use WhatsApp, Skype, Zoom, and everything else you can do to give your parents the *nachas* they want and, I might add, deserve.

Whether you are twenty or fifty, as long as your parents are alive, they need the satisfaction, attention, and the sense that you are there for them. True, you may not live nearby for whatever reasons, and may not be able to take care of all their physical needs when they grow old and infirm, but that is not the issue. The issue is whether or not you are giving over the sense that you still belong to them.

Do you call when your child says his first words, or let them share in the new developments in your life? Do you call just because you are their child? These questions must be honestly addressed.

It's Never Too Late

Over the years, however well intended, those feelings might have grown to the extent that enormous gaps in your relationships have developed.

Please do not give up. The Torah teaches us that it is never too late to repair the relationship between a child and his parents. Hakadosh Baruch Hu is the ultimate father. Chazal explain the nature of fatherhood, and the Gemara discusses the concept at length.[1] The Torah says,

---

1   *Kiddushin* 36a.

"You are children of Hashem, your *Elokim*."[2] Rabbi Meir explains: you are always children to Hashem, your God.

We interpret this to mean that no matter what happens, we never lose the status of a child to our parents. We learn from our relationship with Hashem that this is an absolute. It can never change.

The Torah describes us in many different ways, not all flattering, but we remain His children. The advantage of remaining a child is that if we have acted disgracefully or horribly, but cease these actions, Hashem automatically allows us back into His house.

If your parents feel understood, they will be able to accept you even though difficult emotions may have erupted and sharp words may have been said over the years. *The relationship between a child and a parent can always be rebuilt.*

Friendships can go astray, marriages can be destroyed, and various stresses can cause unbridgeable chasms in relationships, but the bond between parents and children is unique; a way can always be found to overcome the obstacles. (Please note that this applies only to emotionally and mentally healthy people; the topic of emotionally or mentally disturbed parents is one on which we will discuss in chapter 21.)

Respect Is the Key

Respect is the key to maintaining a good relationship with relatives who have a different lifestyle, and the secret ingredient needed to live compatibly with all kinds of people. Once again, the Mishnah offers a very interesting insight into how this works.[3]

"Who is a respected person?" asks the Mishnah, and answers, "One who respects others." The nature of respect is such that the more I have for others, the more they will have for me.

This sometimes seems counterintuitive. Parents often think that they should demand respect. Teachers believe that they should command respect. Politicians and others in positions of power have similar

---

2   *Devarim* 14:1, "בנים אתם לה'."
3   *Pirkei Avos* 4:1.

assumptions. The kind of deference afforded us by our position in life is nothing but lip service. It is not the kind of regard we really want.

Rabbi Yechiel Bamberger, *shlita*, the head of the Haifa Beis Din, told me the following story:

> Yankel went to visit his cousin Beryl in a different town but didn't know his address. He asked the first person he met, "Where can I find Beryl, the shamash [sexton] of the shul?"
>
> "Beryl the shamash, Beryl the shamash? That thief, that low life, that…"
>
> "Where does he live?" Yankel persisted.
>
> "Just go straight, make a right, and ask somebody."
>
> Yankel did as he was told, and asked the next person, "Where is the home of Beryl the shamash?"
>
> He was again surprised to hear, "Beryl the shamash? That liar, that deceitful, hateful man?"
>
> He met another person and another, until he had spoken to five more people on the way, each of whom cursed his cousin so badly that he did not want anyone to know they were related. He finally reached the house, and his cousin welcomed him with coffee and cake. As they were catching up on the family news, Yankel finally got up the courage to ask, "So, how is your job?"
>
> "Oh, you know, it is a little hard…not everything goes the way we want…"
>
> "Tell me, if it is so hard, why remain in the position?" asked Yankel.
>
> His cousin was surprised at the question.
>
> "…And prestige is nothing?" his cousin asked.

Kavod, honor or prestige, is of no value if it is not real. The *kavod* shown to someone in his presence because he is needed is faked. Behind his back people may speak ill of him, but he still has the illusion of being respected.

The Mishnah tells us that true *kavod* is shown when we appreciate the other person, who will automatically reciprocate the feeling. In order to truly appreciate the value of another person—not in terms of flattery but in true appreciation of his significance—I have to recognize my own worth, my own humanity.

When I have an understanding of that, I can appreciate others. Even if there are some things about them that I don't like and that may irritate me, I can still value them as human beings. This becomes possible only when I know my own worth. If I am honest with myself, I probably know that I have a very long list of faults, possibly even more than someone else's, yet I believe that I am a human being who was put here for a reason.

My faults are my challenge, giving me purpose, something to work toward. I am unique in the history of mankind. From the time of Creation through eternity, there will never be another me!

The whole world was created for my sake.[4] Hashem would not have put me here if I did not have innate value. When I internalize this, I can understand the significance of others as well. A respected person, a person of value, of essential worth, is one who respects others.[5]

Respect and Appreciation

Respect is similar to appreciation. After recognizing and accepting *emes*, beginning to live for a real purpose, you may have regarded others as shallow and misguided. In your interactions, you may have involuntarily regarded them with somewhat less respect. It is very sad when your own parents, sensing this, lose their esteem for *you*. Should that happen, something will be missing in your ability to appreciate the people who brought you into the world, providing almost everything needed to become what you are today.

The Torah teaches us that every person, Jew and non-Jew alike, is important in the scheme of things.[6] Hashem expressed a special love

---

4   This was discussed at length in chapter 5.
5   *Pirkei Avos* 4:1.
6   Ibid., 3:14.

toward man, who was created *b'tzelem Elokim*, in His image. Although this requires us to show regard for all people, it is absolutely necessary to show much greater appreciation to our parents, no matter who they are, how they live or what they do, than to anyone else.

Showing your parents the respect they deserve and accepting them for who they are does not mean that you agree with their lifestyle, nor does it imply that you condone everything they say or believe.

We all have friends whom we value for the good we perceive in them while not agreeing with their taste or priorities. Your parents can only accept and respect you if there is reciprocity. It is you who needs to begin the process, because you are the one who made the changes!

Open-Mindedness

You may feel that I am a little too open-minded. Is this an advantage or a disadvantage? Rabbi Dovid Refson, founder of the Neve Yerushalayim College for Women, is fond of saying, "Some people are so open-minded that their brains fall out."

The open-mindedness to which we are referring, however, is the understanding that there are over seven billion people in the world, and each is different. It means that I can hear another opinion without being swayed or becoming angry, that I do not lose my presence of mind because I hear that there is a way of thinking other than mine. I do not have to agree with it, but I can listen.

In a discussion with relatives or other people with whom I am close, open-mindedness simply means that I understand their position, and that any disagreement I have with it is not going to affect the way I relate to them.

Your family members are who they are; they gave you what they could, and only if they feel respected will they be able to accept who you have become.

Serious Opposition

A more serious problem arises when dealing with parents or other family members who are diametrically opposed to your decisions. They may feel threatened or hurt, or be emotionally unhealthy, and you need to learn how to react to these difficult situations.

Please understand the difference between feeling threatened or hurt and being emotionally unhealthy. In the latter instance, there is very small chance, if any, that you will be able to resolve the damaging situation yourself. Where parents or relatives feel hurt, estranged, or rejected, there is something that can be done to mitigate those feelings. Challenging relationships can be repaired because most of them, certainly when they involve parents, are worth the investment of time and effort.

Beverly was a model for a large clothing company. Mike, her twenty-one-year-old son, had always shown her off to his friends. As Mike began to become religious, however, he no longer brought his new friends home. He would go to classes at the local kiruv (outreach) kollel where he had a chavrusa with one of the rabbis. Beverly was distraught; Mike not only stopped showing her off, but he seemed ashamed of her. When she asked him to bring his friends over for a drink, he stammered, hemmed, and hawed.

Then there was a Chanukah party at the kollel. The very eager young kollel wife called the house and invited Mike and his family. Mike did not want his mom at this party, knowing exactly how she would dress and not knowing how to direct her otherwise. His attempt to explain tz'nius (modesty) to his mother fell flat, especially as he himself was still dating his not-very-tzanua "half-Jewish" girlfriend (even though he already knew he would not marry her).

In a class a month or two earlier, another new student had asked one of the kollel members if his beautiful wife had ever considered becoming a model? The kollel man had explained that his wife would consider that as just another form of selling one's body. Mike deeply respected the rabbis at the kollel and had begun to understand the dissonance between their views and his mother's chosen occupation.

Beverly was beside herself. Mike was going crazy on her! They argued for days, insulting and hurting each other. Finally, Mike stopped going to classes, went off to college and did not speak to his mother for the next four months. During midwinter vacation, he came home even more observant, unwilling to eat his mother's food or stay at home for Shabbos. His mother told him that he was no longer welcome at home, and that he could pay his own way through his master's program.

He met his former chavrusa, the local kollel rabbi, at the kosher bakery two days later. He told the whole story and shame-facedly admitted that he had been too taken up in his own conflicts to call for help. The rabbi invited Mike and Beverly for coffee with his wife, Chaya. Lo and behold, this very sensitive and intelligent rebbetzin figured out exactly what to say and how to say it. After complimenting Beverly on her beautiful appearance and admiring her outfit, they sat down for a friendly schmooze. Beverly asked Chaya about her family and they had a great time comparing notes on the antics of their children. Eventually, they spoke about Chaya's upbringing, her younger years and the choices she had made. Chaya told Beverly how she had grown up as a very beautiful young woman who often received catcalls and remarks. When she was eighteen, she was offered the chance to be a model for a local business in the city where she lived. She discussed how torn she had been; on the one hand the adulation and money, on the other hand she felt a sense of being exposed and objectified. In the end, she decided that she wanted to work on her inner spiritual self rather than on her physical appearance. She married her husband and is very happy with her role as a mother and teacher. Beverly left feeling respected and understood. She admired the young rebbetzin and her beautiful home and hospitality. The visit broke the ice between Mike and herself and despite the previous anger that had been unleashed between mother and son, the intense hurt slowly dissipated, and a respectful relationship evolved. It took a couple of years and lots of work on both sides to completely erase what had transpired, but Mike, who never went to yeshiva, finished his MBA with a kippah on his head, tzitzis on his back, and his mother at his side.

Unhealthy Relationships

There are parents whose antagonism comes from the unfortunate fact that the relationship was never a healthy one. People who are emotionally unhealthy cannot relate normally to their families. Some may be extremely controlling, unable to let go of those close to them.

There are those who actually ran away from such parents, becoming *frum* and changing their lifestyle in no small part attempting to escape that home. This type of parent will never accept and never forgive, because he or she was incapable of doing so before the child became religious as well.

Such behavior has nothing to do with religion, but stems from the parents' own personality, problems, and issues. Their child's relationship with them now is solidified by the fact that the child has physically broken away to live a different life, with a spouse and children, which is deemed unacceptable.

There are situations where a child, who does not even realize how controlling his parents are, has never moved out to avoid conflict. The child stays at home and keeps the relationship going on whatever unhealthy but familiar level it has always been. Should the child develop the emotional fortitude to get married and build a family, the conflict stemming from the earlier unhealthy relationship will be exacerbated.

The general rule for relationships with unhealthy people is to limit or outright avoid contact. The Gemara teaches us that when one cannot fulfill the command to respect his parents, it is best to remove himself from the situation completely, even if it means leaving the country.[7] Unhealthy relationships are rarely sustainable. It is better to have one

---

7   *Kiddushin* 31b.

serious breach than to be in a state of constant conflict. As much as we wish that the relationship could change, the chances of this happening are extremely small unless both parties are capable of serious work. When we continue relationships that need to be curtailed, we end up hurting others and ourselves far more than had we drawn the necessary lines at an earlier time.

Abusive Parents[8]

The same rule applies when parents are abusive. Children need to leave such parents and move to a safer and healthier environment. The mitzvah of honoring one's father and mother does not apply to a *rasha*, a wicked person.[9]

Nonobservant parents certainly do not qualify as wicked.

An abusive parent, on the other hand, is considered malicious even if he was once a victim; as an adult now, his interaction with his children is that of a *rasha*, and as such, he is not included in the commandment to be honored. The child's responsibility is to leave and find a healthier place to live.

"If it is impossible for a man to show respect for his parents any longer because they have reached extreme levels of abnormal behavior," says the *Ralbag* in his exegesis on the Ten Commandments, "he should do what he can to help them through others, and he should avoid contact with them...because the Torah does not command us to do the impossible..."[10]

The *Pele Yoetz* adds that if you cannot achieve the minimal fulfillment of the mitzvah with such parents no matter what you do, especially if your changed outlook is one of the barriers between you, you have

---

8 I am not a *posek*, halachic authority, and one should consult with a *rav/posek* who is experienced with mental health issues before making serious decisions as to the definition of a *rasha*, as this is a very delicate situation. See "Important Note" in the Preface.
9 *Shulchan Aruch, Yoreh Deah* 240:18.
10 *Ralbag*, commentary on the Chumash (Jerusalem: Mossad Harav Kook, 2000), *Bamidbar*, p. 186.

no choice.[11] You must remove yourself from their presence as far away as you can, having as little to do with them as possible. If proximity is going to cause conflict on a regular basis, it is our responsibility to remove ourselves from the situation in every way feasible.

---

11   Rabbi Eliezer Papo (1786–1827) was a rabbi, *posek*, *mekubal*, and advisor in Bulgaria; *Pele Yoetz*, "*Hakaah*" (*Toras Chaim*), vol. 1, p. 173.

Chapter 12

Danger!
Outreach in Your Family

Children's attempts to improve their parents' religious observance often end in disaster. They do not work because it is the parents' job to teach their children how to live, not the reverse. While often proud of children who achieve more than they in any other sphere, parents rarely appreciate being challenged in their own area of weakness. If my father is a lawyer and I am a better lawyer, my father will be proud of me. If we are both lawyers and I go up against him on a case, however, there is probably going to be bad blood because I am challenging him.

I once had a discussion with Rav Noach Weinberg, the visionary founder and Rosh Yeshiva of Aish HaTorah. He was a rare and extraordinary man, a true *tzaddik* who influenced and shaped the entire *kiruv* movement. Part of his greatness was his tolerance of people like me, who did not always accept what some considered his idiosyncratic approach to life. Despite occasional differences, and although I considered myself a midget in his presence, we shared a very close and warm relationship that spanned almost thirty years.

We once had a discussion about whose job it is to help the parents become *frum*. I claimed that it is not the job of a child, and he said that it is the job of every Jew to help every other Jew keep the Torah, including parents.

"But the minute the child takes on the job," I said after a short exchange, "he will only cause trouble and be unable to accomplish it."

"That is true," he replied.

These seem like two opposing values. Although it is certainly not our job to make our parents keep the Torah, it *is* our job to bring Hakadosh Baruch Hu's love to all of Klal Yisrael. The *pasuk* says that just before Mashiach arrives, "the children will bring the hearts of their fathers to Hashem and to Torah."[1] It is going to happen, so is it our responsibility, or is it not?

Rav Noach was not contradicting himself. I believe that the following is the resolution.

I learned from my *rebbi* that the only way to fulfill our responsibility to teach our parents is through example. We must *never* lecture them! We must be the kind of people that all other Jews will look at and say, "That's a good way to live!"[2] If they see it, our parents might recognize it as well.

A closer look at the *pasuk* shows that it says that children will draw their father's heart to God. It does not say that they will teach their parents. They will inspire, not preach.

Picture a person coming back to visit his parents in their house. (I have seen this happen with people who have been *frum* for twenty-five years). The son is still reminding his parents to wash their hands and make a berachah. The parent reluctantly goes to the sink and the fifty-year-old son is saying, "*Baruch…*" The father mumbles the words after him in embarrassment. After all this time, the son is still fighting with his parents!

Just as it is not your job to force your adult children to do mitzvos, you should not attempt to use coercion with your parents. Doing so will only ensure that they will *not* want to do them. It is wrong, it is counterproductive, and an already shaky relationship becomes even more untenable.

You have to be a good, *frum* Jew and show by example how happy you are with your lifestyle. Let them ask you questions. Let them urge you to explain what you are doing and why. No pressure. You can then

---

1   *Malachi* 3:24, "והשיב לב אבות על בנים ולב בנים על אבותם."
2   *Yoma* 86a.

answer their questions gently, responding to their inquiries without making demands. Don't expect them to say the entire *bentching* after eating, but buy *bentchers* with an English translation and casually put them on the table. Leave the decision of whether or not they will be used up to the family.

None of us likes to be told how to conduct his life. Just as your children learn how to live their lives by observing what you do, you learned many good things from your parents as well. Similar tools have to be used when teaching values.

One of my students had a very hard time with any form of stringency in halachic rulings. Whenever someone would suggest taking on a stricter form of mitzvah performance, she would get all bent out of shape. I casually asked about her extreme reactions in a conversation one day, and her response really shed light on this matter.

Her family had lived in a small, mostly Orthodox community in the United States. When she turned eleven, her parents, both *baalei teshuvah*, decided to move to a large, strong Torah community where they felt they would be able to give their children a better, stronger Jewish education. Once they moved, this young lady had to give up riding her bicycle, change all her clothes, and wear her hair differently, while her parents took on *chalav Yisrael* and *yashan*; there went the Entenmann's donuts, her favorite nosh. Out went her most beloved outfits, and before she could say, "I love Brooklyn" three times fast, she was not allowed to do many things that had been acceptable in their previous life.

Her parents, in their intense desire to fit in and be accepted, demanded full compliance so that all the children would be accepted in their new schools. They neither eased her along nor helped her with the process. Instead of encouraging growth, they pressured, forced, and demanded changes and conformity.

We should not have to nag or push. The proper way to transmit vital ideas and ideals is to take the path that conforms to the dictum "The ways of Torah are pleasant, and all its paths are of peace."[3]

---

3   *Mishlei* 3:17.

This is the reconciliation of my position and that of Rav Weinberg. Rav Noach taught, and of course, he was correct, that it is every Jew's job to make sure that every other Jew becomes a lover of Torah and mitzvos. My position was, and remains, that an observant Jew has to be the kind of person who will encourage others, parents included, to be interested in becoming *frum*.

There is a subtle difference in wording, but the difference in approach is vast. I am happy to report that at the *sheva berachos* of one of my sons, Rabbi Weinberg accepted my explanation and wholeheartedly agreed with me. With that huge smile that came from his even huger heart, he said, "You can only do what works, and there is no way that pushing parents will work."

It is clear that if parents are interested and are asking questions, you have a responsibility to help them move forward *at the rate that they can accept*.

I had an interesting experience a number of years ago. We spent Shabbos with an older couple whose child had become religious many years earlier. We spent a pleasant few hours chatting. A day or two later, the elderly gentleman came to me and said, "You know, it's really interesting. I didn't know that religious people could be so friendly and happy."

Oh my, I said to myself, *hadn't his own son become religious?*

I found out that there had been, and still was, great tension between them about the son's observance, and they had never once been able to relax and enjoy each other's company as in the past. After he became religious, the boy, in the father's perception, had become a recluse. Although his son had been outgoing, and their relationship had been very close, once religion entered the picture, he seemed to turn into someone else.

Young and idealistic, he wanted his folks to become religious as well, so he tried to encourage them to make changes in which they had no interest.

This tension took over the relationship, and the son did not have the sense to comprehend what had gone wrong.

Honoring Parents[4]

By carefully studying the laws of honoring one's parents, we can learn something valuable about combining interaction with our parents *and* our enthusiasm for keeping Torah and mitzvos. The laws of *kibbud av va'eim*, honoring one's father and mother, provide clear guidance in a case when both a father and his son are knowledgeable about the Torah and mitzvos, but the father is about to do something wrong. The son is not allowed to say, "Daddy, that is prohibited."[5]

The Torah tells us the correct way to do it. The son may hint to the father by showing him the words of a halachic authority about the matter, as if he is asking the parent to interpret the meaning for him. The father will then realize what he is doing wrong. Telling him outright that he is mistaken is against halachah. Even though the father is observant, and would want to understand his error, there is a correct protocol.

How much more careful must we be when a father does *not* want to hear that he needs correction. This is a delicate situation because even when he is unable or unwilling to hear that he should change, the child still needs to respect him. The mitzvah of honoring one's father and mother applies to almost all situations in life.

The primary exception is that if a parent commands a child to violate the laws of Torah, the son or daughter does not have to listen.

There are rare cases, as explained earlier, where honoring parents is adjusted, when the child isn't capable of fulfilling the commandment because of the parent's inability to function normally. In such a case, the mitzvah is to put distance between them.

Even then we are not allowed to be disrespectful. We would hesitate to tell a parent how to operate his business, so why should we think it suitable to tell him how to run his life?

Good human relations require that a child find a way to preserve whatever areas exist in which his parents can still relate to him. Asking

---

4   Please see "Important Note" in the Preface. All discussions that have halachic consequences should be followed up with a rabbi to deal with your particular situation.

5   *Shulchan Aruch, Yoreh Deah* 240:11.

your parents for advice about things in which they are knowledgeable or experienced is essential to building a better relationship. Try to keep it going on the level that is most satisfying for both of you. The better your relationship, the greater chance you will have to influence them. The more honest you are about your search, the more likely they will be to join in.

None of us has the whole truth packaged and ready to give to anyone else. Not everything that works for me will work for someone else. In the vast majority of cases that I have seen, however, if you modestly and humbly continue your search for growth and truth, your parents will have a role model from whom to learn.

Chapter 13

Parents, Continued

Acceptance and Respect...and Denial

One of life's difficulties is learning to see things as they are, as opposed to the way we want them to be. No matter how uncomfortable or challenging a fact or situation makes us feel, with acceptance we can then decide how to deal with it. It may be painful, but so be it.

The opposite of this acceptance would be denial.

When someone changes around his entire life, it is often the response of their parents to react with denial. Denial is one of man's initial, instinctive responses to challenging situations. It may take the form of fighting the fact, ignoring it, or making believe that it doesn't exist at all. We must be aware of this impulse and work against it. By refusing to recognize their child's decisions or values, it becomes OK to force him into a different mold because they cannot accept who he has become, This, of course, will not help him be what they want him to be.

If those who made the changes are understanding and respectful of their parents, it will help the parents be accepting of their children despite their new lifestyle.

Your parents might be in denial, and you therefore need to understand them and help them through this.

When Parents Feel Threatened

Rabbi Dovid Refson tells a story involving a very well-known Jewish political activist from the United States. Her extremely vocal liberal views were her trademark, and by some quirk of fate her daughter ended up, of all places, in Neve Yerushalayim.

The unhappy lady telephoned Rabbi Refson, unleashing a tirade of anger and frustration.

Rabbi Refson, in his very restrained British manner, said, "Excuse me, with whom am I speaking?"

She gave her name.

"Oh," he said, "is this Mrs. __? I really enjoyed your article last week in which you wrote that people must be allowed to adopt any lifestyle they wish!" He went on to quote the various positions that she was known to espouse.

Suddenly, all her liberal views and beliefs were challenged. Had her daughter decided to marry an aboriginal pygmy or live in a Buddhist ashram, this woman would most likely not have voiced any objections—people can do whatever they want, can't they?

Becoming *frum* is entirely different, however; this was a decision that she could not accept. The values that she held dear, and with which she had brought up her daughter, were being challenged! When her child questioned *the way her mother acted as a Jew*, it was a criticism of the parent's lifestyle and beliefs.

Such a challenge evokes the fear of being abandoned. Our parents feel, "I am the same person I always was; *I* haven't changed. Why has my child changed?" Since we are the ones who have changed, it is up to us, the children, to allay our parents' fears. We have to realize that our parents, as much as their love is reciprocated, often cannot understand that which has so deeply affected us.

Think about it for a moment and put yourself in their shoes. They feel they did a pretty good job raising you. They gave you an education, did all the things a father and mother are supposed to do, and then one fine day you come home with a whole new set of rules. You can only eat this, cannot come to visit on certain holidays, can't do some of your former activities, etc. When you come to their home, certain subjects are taboo; their grandchildren's vocabulary has these strange words; they may be asked to dress a certain way when they visit.

Before you tell yourself that your parents are not being understanding, you have to consider who is really suffering in this situation. You have hit them with an entirely new set of rules. Without your help they have no information, and no way to deal with these all-encompassing changes in a sensible way.

As a loving child, what are your options? You can be upset that they are unable to understand you or be compassionate. They have always said, "We just want you to be happy," but now they really think that you are being unreasonable. They are afraid that you are *not* going to be happy with these extreme customs; that you "must have been brainwashed."

Every year, there are many parents who fly to Eretz Yisrael, sometimes accompanied by deprogrammers, to rescue their children. Some rabbi at the Western Wall has spirited their child away to a yeshiva, and now he is lost to them.

What did we do wrong, for goodness' sake? What prompted this? Is he actually telling me that I am not religious enough, that the way I serve God or the way I conduct my life is wrong? That must be so because now he is making moral decisions that are different from the ones I made. Now, he cannot kiss Aunt Tillie; Cousin Amy is all upset; and our best friend, Chris, is totally baffled.

The whole family feels alienated, and you expect them all to *understand*. They do not realize that these decisions were not made overnight, but after much study and thought. And you may not realize that these decisions are affecting the lives of those closest to you, their comfort level and sense of security, the confidence that they did a good job of bringing up their family, and sometimes their dreams, hopes, and aspirations.

I thought he was going to go into the family business...That rich doctor wanted to marry her, and I can't understand why she turned him down...I saved for years so my grandson could become a lawyer...I already bought the 27-inch flat-screen television for my granddaughter and then she refused to take it...We put away almost every penny we earned and looked forward to that great day when our son would come home and settle down and be someone we could be proud of, and now he's decided to go off to some yeshiva and become a rabbi. What is this world coming to?

In their eyes, *you* went off the *derech*; it is *you* who strayed. Consider how it would feel if, Heaven forbid, your children challenged the way of life that you are passing on to them. It's a terrible, even frightening, feeling. You would most likely have a reaction very similar to that of your parents, who have to be helped to appreciate, understand, and love what you are doing. Even if that doesn't happen, you will hopefully help them to understand that what you are doing will make you a better and happier person. If they are able to see this actualized in you, it will be easier for them, but if every discussion ends up in hostility and disrespect, they will have legitimate questions about this new moral system.

Although your values and lifestyle are different now, there are elements that should remain the same, and one of them is your basic personality. You may now be a bit more subdued, or less excited about certain things in which you have lost interest, but that is not an essential change. Feeling the necessity to present yourself as basically different in order to prove to your parents, siblings, and old friends that something real has changed can be unhealthy.

Some *baalei teshuvah* adopt a rabbinical facade, while others may feel the need to go to extremes so the people they know will "get it," which only increases their sense of being challenged. If your decisions have made you a better human being, old friends and family may more easily accept the new you. If others remember the good aspects of your personality from before you changed, *you* should remember them as well. Personality is a trait that stays with you even after quantum changes, and sometimes it's necessary to take a good look at the baggage you are carrying, as much of it may be worth keeping.

Most people can respect high standards and lofty moral values as long as they feel accepted as equals. If there are activities you can't pursue now because they were always done on Shabbos, there may be other options. If Dad wants to take some of you bowling or Mom wants to take you and the family to the mall on Saturday, try, "That's a great idea, but I was really hoping we could do it on Sunday."

You want to convey the message that you still enjoy their company, want to spend time together, and maintain a close relationship. "I remember the great times we had hiking, Dad. If you can possibly take a day off during my vacation, we can do it again!"

Although there may eventually be limitations of marriage, work, and children, you want your parents to feel that they can still identify with you. Get rid of the tension! Show your love! You must thank them for providing you with the tools to improve your life. Many experienced and professional mentors give this advice to young people who are beginning their process of change.

Sometimes parents are correct in their concerns, they see things that are off and recognize aberrant behavior.

> *A seventeen-year-old girl who had decided that she wanted to become religious used to hang out in our home. She had previously lived in a completely nonreligious way, at risk of doing every single extreme thing that a seventeen-year-old girl could possibly do. When she became frum, she remained true to type and also carried that to extremes. Eventually, we were not religious enough for her, either.*
>
> *Before she actually stopped coming to see us, she came to me one day and said, "Rabbi Greenwald, my father asked me for your telephone number. He wants to visit you, and I am afraid."*
>
> *"What are you afraid of?" I asked.*
>
> *"He wants to kill you!"*
>
> *"Why would he want to do that?"*
>
> *"Because he says that you made me frum and he is very angry."*
>
> *"OK," I replied, "tell him to call me and I will make an appointment to see him."*

"Rabbi Greenwald, aren't you scared?"

"No, I am not scared."

"But really, he is very angry."

I just said, "OK."

When I opened my door at the appointed time, I saw a man whose face announced his unhappiness. With a warm smile and a hearty welcome, I greeted him.

"It is so nice to meet you. I have been waiting for this opportunity because I need to talk to you. It's good that you came to see me."

He was totally nonplussed. I showed him to a seat, and my wife brought him something to drink.

"Mr. Cohen, I don't know what to do about your daughter. Is this tendency to extremes a family trait? What is the source of this?"

"What?"

"Your daughter is really extreme. Are you or your wife like that? What is going on?"

"Yes," he admitted. "My daughter is extreme…"

"What are we going to do about it?" I asked. "This is not in consonance with Torah living. 'The ways of the Torah are pleasant, and all of its paths are sweet.'[1] She is really taking things too far and I don't know what to do about it. When I see certain traits in children, the first thing I do is look at the parents. I need to know what is going on at home. Are you fighting her, or pushing her? What was she like before this? I guess you must be very happy that she is interested in being observant, because I can just imagine what she would be doing now if she hadn't become religious!"

---

1   *Mishlei* 3:17.

Mr. Cohen was quiet for a moment, obviously remembering things.

"You know," he said thoughtfully, "my daughter has always had an extreme personality. What can we do?"

When he had stormed in to see me, he had been prepared to burn down all the *frum* schools and yeshivos in the world, but we parted as great friends and he left with a changed perspective. I advised him to send her to a *frum* summer camp in America because religious institutions tend to be a little bit more relaxed there than in Israel. I thought that the atmosphere there might help her to unbend, to be more accepting of others. He was so happy with the idea that he paid for her to go to a *frum* camp overseas! She was convinced that he was angry that she was religious, while he was scared of her extreme take on religion.

Unfortunately, the experience did not affect her as I had hoped, and she came back terribly upset at the religious laxity of American camps. "American Judaism is so diluted," she complained.

This young lady somehow married an extremely *frum* man who gave her a Yiddish name, and she sent her children to Yiddish-speaking schools. I wish that the rest of the story would be upbeat, but I recently learned that she is having health and marriage difficulties, along with many other challenges. May Hashem send her a *refuah sheleimah* and good advisors. She could not see her parents in the picture and her father was correct about her extreme behavior.

Helping Parents Accept Our Changes

Judging by the strength of character it took to change your life, it is only logical to surmise that you have inherited your determination and fortitude in the face of opposition. Someone in your family is evidently stubborn, strong-willed, and tough enough to make a decision and go with it. It may be these same traits that are making it difficult for your parents to make any changes now, as they are accustomed to living with whatever choices they made many years ago.

It may be time to focus your efforts on helping your parents understand that you see the good in your life now as a part of what they passed on to you, and that you are thankful for it. This attitude may change your parents' perspective of you from that of an ungrateful child who is rejecting their values, to someone who embraces their goodness and appreciates it.

I suggest to students that they share the following message with their parents.

"You know, Mom and Dad, these decisions I've made to change my life were not easy. It required integrity, a lot of thinking, and a great deal of internal strength. I really have to thank you both for giving me the intellectual and emotional fortitude, the education, the self-confidence, and all the other traits I needed to do it because I would never have been able to go forward if I hadn't learned these qualities from you."

If you can show your parents that your strength of character is a product of who they are and who they raised you to be—that you are proud of it, of them, and also of your Judaism—then you will have made it easier for them to understand where you are coming from and what you are doing. In this way, your parents may come to understand that you view your life as a positive result of their contribution to your success.

Their initial disappointment does not necessarily derive from your being religious. Parents in all walks of life must often face the fact that their children have differing goals. I had friends in yeshiva with *frum* parents who put funds away from the day their children were born so that they could go to college or law school or set up a business.

Unfortunately, too many of these individuals are unhappy today because they lived up to their parents' expectations instead of fulfilling their own personal aspirations. A parent's presumed ability to choose a vocation for a six-month-old child has always puzzled me. It obviously has nothing to do with altruistic thought processes, and most certainly nothing to do with the thinking or talents of the child. Some parents just have a need to live vicariously through their children.

This issue is no different from having to deal with parents who want their child to be a *talmid chacham* when he really wants to be a businessman, or a father who hopes his child will take over the family business when the child wants to become a *talmid chacham* or doctor. These are issues common to many, and the solution is common to all: we, the children, have to help our parents accept the fact that, although we have great respect for the sincerity of their hopes for us, we have different aspirations.

"I know you really wanted me to do such and such with my life because you wanted me to be happy, or live up to my potential. I can understand that you decided what was best for me when I was very young, but as I get older and find my own way in life, it is only natural that my decisions do not necessarily fit your dream. I am not acting out of disrespect for you, Mom and Dad, or for your goals. On the contrary, I would hope that you would be happy to see me find myself and live according to my values."

This process of becoming an independent individual is something with which every young person in every society needs to deal. It must be removed from the "religious" pigeonhole and placed in the one labeled, "I need to feel self-fulfilled."

We take our seminary students to a hotel in northern Israel when the weather gets warm. The hotel owner's only connection with religion is when he greets his religious guests. Although he has a mashgiach there all year round, his job is just to make sure all the food is kosher.

The owner is a terribly disappointed man. He has two children, neither of whom is interested in helping him run the hotel that he has built up for the past forty years. It is becoming more difficult for him to handle the work as he ages, and he begs them to come and fill in for a night, but they hate the place. One is an artist, the other is studying law, and neither are interested in the business.

The distress that this man is suffering has nothing to do with religion. It comes from raising children and learning that they made life choices other than what he had anticipated. Although

he wanted them to be able to do what they believe is right
and be happy, he can't accept the fact that they are finding
their own way.

They Are Not Young Anymore

Most of you went through your process of introspection and change
at a relatively young age, teens to mid-twenties. Your parents, if they
are inspired to change, will require a different process more suitable to
their age and life situation.

When I was nineteen years old, I went to Minneapolis, Minnesota,
to teach during the summer. When I had free time, I would go to the
Jewish bookstore to interact with the customers. Most of the time, I was
the only one in the store with a yarmulke, white shirt, and visible tzitzis,
so people would ask me for guidance in choosing reading material on
various topics. I would help them to buy a good book while hoping to
raise their interest level in Judaism.

A charming middle-aged woman who worked in the store had many
conversations with me about all these discussions.

"I cannot talk about this anymore," she said to me one day, and began
to cry.

I was not quite ready for a fifty-year-old woman's tears; it was a bit
too much for me. I asked her what I could do to help.

"You don't understand," she said, "I can't make these changes. I know
that you are right, but I am not able to do it."

"What can't you do?" I asked.

"Fifty years! What do I do, just throw them in the garbage?"

Because I was only nineteen and not so experienced or politically
correct at the time, I replied, "So, do you want to just throw away the
next fifty years after them?"

That was a little too honest for her. She did not become *frum*, but
I don't know whether it was because of what she said or because of what
I said.

This woman expressed quite frankly the difficulty of making changes
in one's later years. When we are young, it is not so difficult to reject the

values of the society around us. Your parents, however, are settled in their lives with children and perhaps grandchildren. They have an established comfort level, secure with who they are until one of their children throws a monkey wrench into the works and starts questioning everything. Even should they want to make changes, the process is going to be much more difficult, and children have to be sensitive to these feelings.

Financial Support

One of the issues that you might have at this point in your life is concern over how your parents spend their money. They seem to have money for vacations, and to buy a new and fancier car, and you can't help but wonder why they don't give the money to you instead. You may have a large family, be struggling to make ends meet, and wonder why they don't think of helping you out rather than spending it on things that you consider less urgent than your needs.

You may have friends whose parents often financially help them out, which can prompt you to wonder why you are not getting more help. The answer is that your parents have a life too; it is their money and their decision how to spend it. They raised you, paid for what they felt responsible when you were younger, and now you are on your own. They are under no obligation to continue to support you.

We have difficulty with this concept when we look at a parent in the role of a provider, and not as a person.

As a child, I was not much of a student. Sometimes, when my children come to me with their homework, although I like to help them if I can, they are usually better off asking their mother. (I appreciate the blessing of diversity in the gene pool. At least there is someone in my house who can help those of my children who resemble the way I was with their homework, and there are even some who do not need too much assistance.)

While I am willing to help, if the child wants me to actually *do* the homework for him, I say, "Excuse me, I finished my third-grade homework, and I'm not doing it again! As your father, I will do anything to help you, but I will not do your work for you."

I believe that this is good *chinuch*, that it is wrong to do homework for our children. But the real message I am telling the child is: This is *your* job right now, just as it is *your* life.

Our parents have been planning to have more time to themselves for their entire lives. Now, they have married off their children and are on their own. Having worked hard for fifty years, they have been dreaming about retirement, taking a real vacation, or doing something interesting together.

Because one of their children has ten of his own and wants them to help him out financially, must they abandon all of their cherished plans? They may rightfully feel that they have already done their share for their offspring. The fact that there are extraordinary individuals who see life's opportunities differently, happily forgoing their own vacations for the sake of their children, does not imply a lack of responsibility on the part of those who do not.

Is it surprising that many parents need and want to devote their time and their resources to themselves? Whether or not they are being selfish is completely irrelevant. We do not know their emotional states, what their *shalom bayis* requires, nor are we aware of other needs they may have. We forget to look at them as individuals, expecting them to just keep on giving, doing, and being there for us. If I need help now, of course they should drop everything for my sake.

But Mom has many things she has been planning to do, in which she is possibly already involved, and is not ready to drop everything right now for her children. Is she responsible for my welfare at this stage in life? No. Does it say anywhere in the Torah that she should be? No. But I have that expectation.

It is possible, although by no means guaranteed, that I might go out of my way to pitch in to eventually help my children, but it would not be my *responsibility*.

Such expectations are grounded in the false values of a service-oriented society.

Can you have a close relationship with someone who regards your problems with an attitude of "It's *your* life and *your* responsibility"?

I think so. When we are living such different lives from our parents, we can have a much healthier and closer relationship with them as independent individuals—*if* we respect one another.

You have your life, I have mine; there are things we do together and others that we do separately. There are aspects of your life that I appreciate, and I hope that you appreciate certain facets of mine.

You want, or should want, to reach a point when, despite having undergone immense changes in your life, you can say to your mother, "You know, Ma, you really need a vacation. Is there any way I can help you to make plans?"

Mom is surprised by the offer. "What do you mean?"

"Mom, you've been working for forty years, and just retired. Take a couple of months off; it's time you did something for *yourself.*"

The relationship is no longer a relationship of *just* mother and child, although it will always be that. It is now also one of adult to adult, and that is the way it must be approached. If you cannot assume responsibility and deal with the relationship on that level, the chasm between you will be perpetuated.

We are now living in a whole new world, in which maturity seems to be optional. In my classes on dealing with adolescents, I tell parents that adolescence used to be the developmental stage between the ages of twelve and nineteen. Today, adolescence in many Western countries continues until about thirty-five! Many adults today are not ready to take on age-appropriate responsibility and, therefore, cannot teach it to their children. It should not be surprising when children follow suit and are irresponsible.

If parents take over the children's task of choosing their profession or making other important decisions for them, their offspring will never become independent individuals. They will still be looking for support as adults. This problem is not restricted to any particular group and is quite common in a society of affluence.

Educating and raising children is a great challenge. Parents who are too giving teach their children irresponsibility: "It's coming to me." Spoiling a child retards maturation, and has the same long-term effect as neglect and control. They are all damaging, leaving the child without coping tools. Spoiled kids, or adults for that matter, *need* to have what they want, and cannot adequately function as responsible people.

Chapter 14

Communicating

Good intergenerational communication is usually the responsibility of parents when their children are growing up. But you are an adult and in the context of your growth and change, its success depends on your efforts even more. Rav Wolbe spoke to us about the concept he called "service society," from which we suffer greatly.

In most of North America, for example, you can walk into a store knowing that someone will smile and ask, "How can I help you?" The salesperson will attempt to show you what you want and, try within reason, to comply with your wishes.

"The customer is always right"—because we hope that he will return and buy something.

Living in a service-oriented society teaches us that we deserve to get the best of what life has to offer. We pay, and people provide. We understand that the world is here to serve us, and we have expectations. The pleasant music we hear upon walking into a store is not there just for our comfort, but because research indicates that when we are relaxed we spend more money than when we are tense. We walk around in a world where everything is wonderful and presented in a good light.

I am waiting in a long line at the post office. Next to the clerk is a huge pile of packages that need to be weighed and sent out, and he weighs three or four of them in between serving each of us.

Now, wait a moment! I will be paying good money for my stamps! This fellow should not be doing his work on my time. I am just about ready to go the postmaster and complain loudly. I finally get to the counter, and the clerk makes a phone call which is clearly private. I am ready to have him fired.

"Do I want to know that he was on the phone because his wife was in the hospital," Rav Wolbe would ask, "and the babysitter called to say that she cannot stay later today, so he must leave immediately after work or his young children will be left alone?"

No. I am not interested in knowing that. I want the clerk to do his job efficiently and quickly because I am a busy person. He is supposed to provide me with service, *and I want that service now*.

When I walk into a store and the salesman stays seated and continues reading his newspaper, I am justifiably upset. If he wants my money, he should be jumping up to earn it.

We have this perception with us wherever we go in this service-oriented society. The hardware store must stock all the things we need all the time. Never mind that the salesman had a flat tire that day. We do not want to hear about anything that doesn't concern us directly!

UPS has us well trained: "Guaranteed to be delivered by 10:30 tomorrow or your money back."

At 10:40, I am on the phone.

"Where is the package?"

It's too bad that the delivery man was in a crash and he is in critical condition; I am expecting my package. I do not even hear what the representative is saying, because the delivery was guaranteed ten minutes ago.

"I want my money back!"

Others do not exist; the only thing that exists is the service we expect.

I was once at a very posh restaurant in Jerusalem, waiting in a long line because I had not made reservations. I was schmoozing with the maître d' when suddenly a fellow came up to him and started screaming.

"Where's my food? Do you know how long I've been waiting to eat?"

"Excuse me, sir," replied the maître d', "as you can see, we are very busy tonight and are trying our best..."

The fellow went into a frenzy. "I just came in from the States, and I am very hungry! I told the waitress that she should hurry! If you guys can't get your act together...this waitress should be fired, and this place..."

"I am sorry, sir, but I don't control the kitchen," said the poor waitress, close to tears.

But the fellow was still livid. At this point the maître d' turned to me and said in Hebrew, "You know, because he pays a hundred dollars for dinner, he thinks he owns everyone who works here."

That is precisely the source of this terrible chutzpah. Because we pay money, we think we own people. We check out of a hotel and are asked to fill out a questionnaire: *Did all our staff perform to your liking? Did anyone not treat you right? Did anyone make your stay especially comfortable?*

We are so well trained!

Holiday Inn promoted its service with a guarantee that if you were not one hundred percent satisfied with your stay, your night would be free. Delivery services guarantee delivery on time or your money back. Almost every store in the United States has rules that allow you to change your mind if you are not satisfied with the merchandise, and either exchange it or receive a refund for your purchase.

Unfortunately, this trickles down into all our relationships, and we end up viewing everybody in our lives as service providers.

A spouse has become a job description and is someone from whom we have expectations. A husband is supposed to provide certain things, and a wife has her responsibilities.

A father looks at his child and thinks, *This child is supposed to give me nachas. Why is he not giving me nachas today?*

The child does not want to go to school because something is bothering him. This is unacceptable to his parents. The child tries to express what is wrong, but they cannot hear it.

"What do you mean, you don't want to go to school?"

In our service-oriented society, a child is not a multisided person; he is just my child, and his job is to give me *nachas*. Likewise, my parents are not independent people; they are responsible for me. It is their job to give me financial, moral, psychological, and emotional support whenever I need it.

There are people in their fifties who still look to their elders to provide for them as if they were seven years old. A rude awakening often occurs later in life if parents become infirm or incapable of functioning in various ways. Sometimes, even then, the children do not accept responsibility. Upset and disappointed, these unfortunate adults have no tools with which to deal with their own needs, let alone those of their parents.

Growing up includes recognizing that our parents may have infirmities, insecurities, fears, and concerns. In the past they may not have been, or are not presently capable of, providing us with the things we want from them. Similarly, our children have their own disabilities or challenges, and at times are just not able to provide us with the *nachas* we were hoping to see.

We have to make adjustments and allowances to deal with whatever situation is current. Understanding and overcoming the challenges of living in a service-oriented society requires the ability to communicate.

Communicating in a Service-Oriented Society

A service-demanding attitude knows no communication other than that of requirements and expectations. *Whoever or whatever you are, I expect you to provide what I desire.*

It must be very clear to us, and this is true whether or not we have made quantum changes in our lives, that our parents deal with their adult children in ways with which we are not always comfortable. However, even if their response is not what we want, it is still our responsibility to show them respect. Our parents are not automatons to be taken for granted but must be related to as individual people with their own set of values.

If we truly explore our relationships, we will probably recognize long-held expectations. If we go a little bit deeper, we will find that some of them are unrealistic and far from reasonable.

It is sad to be so disconnected that we think parents must still play the roles we assigned to them when we were children.

Expectations are the sole source of disappointment in life. Every disappointment we will ever experience is the consequence of an expectation.

When we expect things from people that they are not really capable of providing, we are setting ourselves up for even greater disappointment.

Rav Wolbe used to say that through communication we overcome differences and come to understanding. Identifying people by the ways in which they differ from us instead of striving to find commonality will always make the other person the "not normal" one, and the differences will be magnified.

Whatever dissimilarities there are or were between you and your parents do not necessarily increase because you are presently observing the mitzvos, but they may now see you as abnormal or worse, as if you are no longer the same person they knew and loved.

Communication is the best way of dealing with this gap. Speaking honestly and openly, discussing and working things out, is really the only way we can break through the normal/not-normal divide.

Harking back to our discussion of wanting to force observance on parents, you will remember that in trying to affect who they are and change them, you are seen as having placed yourself on the other, not normal side. If you try to make them feel more comfortable with the relationship, adding to the quality of their lives by giving them *nachas*, helping them to understand you in a way that they can consider reasonable, they will hopefully be able to perceive you as normal.

Sharing new information with your parents and siblings requires an artful approach that lets them know that *you* are comfortable with who *they* are. We accept that they haven't changed, and that's OK with us. We tell our parents how important it is going to be for us that our children will have grandparents of their caliber.

But what am I going to do, you may be thinking, *when my child goes to his grandparents' home and they see cable television, internet, and 46-inch flat screens with a surround-theater sound system? What am I going to do when my children visit and not everything is a hundred percent kosher? Here I am telling them how much I want my children to have them as grandparents, and inside I am thinking, oh my, what am I going to do about these grandparents?*

Whether we are convinced that it's going to be a challenge because we know our parents' mindset or because it's already happening, in most cases the real problem is that we have not built up a relationship of trust and understanding. You are afraid of what will happen when your babies grow up and you are going to have to take them to visit.

While your children are young, you probably have enough time to develop a new kind of relationship with your parents. You will need to show them that your present life is a good one, and that even though you have acquired a new set of values, there are probably quite a few with which they will agree. If you have already tried to remake your parents or turn them into what you would like them to be and things are tense between you, it is time to step back, consider all that has been said, and think about what you can do to build up a more understanding relationship.

How can you talk to your parents from here on in to help them understand who you are? Talk about your dilemmas and challenges. You don't have to ask them for advice on halachic questions, but you can share that not everything is easy. You can admit that there are things about which you do not really know so much yet, and that not only do you still have to ask questions, but that it is sometimes embarrassing to do so.

With this approach, your parents, who may still disagree about the whole matter of *kashrus* and do not understand why it is so complicated that you still have to ask questions about it, might find themselves saying, *Yes, well, if that is what is important to you, then you have to find the answers.*

Drawing your parents, as every child can, into sharing in your problems, instead of dwelling on what you want from them, will likely elicit a positive response. You can do this *now*, even if communication was never very easy in your home, and your relationship when you were younger was never close.

A poll was taken a while back in the United States to discover the preferred way of getting a message through to the respondent's spouse/child/parent. The most common answer was, "Hang a notice on the refrigerator." The refrigerator was the center of family life in the United States for a long time because everybody needed it at some point in the day. Nowadays, of course, most people will just WhatsApp the child to come down for supper, or send an email: "Supper is hot, come down before it gets cold!"

Let's consider the empathy between family members. When parents are not understanding, you might be faced with the following dialogue:

Daughter: "*Oy*, it's been such a long day and just look at the mess in the house!"

Mother: "Well, you're the one who wanted five children."

Your first reaction is to say: "Thanks, this is the last time I'll share anything that's on my mind with *you*!"

Before you do that, think it through for a minute. Could it be that when you talk about difficulties you are having to your parents, they might be seeing it as a criticism of *them*? Is it possible that they assume your comment was a hint for economic assistance rather than a plea for their advice? Your mother might even be subconsciously thinking that she should be helping you more, and your comment has just touched a nerve. In the face of perceived criticism, parents can easily go on the defensive.

Think carefully before you choose a topic of conversation. Sometimes, there are elements of our lives with which parents are not only *not* empathetic, but to which they are unable to relate. Stick to what interests them.

In those areas where they think that they know better and you disagree, you can explain your position without asking their opinion. If they offer their opinion anyway, you need to learn to hear it without arguing, or to discuss it without making a decision on the spot. There are many areas in which conversation is food for thought, not a halachic stringency.

We began this chapter with the necessity for better communication to remove the barriers in your relationships with close family. You have seen that it is not necessarily your parents' fault that they cannot understand your new world of observance and commitment. Perhaps you haven't admitted them into it with your responsibility to build solid channels of communication by judicious sharing.

When we see our spouses after a day spent apart, the words and tone of what we say are crucial; saying one thing will cause a certain reaction, while another will assuredly bring about differing results.

We often know, even before the words leave our mouths, that a specific comment is going to cause an explosion, but we have neither the good sense nor the self-control to stop and think of a better way to say it. Consequently, out come the words that cause the expected eruption. For any kind of successful personal relationship, whether it is at work, at home with our spouse and children, or with our parents, intelligent communication is required.

This comprises knowing what to say, as well as when and how to say it. I remember my *rebbi* telling us many years ago how elements as small as tone of voice can completely change a situation.

It makes no difference whether you are the husband or the wife in the following scenario:

> *A child went away to yeshiva and sent a telegram to his father, who received it in the middle of a business day while he was harried and stressed out between customers, deliveries, payments, employees, and all his other responsibilities. His secretary came in and gave him the telegram from his son. He tore it open and hurriedly read the letter.*
>
> "*Dear Dad, hope that everything is OK. I really need a hundred dollars, please send it right away, Sammy.*"
>
> "*That is the way you ask?*" *the father said to himself.*
>
> *He stuffed the letter in his pocket, where it remained until he went home at the end of the day. Putting his jacket on the back of a chair, he sat down to eat supper. His wife saw the telegram sticking out of the jacket pocket, and cheerily read it aloud.*
>
> "*Dear Dad, hope that everything is OK. I really need a hundred dollars, please send it right away, Sammy.*"
>
> "*Ah,*" *said the father as he sipped his soup,* "*now he is asking like a mensch, a decent human being.*"

The way messages are interpreted will often depend on how they are heard. If one or two words are taken out of context, an unexpected response can ensue.

"How was your day?" can be asked with love, indifference, care, or anger. The words are the same, but the emphasis or intonation makes a huge difference. If we take the time to think about how our words are going to be received, our communication will surely improve. The basic law of communication is that it doesn't matter what one *says*; it's what the other person *hears* that counts.

Communication does not always have to be spoken.

I often use a parable from another field. In the vocational yeshiva high school for boys that I had the privilege to found and head for several years, I worked with a highly professional general manager. Sometimes, he would comment about how much money we spent on food, as we wanted to give the students the best food possible. He could not understand why the boys sometimes kvetched about the meals.

"If you want to know how you are feeding the students," I told him, "go into the lunchroom five minutes after lunch is over. Sometimes, it's just a vocal minority that complains. If five minutes after the meal, however, you see all the fish patties still piled in a pyramid, you will know that you'd better not make them again. You may have bought the most expensive fish and used the freshest breadcrumbs, but if the students are buying pretzels and potato chips after lunch, they are telling you that you didn't feed them. Go into the dining room every day, see what is eaten and what is not, and stop making food that the students do not eat."

Every yeshiva thinks you have to have a fish day once a week because fish is less expensive. But fish is much more expensive when you throw it away. To throw away money is a sin. Do not use the excuse that fish is healthy. If the students don't eat it, can you claim that you fed them?

When you speak to someone, you are sending a message. That is communication. But if I speak Chinese, and your only language is French, can I say that I passed on a message?

Speech should not be just what I want to get off my chest, it must be what I want you to hear; communication means that you understand what I have told you. When I know that a certain topic will disturb the other person, whether a child, friend, parent, or spouse, I should consider well what I am about to say before I speak.

If you know that your parents worry about your ability to cope with many children, for example, it is a mistake to speak to them about the difficulties involved in doing so.

When parents react unfavorably, we think they are angry with us, but usually they are just worried. Raising an issue about which they already feel frustrated means we're increasing those feelings. When you complain, your parents feel responsible for helping with your problems. In most cases, not only don't they know how to help you, but consider that they don't think you should be living this way in the first place!

There are plenty of issues you *can* share, from the tomatoes growing in your garden to the new stage of development your two-year-old has just reached. You can talk about a teacher with whom you are happy or even something you are unhappy with in the school your children attend, as long as your parents are not antagonistic. There are many areas of mutual interest where our communication skills can serve to bring us into a closer, more satisfying relationship with our parents while avoiding areas that can be hurtful.

Intelligent Communication

A number of years ago, a young lady consulted me about her schooling options for the coming year. Her parents were more or less set on a certain school near home that they thought suitable for her, but she wanted to apply to a school in Israel and didn't know how to broach the subject.

"Think about your parents," I advised her. "They are worried about the fact that if you come to Israel, you may be brainwashed, that you will not be thinking for yourself, and won't be able to make mature decisions based on important concerns.

"Mommy, thank you for helping me to plan my next step," I advised her to say. "I hope you sent in my application for the school you liked, as I don't want to lose that option. I've also heard about some other very good programs I would like to think about as well. I'm not ready to make up my mind right now because I don't want to rush into a decision." She validated her parents' wishes and allowed them to know that she had other options to consider in a thoughtful way.

It is always essential in such a situation to avoid becoming defensive and negative. When children say, "I don't want to go to that place," or "I don't want to do what you are telling me to do," it indicates that they think they have to fight for their preferences. At the same time, the parents feel disrespected and unappreciated.

If there is a fight or disagreement, everything that ensues is usually the fault of the child (we are talking about older, mature children here) who did not consider how to communicate properly. This is not being manipulative; it is being intelligent.

You wouldn't walk into your boss's office, slam your hand on the desk, and say, "I have been working here for two years, and I want a raise!" Even if your boss had a letter in his drawer that he was about to put on your desk that day, telling you he is so happy with your job performance that he wants to increase your salary, he would tear it up. You would be lucky if he didn't fire you.

When you think before you present your views, you are not being calculating; you are being smart. In communicating with parents and siblings who are not observant you have to be intelligent. Recognize their ideas and the source of those ideas—what is central in *their* lives, not just in yours.

Obviously, you are going to prioritize the things that are significant to you, but it is no less a priority to show an interest in what they deem important. Ask yourself if you are demonstrating that you care about them, or if you are only pushing your agenda, e.g., convincing them to take on mitzvos. What messages are they continually hearing from you?

Are you looking for sympathy, talking about the difficulties of your new culture? If so, they'll probably say, "I told you so." It's far better to give over messages of what is good in your life, what makes you happy, and what *is* working. If you want to convey the beauty and vitality of your way of living, you must communicate in an honest and open *but intelligent* way.

What might help the rest of the family take up the process of change? Be the example that may inspire them to decide that what you are doing is something worth looking into. Only by communicating the *simchah* and beauty, as well as the personal satisfaction and fulfillment in living a life of Torah and mitzvos, will you avoid spoiling your rapport.

I have known many young people who followed this advice. Their parents were usually much more understanding of them, and the relationship improved. On the other hand, those who tried to change their parents with demands and negativity ended up not only *not* changing their family but damaging their connection.

In summation: The key to proper communication begins with acceptance of others as real human beings. Understand where they are coming from and what drives their ideas, and respect them as individuals with the right to think and feel differently. Last, but most certainly not least, is positive communication, making sure to neutralize land mines and prepare alternatives without negativity toward their ideas.

Chapter 15

The First Year and Beyond

F or those who have not yet begun the building of their home, it is vital to consider before marriage, and certainly prior to raising a family, the atmosphere you want to create. (This perception will almost certainly evolve, and even change, with time.)

The Torah clearly delineates a period in marriage called *shanah rishonah*, the first year. Let us consider how the Torah describes this special time, and the relationship between this concept and building a home.

The Torah says, *"V'simach es ishto*—[A man has to] make his wife happy."[1] The first year of marriage is defined by the Sages as the time for building understanding and learning to share. A man and a woman need to invest that first year in building a relationship of *simchah*. In this all-important period, when the foundations of a lifelong relationship are being laid, our goal is to become more understanding and accepting of each other as time goes on.

If we do not bond together during the first year of marriage, an investment of much time and even greater effort will be required afterward. It takes a long time to make up for a poor beginning, but husband and wife working together have the ability to build a relationship of joy and happiness. The challenges of building a home and starting a family are many, and doubly so for people who have made such enormous changes in their lives.

---

1   *Devarim* 24:5.

Roles and Role Models

One of the difficulties facing the young newly religious couple is the lack of role models for building a religious home. If neither set of parents were religious, even if they enjoyed a wonderful, peaceful marriage and mutual respect, their homes were doubtlessly influenced by prevalent social and moral values. To put a finer point on it, statistics show that today less than 50 percent of the heads of households (in the USA) are married,[2] which implies a "family" life without shared responsibility or commitment. The figures predict that more than 50 percent of marriages will be broken by divorce.[3]

"Marriage," wrote Rav Wolbe, "requires flexibility, understanding, and commitment."[4]

People who do not understand the concept of commitment falter when things get tough, and the peace in their home is inevitably shattered. It is difficult to achieve the devotion and mutual responsibility of the domestic unit in the secular world today, as for many people, having a family has no intrinsic value. Our newly religious young couples, therefore, even when they come from moral families whose members are kind to one another, often have no actual role model on which to base their future homes and families when their goal is to build a Torah-oriented home.

The Torah perception of *shalom bayis*, peace in the home, is that all fulfill their roles according to a certain time-honored and prescribed structure. In some happy secular homes, this may well have been achieved by everyone doing so in alternative ways not in consonance with the Torah. Sometimes the parents maintained the peace by allowing each other a kind of freedom or other outlets that are not acceptable in a religious home. Our young couples are challenged by the need to

---

2   US Census Bureau R1101, "Percent of Households That Are Married-Couple Families," 2005 Universe, Households Data Set, 2005 American Community Survey.

3   US Census Bureau 2010.

4   Rabbi Shlomo Wolbe, *Kuntres Hachassanim*, ch. 1.

build a home based on new values and codes for which they must find their own building blocks and set their own boundaries.

How are they going to accomplish this? The natural assumption is that they will have to find alternative role models. When they were young and single, they could spend time in other people's homes and observe how these role models conducted their lives. Young people who are just beginning the process of change have many opportunities to do that.

"Yes, you can go to many homes and observe," I often tell them. "But choose one or two where you find particularly impressive role models for your life. Try to visit these families as often as possible, investing time and effort in establishing a relationship with them."

Even when newly married, it is not too difficult to build relationships with others who have the sort of homes you admire. They do not have to be rabbis or *rebbis* or *rebbetzins*. They can just be healthy, warm people with children who seem to be well-adjusted, and whose close-knit family life appeals to you.

Families deal with situations in varied ways. If you are active, vibrant, and of a tumultuous nature, you might love being in the home of the calm, patient, and soft-spoken friend, but you will not be able to build this type of home. You need to find the path that resonates with you and seems to fit with your personality and nature.

We live in a busy world, yet it is worth a little investment to develop relationships with others whom you hold in esteem. This will provide you with friends with whom you can talk about family life, discuss what is and is not acceptable, what works for them, and what does not. Investing in those relationships means making the effort to be a desirable guest by interacting with the children and other family members, bringing small gifts, helping with the serving and cleaning up, or doing errands. Another set of helping hands, when offered generously and genuinely, will be warmly received.

Couples often feel tense when they come up against new situations. Variations in upbringing and personality may bring out differences in the way in which each of you views others and the world in general.

How can you manage with these dissimilarities, especially when placed into new circumstances?

Until you have learned to develop attitudes and reactions that are more in tune with your new way of life, you may react spontaneously, if not automatically, without thinking about it. Over time, you will question these responses and cultivate your own, mutually satisfactory alternatives to deal with situations that your parents never faced. It is both normal and beneficial to fall back on the experience of your new role models. You and your spouse should reach out for those options because, as your children grow, you can always see ways to improve.

If you've missed a few tricks along the way, don't let frustration get the better of you! Look for new alternatives. When we consider that the increase in the general divorce rate is affecting the religious community, it is even more important to seek role models with whom to build a close relationship. We can always learn. In addition, there are usually good things that you **can** and **should** learn from your parental home; do not lose the chance to do so. Some people can learn from the way their parents handled the finances, others from their friendships. Still others from the how they treated each other. Honesty, integrity, responsibility, or dedication. Take what you can from your parents because they are the most natural place to learn from.

Distinct Male and Female Roles

The traditional distinction between the roles of husband and wife is a concept that contemporary Western civilization has a difficult time accepting. Those who were raised with the gift of Torah are aware of its clear lesson that men and women were created with their own tendencies. We have our own frames of reference, divergent proclivities, and different mitzvos and responsibilities to fulfill. People living in a Torah-based home can better accept this notion. We were created to appreciate that which we have without looking at what someone else has, and certainly not to look over our shoulder with envy at the other gender.

I have had the honor of teaching in a post–high school teacher's seminary for *frum* girls from Bais Yaakov schools for over twenty years.

When I talk about the different roles of men and women, I do not have to be apologetic, and my students feel comfortable with the discussion almost without exception. When I lecture to other groups, however, even in some religious communities, especially in those with a slightly more assimilated perspective, the reaction is different.

When teaching about aspects of *tefillah*, we speak about the morning blessing where men recite "*She'lo asani ishah*—That I was not created as a woman." This is a berachah of appreciation for the added opportunity afforded by the extra mitzvos men have that women do not. Women say, "*She'asani ki'retzono*—That I was created in accordance with His will." This gender-differentiated berachah, which creates so much irritation in schools of higher learning for people who are just coming to a Torah way of life, is taken in stride by my students.

There is interest as to what it means and how it can be understood, but my students know that there are different roles in life. Because of all the frustration engendered by that berachah, however, along with feelings of indignation and perception of unfairness, I think we need to try to understand what it is meant to teach us—the unique opportunity for which women are expressing their own appreciation.

I heard a very beautiful explanation from Rav Wolbe, in the name of Rav Chaim Volozhiner, of the meaning of "*she'asani ki'retzono*—that He made me in accordance with His will."

Rav Chaim Volozhiner[5] takes note that the words *she'asani ki'retzono* appear in one other place in our prayers.[6] In the magnificent *tefillah* of *Kaddish* that we say numerous times every day, we recite, "May His great name be exalted and sanctified in the world that He created, *ki're'usei* [Aramaic for *ki'retzono*], in accordance with His will." The implication is that while we cannot understand why Hashem wanted to create this lowly and physically limited world, would it not have been

---

5   Rav Chaim Volozhiner was the greatest student of the Vilna Gaon. He was the founder of the Volozhiner Yeshiva, which is the prototype followed by all yeshivos until today, and is the author of the masterpiece *Nefesh Hachaim*.

6   In his work *Ruach Chaim* on *Pirkei Avos*, end of the fourth chapter on the words, "You were created against your will."

more befitting for Him to be praised and exalted by universes full of extraordinary spiritual beings?

Rav Chaim explains that these words state that Hashem created this world especially so that His name might be exalted by us, specifically in this physical world. We wonder why Hashem should "need" or desire His name to be praised here, when He has myriad angels and the highest levels of exalted beings who praise His name constantly. It is because it is His will that His name be exalted *here, by us*. This is *"ki're'usei*—in accordance with His will."

Similarly, the woman says the blessing that she was created *"ki'ret-zono*—in accordance with His will." In the physical world, as well as in the spiritual realm, Hashem has chosen her to be the vehicle for exalting His name, for woman is the medium through which every Jewish soul comes down into this world.

This berachah, like that of the man's, is a blessing in which a woman recognizes and appreciates her unique responsibilities. The man says a berachah accepting his greater responsibilities, and the woman says a berachah that accepts her extraordinary task as the facilitator of the Jewish soul.

This is an awesome responsibility. Were the world's greatest *tzaddik* to marry and have a child, and then find out that his wife was not Jewish, the child would not be Jewish. This rule applies no matter how great the man is. On the other hand, were the lowest, non-Jewish character in the world to father a Jewish woman's child, the child would be Jewish.

This means that the life of the *neshamah* in this world is going to depend on the woman. Will this new life have a Jewish soul that can fulfill Hashem's will, perform mitzvos, bring holiness into the world, and exalt and sanctify His name?

This is one of the concepts that is beyond our understanding, because we would think that the *Kaddish*, the praise of Hashem, should be said on High, and we would opine that the man who learns Torah and does the most mitzvos is the epitome of creation; it is *he* who should determine the transmission of the *neshamah*. But that is not the way it works. The will of Hashem is that the woman is *specifically* the one chosen to undertake this tremendous responsibility. Woman is the creation that He made in accordance with His will. The father's spiritual qualities will affect the level of the soul, but not the essence of it. Hence the special blessing of "…that He made me according to *His* will."

The first morning berachos are our recognition and appreciation of the opportunities and responsibilities that we have been given. Each berachah we say is an acknowledgment that addresses another level of responsibility and opportunity. The woman's berachah fits into this well, as she recognizes that she is the channel through which a Jewish *neshamah* is going to be delivered. It is, to say the least, an awesome responsibility for a woman to contemplate: *What kind of vessel am I preparing for this new neshamah, and how can I prepare myself to be the best recipient I can be?*

In a home where the parents are comfortable with their Judaically defined roles, there is little need for men and women to prove the worth of their gender. It is Western civilization that has confused us in this regard, causing many women to feel the need to measure themselves against men.

Hierarchy of Roles

In today's *frum* community, most people are not willing to settle for a lower standard of living. As men remain longer in learning, many women are seeking not only work, but careers. They expect and aspire to have the same income as if their husbands were working full-time, a standard that can only be achieved with more high-powered career options.

Shalom bayis is becoming the sacrificial goat in the *frum* world in our generation. When the hierarchy of roles is partially reversed, confusion often accompanies the blurring of the lines between who does what and why in the home.

"Hierarchy of roles" almost sounds like "Who's the boss?" another concept that seems threatening from the secular perspective. How can we discuss hierarchy if we are all equals? In every business and family, it is necessary for there to be an ultimate voice of authority.

Although, practically speaking, someone has to carry the ultimate weight of decision-making, in marriage, conclusions can and must be made together. Any good leader or person in a position of authority must possess the humility to be willing to listen, to seek understanding, and share the decision-making. The greatest leader the Jewish people ever had was Moshe Rabbeinu, and it is well-known that he was also the humblest man who ever walked the earth.[7]

Good leadership in Jewish thought is not described with concepts of power and control, but with humility, understanding, and sensitivity. Leadership is looked upon as "slavery," i.e., subservience and responsibility to those whom you lead.[8] The Talmud tells of the lesson Rabban Gamliel taught to two of his students who had been appointed as leaders and were trying to avoid the honor.[9]

"Do you think you have become rulers?" he asked. "You have become slaves!"

The concept of leadership is that you are now committed to taking care of and being concerned for those in your care. It is about responsibility, not rights or power. The hierarchy of authority in a Jewish family is one of the built-in safety features of the home. There is one joint voice, with the husband and wife acting together with mutual respect and understanding of each other's role and obligations—and it works!

A couple has to discuss every issue that arises between them in order to come to an understanding. When Hashem created the partnership of marriage, He said, "It is not good for man to be alone, I will make him [someone to] *help against him*."[10] This description seems to be a contradiction in terms, but the Gemara explains, "If he merits it, she will be a help...if he does not merit it, she will be against him."[11]

---

8   *Melachim I* 12:7, "אם היום תהיה עבד לעם הזה."
9   *Horayos* 10a–b.
10 *Bereishis* 2:18.
11 *Yevamos* 63a.

"There were those who listened to their wives and gained," the Midrash says, "and those who listened to their wives and lost out. Adam listened to his wife and lost out. Avraham listened to his wife and gained."[12]

Rabbi Ezriel Erlanger, the *mashgiach* in the Mirrer Yeshiva in Brooklyn, pointed out that Adam and his wife were in total agreement regarding the forbidden fruit, while Avraham and his wife disagreed over dealing with Yishmael. The lesson is clear: a helper is not necessarily one with whom you always agree, and going against someone does not necessarily mean disagreement. The inference is that there should be both a discussion of an issue and a method of coming to an agreement.

When Avraham and Sarah disagreed, they went to arbitration, as it were, instead of trying to force the issue. They asked Hashem, who responded, "Anything that Sarah tells you, you should do."[13] It was a clear method of resolving a conflict of opinions. Adam and Chavah, on the contrary, did not hold conflicting opinions, yet she was undoubtedly against him, as she did not have his best interests in mind. In the situation that unfolded, they both lost out.

Sharing Responsibility

We live in a world where leisure is a central part of life in every home, religious ones included. In the secular home, however, the wife might be doing the dishes and laundry while her husband is watching television. He can sit back with a beer in hand and watch the ballgame without a thought as to who should be doing household chores.

"I put in a hard day," he says. "I worked and brought home my pay, now I'm entitled to take it easy."

In a Torah home, there is a more equal division of responsibilities. There is, of course, the husband's responsibility to learn Torah, and often the needs of the community will take precedence over almost everything. But there is no such thing as one person who sits back while the other person works. Everyone has to be responsible. *If it*

---

12   *Yalkut Shimoni, Bereishis, perek 3, remez 32.*
13   *Bereishis 21:12.*

isn't exactly my job, then I ought to lend a hand, unless I am fulfilling other responsibilities. If you are blessed with the large family for which you both hoped, there is plenty that must be done.

The more external responsibilities the husband has, however, the more household duties the wife will have to shoulder. Whether or not his activities comprise full-time learning, as long as they both live up to their agreed-upon tasks, there can be tranquility in the home. There are times when the woman's responsibilities are overwhelming, and the husband needs to accept a greater share of duties in order for the family to function properly.

If one spouse is enjoying entertainment or leisure while the other is working very hard, it will certainly create dissatisfaction and resentment, a sure recipe for marital disharmony.

Chapter 16

Love and Marriage

Ⅰn your previous exposure to life in the secular world, false perceptions of love, marriage, and family relationships were certainly imprinted on your unconscious mind and accepted as "normal."

Contrast those perceptions with the observations of children who have never read a romantic novel or seen a popular movie, whose impressions of love and marriage are based on their family life. If they have grown up with a stable, responsible set of parents, their chances of going into marriage with a clear and healthy view of what it takes to build a home are great.

For those who have had former relationships without any real commitment or responsibility, forging a bond based totally on dedication and trustworthiness is going to be a difficult challenge. Adjusting to the first year of marriage will likely be complicated, and continued commitment even harder. In some cases, the challenge is even more daunting because past relationships still haunt the present one. Learning to deal with that unfortunate problem is an issue that is necessary to include in our discussion.

The Talmud mentions frankly that "when two divorced people marry in the lifetime of the former spouses, there are four minds in the bed."[1] Chazal, with great sensitivity, recognized the fact that former relationships leave impressions that can linger in the lower levels of our

---

1   *Pesachim* 112a.

consciousness. It is imperative to know that since this is normal and only to be expected, guilt is not the remedy.

We must focus on positive strategies to overcome, or at least lessen, the lingering background interference. After speaking to Gedolim regarding this delicate matter, I have come to the understanding that there are two things one can do in such a case.

1. Work hard to build your new relationship through *chessed*, giving. An intimate relationship should be based on this. If you focus on making your spouse content, it will go a long way toward blocking out the background noise and cementing the present relationship.

2. Work on retaining a pure lifestyle. Avoid reading licentious material and be careful of what you see and say.

These two actions will bring added *kedushah*, holiness, into your life and lessen the hold of past influences on your thoughts.

Love Means Commitment

The Chazon Ish is quoted as having said, "Their *ahavah* is our *kareis*. What the world considers love, in our world is *kareis*, death at the Hands of Heaven, the punishment for adultery."

Love in the world around us refers to something that is expressed physically. Love as *we* know it is expressed in giving, caring, commitment, and responsibility. *Rashi*[2] comments on the verse "*V'ahavta es Hashem Elokecha*—You shall love Hashem your God,"[3] saying, "*Aseh mitzvosav b'ahavah*—Do His commandments with love."[4] This is not just a description of a feeling, it is a depiction of what we do and how we act toward the one we love. We want that person to be fulfilled and content.

---

2   Rabbi Shlomo Yitzchaki (1040–1105) is generally known by the acronym *Rashi*. He was a French rabbi and author of a comprehensive commentary on the Talmud and Tanach, and is best known for his ability to present the basic meaning of the text in a concise and lucid fashion.

3   *Devarim* 6:5.

4   *Rashi* on ibid.

While I was engaged, I wrote a little poem about love, which I showed to my *rebbi*. I thought it was a very deep, sensitive, special piece. Since I used to show him all my writings to receive his critique, I showed him this one as well. It comprised my philosophy of love and described the depths of my feeling toward my fiancée. I thought of giving it to her after our wedding and wanted to hear my *rebbi*'s opinion of my thoughts.

Rav Wolbe looked at it. "I do not understand it," he said,

I said, "Excuse me, but isn't it quite clear?"

"To me," he said, "*ahavah* means that you take off your shoes before you walk into the room late at night, and you make your wife a cup of coffee in the morning. That is what it means. What I know about *ahavah* is that you are careful with each other's needs and feelings, and that you take care of each other."

After that brief discussion, I decided I no longer needed the poem.

The *Meiri* sums up this idea beautifully: "The definition of love is the unifying of the will of the lover with the will of the beloved."[5]

In so few words, he says so much. The word "*ahavah*," love, in the holy language has the same numerical value, thirteen, as the word "*echad*," one. Unity is the key to love, but the lover needs to understand that this means making his will fit that of the one he loves, and not vice versa.

When we think of love, we tend to think of the feelings of the heart, but true love—and I cannot emphasize this enough—is commitment and responsibility to the beloved. Doing for your spouse what is good for her, being concerned and thinking about how to make her happy, is true *ahavah*.

So many of us, however, come from a world where love is a description of feelings and intimacy that it is difficult to implement this new concept. Years of erroneous conditioning do not dissipate with a deepened appreciation of Yiddishkeit.

---

5   *Meiri*'s commentary on *Tehillim* 26:8 (*Meikitzei Nirdamim*, 1936), p. 60. Rabbi Menachem ben Shlomo Meiri (1249–1315) of Perpignan, France, was known as the *Meiri* and was the most prolific of the latter Rishonim.

When I say, "I love Pringles," it means that I love the way Pringles taste because the taste pleases me. When I say, "I love duck," what I am actually saying is, "I would like the duck slaughtered, plucked, and cooked," which really means that I love the taste of roasted duck and the satisfaction of eating it. If I really loved a duck, I would put it in a pen, feed, and guard it, and make sure that it lived out its life in dignity.

Loving a person cannot refer to the way that person makes *me* feel, for that is tantamount to loving myself and making sure I get what I want. It needs to mean thinking seriously and working hard to make my spouse feel wanted, special, secure, and cared for. It means applying the concepts of commitment and responsibility upon which our marriage has to be built.

Marriage Is a Partnership

In our Western society, it is not uncommon for a married woman to retain her own family surname, maintain a separate bank account, and basically live a somewhat separate life, except for when she is at home with her husband. Though the couple lives in the same house, occasionally shops together, and files joint taxes, it is often just a relationship of convenience: living alongside one another, but not truly together.

In a Torah home, marriage is a partnership—all the way. Individual bank accounts really mean that he does things *his* way and she does things *her* way. In a Torah home, they might have different accounts for different needs, or a home account that the wife manages and a business account that the husband takes care of. In joint accounts, there is partnership and shared responsibility. Dividing up responsibilities is fine, but in a Torah home there should not be "yours and mine." Husband and wife may have separate responsibilities, but the entire burden is shared, with occasional exceptions for specific and valid circumstances.

Blending Cultural Differences

The *teshuvah* movement has contributed to the admixture of widely varying cultures in Klal Yisrael. At institutions of higher learning, and through the many existing community and campus outreach programs, students from all over the world have had a heretofore unequaled opportunity to be exposed to Yiddishkeit. Jews from many different cultural backgrounds, Sephardim, Ashkenazim, Americans, Russians, South Americans, Ethiopians, Syrians, Iraqis, and Persians have been learning and becoming committed to their heritage. Nuances from all these cultures are entering mainstream religious communities, bringing with them a great deal of variety. Jewish marriages today are much more culturally mixed than they were fifty years ago.

Rav Yaakov Yisrael Kanievsky, the Steipler Gaon, a leading rabbi and Talmudic scholar of the previous generation, was asked about the "intermarriage" of a couple from two extremely diverse cultures.

"I do not know of anyone who did not make a success of marriage because the spouse was of a different background," he responded. "I don't believe that this is the reason for the failure of a relationship. If you are a mensch, you can overcome anything, and if not, then you can both be Polish, or come from the same town in Hungary, and it will not help."

He did not deny that there are more differences to overcome when the husband and wife originate from diverse backgrounds, but this is integral to the building of any relationship.

Advance awareness of the building process will help us recognize the need to understand, appreciate, and deal with each other's differences. There is a cognitive progression necessary to prepare us to overcome those that will surface. We can be determined to accept our spouse for who our spouse is, as well as our spouse's family with all their different customs, outlooks, and values.

The first problems can arise even before the wedding, when the groom's side feels that all his many cousins must be invited. The bride's side doesn't understand why. For whatever reason, extended family is not meaningful to them.

"How can we have an elegant wedding with so many people?"

Diverse cultures do create dissimilarities that need to be addressed, but that is what marriage is all about. There are many forms of diversity: some families are warm and loving, others are cold and distant.

Some are intellectually oriented, while others easily express emotion. Dress codes and different languages play their parts as well.

In marriage we learn to accept one another, to discuss and come to understand our differences, and be able to laugh about them instead of becoming tense.

Without this acceptance and flexibility there will always be stress and resentment—elements no one wants in marriage. The ways we communicate our thoughts and feelings, and the intentions behind our words, are all affected by our personal backgrounds. This is part of the commitment to the responsibility of building a family, which will help overcome nuances of culture, habits, or temperament.

There is a type of family that maintains a somewhat military chain of command in decision-making, which does not include real discussion. Their children know that it's best to discuss things first with Mom because she listens, hears, and understands. She will not decide anything, though, since they all know that what she thinks is irrelevant; Father is the one who gives, or does not give, his OK, after which there is no discussion.

The reverse is true in other families, where Mom is the boss. In still others everyone is pretty much free to do as he or she wishes. Sometimes, even after marriage, children are expected to ask all questions to Father and obey him. It will require time and patience on your part to learn whether or not this type of situation is an unhealthy form of control or merely a healthy type of respect. In the latter case, having a patriarch or matriarch in the family whom we honor and whose opinion we invite can be a great benefit.

Such radical differences in background mean that we, as a couple, need to make those decisions for ourselves, leaving other family members out of the discussion entirely. Meddling relatives more often than not jeopardize our budding relationship.

New couples must understand which type of authority was the style in each of its families, and either accept or reject it as an example to follow in their own homes. This also has to be done with sensitivity and understanding, especially if we become aware of a negative pattern.

Difficult behavior or unhealthy control will cause tension and create an impediment to *shalom bayis*.

All the above are types of issues that need to be worked on and resolved as partners. These subjects of concern may prove to be volatile. Most of us tend to defend our family with a vengeance against anyone who attacks them, even if our own relationship with them hasn't been so good.

"I have a right to speak negatively about my family, but you have no right to do so."

If we think something negative, we need to learn to bite our tongue before saying anything because it will *always* be hurtful. Instead of criticism, we must try to help our spouse recognize the challenges caused by dictatorial authority, unhealthy control, meddling tendencies, and so forth, and then work together as a team to overcome the problem that is not "yours" or "mine," but "ours."

Unique Challenges

While establishing *shalom bayis* can be challenging to any newlyweds, and even more so to those from different cultural backgrounds, it may be doubly or triply challenging to a couple who has made fundamental changes in their lives. Let's consider why this is so.

Serious changes made when we were younger were often the beginning of a prolonged period of adjustment, which we usually had to face pretty much on our own. With marriage, a new process is initiated.

It often marks the first time we objectively confront our upbringing and weigh its impact on the future. Although we were able to identify the facets of our lives with which we were happy and those we wanted to change, as singles our objectives took into account *our* happiness and *our* values.

The extreme individuality of our own existence is not truly confronted until we face the prospect of a commitment to one partner for life. The all-encompassing aspects of marriage, the inability to leave it without tremendous upheaval, questions, and pain, force us to examine our source and our goals in an entirely new light.

Young adults studying in a yeshiva or seminary, or seriously dedicated to taking classes for any number of years, are absorbed in progressing in davening, becoming acquainted with the mitzvos, and negotiating the sea of Torah study. They are relatively cut off from the problems of life in the outside world.

Marriage takes them out of this supportive, sheltered framework into an unprotected, "real" world situation in which they must begin to build something of great significance.

Take a twenty-two-year-old who, after reevaluating his appreciation and usage of time, decides to divest himself of many forms of media. When he begins to build his home, he faces a new reality called family down time or family together time, which in his younger years was completely centered on the media that he thought he left behind.

Most often, neither partner will have the family background to help build the kind of home they desire. This will probably be the first time that they have had to deal with the long-term consequences of their chosen lifestyle, which differs so greatly from that of their childhood.

In the creative framework of yeshiva, seminary, or study groups, they were forced to look objectively at the backgrounds from which they came, to acknowledge what they were leaving. Now, together, they have to build a fresh relationship in a new home of their own. In some cases, this is their first real confrontation with who they are, which may be painful.

Although they've succeeded in making many changes and have adjusted to many new behavior patterns, their basic characters are very much the same. They haven't yet learned new relationship skills; perhaps, they never focused on developing these areas as much as they did their spiritual growth.

Those individuals who *did* work on improving their character, who built new kinds of relationships with positive role models, and spent time in other people's homes because they realized that they needed to add these experiences to their background, are obviously going to be more enriched and better prepared for marriage. There is not always enough time, however, between choosing to change and getting married to accomplish all that, and this is another reason that building *shalom bayis* is an inordinately great challenge.

There is yet another hazard of the creative building process that we call *teshuvah*, and that is the tendency to suppress previous emotional issues having to do with family, parents, and siblings. "Everything is changing, I am becoming a better person, things will work out."

Before marriage, while still in a sheltered learning environment, the couple was not constantly forced to confront those issues, which may well have been ignored. They will not disappear, however, and sooner or later will surface and need to be resolved.

Beginning the *teshuvah* process while still single is a personal voyage, one of self-discovery and self-fulfillment; it all has to do with *me*. Marriage is not only a challenge, but, sometimes, a real shock. It's not just reaching the ticket gate and having to say, "Two, please." It can be a startling revelation that life is no longer personal, and that *you are not the only one here*.

Life with a partner is a whole new way of living, and you may find that you are not well enough equipped to cope. You may be, not surprisingly, filled with a strong sense of inadequacy that can undermine your self-esteem. Your high expectations have been knocked down, and you may become locked into some very bad feelings about your perceived inability to build a home.

To counter these feelings, you must remember that the *teshuvah* process is a creative one of constant growth and development; that creativity is what kept us going and gave us the ability to get through those first years of change.

Marriage is exactly the same. Your approach to it, especially if you are both undergoing the process of *teshuvah* at the same time, has to be that this is a creative and growing learning experience. Even in the best scenario, marriage cannot be approached with utter confidence that you are going to do it right. When the inevitable difficulties arise, you should not feel frustrated and just give up.

A new beginning requires different tools and a lot of fresh learning. It is a challenge that should not be approached with preset expectations.

"My husband has learned and studied for the past few years, so he should know…"

"My wife is FFB, so it shouldn't be a problem for her to…"

It is a new adventure, a new position in life, which must be approached with open eyes, hearts, and minds prepared to learn and grow together. Those who think they possess all the tools they will need are in for some shattering, frustrating moments. If you both accept that you are not automatically prepared for this new relationship just because you spent a lot of time studying, your expectations will be more realistic. When you are grounded and modest, you can admit to, laugh at, and rectify your mistakes, taking them in stride as part of this joint continuing process.

I will say it even more strongly. The *teshuvah* process has two parts: building yourself and building a family. Just as you had to make a quantum leap in changing your life, values, and behavior when you were single, the process will need to start almost entirely anew in marriage. This has nothing to do with repenting from sins or becoming righteous, but learning things of which you were previously unaware.

The Talmud says that one who transgressed Shabbos many times inadvertently only needs to bring one sin offering. This means if a person first learned about Shabbos when he was thirty-three years old and had transgressed it a thousand times in the twenty years since he was thirteen, he probably made over one hundred thousand individual transgressions of halachah—but he only has to bring *one* sin offering for all of them.[6] Part and parcel of *teshuvah* is learning new things and understanding new responsibilities. Sometimes, we are afraid to learn how much was wrong; this passage teaches us to face the new and throw out the old knowing that we are not responsible for what we did not know. We are responsible to learn and know; therefore, once we know, we only bring one offering.

New challenges should be viewed with freshness and excitement. For what is intimidating, you need to have the understanding that you can

6   *Shabbos* 67b.

and should seek direction and ask for help. The first year of marriage is the best time to begin discussing and working through problems together, deciding on the best solutions.

Some Ground Rules for Marriage

There are a few things that we can do to protect our marriages and families right from the beginning.

- In contemporary society, making comparisons is a given. Don't do it! Do not look at another couple's success or their lovely family as opposed to yours, unless you do it purely for learning's sake. The moment a man compares his wife to other wives, the moment a woman begins to judge her husband in regard to others, is the moment that problems will arise in their *shalom bayis*. Your wife is the best wife you will ever have; your husband is the best husband you will ever have. She is who she is, he is who he is, and you will learn to live with each other in full acceptance of your differences. *Pirkei Avos* (Ethics of the Fathers) tells us to be content with our portion, whatever we have, and not focus on that which we perceive as lacking.[7]

- Keep a strong line of communication open between you and your spouse. There is a book called *Men Are from Mars, Women Are from Venus* that has a very intelligent theme, which I would like to adapt to a kosher version entitled, *Men Are from Yeshiva, Women Are from Bais Yaakov*. I cannot agree with everything John Gray writes in the book, but his main point is undeniably accurate: there is an essential difference in the nature of a man and a woman, and this dichotomy affects the communication between them. His chapters on communication say something we can apply to our own lives, although his comments on relationships are in some places inappropriate and off the mark. It is remarkable, and a major fault of the book, that the author exhibits a total ignorance of the concept of self-improvement, the

---

7   *Pirkei Avos* 4:1.

ability that man and woman have and must invest in to attempt
to become better people.

- Take care of yourselves. Our lives are very busy and extremely
demanding. Raising a family usurps great quantities of our en-
ergies. Praying at set times and going to an occasional class or
having a regular study partner will keep you alive spiritually, and
both you and your family will benefit. Physically, too, you must
take care of yourself even though it is hard to find time. A little
reading, resting, eating properly, and regular exercise will go
a long way toward maintaining good health and sanity. My wife
shared something with me that she had read about a Yerushalmi
mother who closed herself in her room every day for three quar-
ters of an hour. When her children asked what she was doing,
she said, "I'm making a Mommy." Be aware that taking even
that small amount of time to strengthen yourself spiritually and
physically will give you the energy you need to give to others.
- Cultivate friends other than your spouse. Although your *best*
friend should be your spouse, it is healthy to have others outside of your marriage, smart people with a positive outlook and
a similar lifestyle who appreciate you as you are, and who want
the best for you. It is good for your emotional stability to be
able to vent to a trusted friend, and it is reassuring to discover
that you are not the only one in the world who is having trouble
getting her children to sleep at night. It is good to know that
there are others who become frustrated when things do not
work as expected. Other children also fight and are jealous.
Other couples also have doubts, concerns, and worries about
the present and future. Other families are also having difficulty
with the local school, etc. Friends can reassure you that the ups
and downs in your family are well within the typical range, and
that you are normal and healthy.[8] Your sense of security will be
enhanced, and many issues will shrink to a less daunting size. It

8   See chapter 10, "Building a Support System."

should go without saying, of course, that one may never discuss spousal shortcomings with anyone other than a *rav* or qualified therapist.

- Flexibility and the acceptance of our differences are the most significant measures of successful marriages. They allow for the inherent differences that must exist between two individuals who together need to work through the obstacles that might otherwise, *chas v'shalom*, cause the marriage to fail.

Abuse within the Family

Responding correctly to situations of emotional, verbal, or physical abuse, whether between parents or between parents and children, is urgent, and we need to be able to identify such a relationship. Abuse is destructive, and we cannot allow anyone to destroy us, no matter who the person may be!

Abuse can reach heights of injury both by having its existence ignored, or by willingness to submit to it.

*If you ever find yourself in an abusive relationship, you **must** deal with it immediately, and with professional help.*

Everyone should be aware of this information. No one should try to ignore the problem and just hope that it will work itself out.

It is not something to push off because you are afraid to deal with the reality of a difficult situation.

We need to find good therapists, psychologists, and sometimes psychiatrists, but **never** may we let things lie. If you found your therapist in the yellow pages, you are very likely to be seeing the wrong person. Finding a psychologist, like finding any specialist, requires research and referrals, trial and error, experience and results. You can use the resource nefesh.org, where you can look for professionals in your area and see which have endorsements; even better is to get referrals from people you know and trust, who know of professionals who succeeded with similar situations.

There are, to our sorrow, children who are born with difficult personalities, who may become challenging individuals as they grow older, and we must not allow their abusive behaviors to continue to wreak havoc on their siblings or parents. Any form of abuse between any family members must be squarely faced and correctly dealt with. The cartoon below depicts the sad truth about abuse when it is not dealt with.

People assume that they would never act as their parents did, but the default reactions to stressful situations are all too often similar to the ones we saw while growing up. Conviction alone will not stop the cycle, which usually requires a combination of professional intervention, the creation of new role models, and the modification of present behavior that will help the process of change.

Chapter 17

Establishing a Happy Torah Home

I t is common that when people have changed their life goals and behavior, the establishment of "family" takes on new meaning. "Building a family is an art."[1] It is a process that requires a great amount of forethought. Although we need a civil license to get married, none is mandated to raise or educate children. Perhaps it should be. There are so many aspects to doing this successfully and so many types of knowledge and understanding are required that just following our instincts may not, and probably will not, provide our children with all they need. How much more effort is necessary in this regard when the home in which we grew up was so vastly different from the home we now intend to build?

If we were to ask the average person to define the most essential ingredient in building a successful family, many would say love.

My *rebbi* taught us, however, that the fundamental quality required of a husband in marriage is accepting the responsibility of having a wife and seeing to her needs,[2] and the fundamental trait needed by a wife is the respectful acceptance of her husband with an understanding heart.[3] Both have a responsibility to invest this basic type of caring in

---

1   Rav Shlomo Wolbe, *Building and Planting: Raising a Jewish Child* (New York: Feldheim, 2000), introduction.

2   Rav Shlomo Wolbe, *Kuntres Hadrachah L'Chassanim* [Guidelines for Newly Married Men], ch. 1.

3   Rav Shlomo Wolbe, *Kuntres Hadrachah L'Kallos* [Guidelines for Newly Married Women], ch. 1.

the marriage, as this will be the key ingredient in building their home. I would like to add that in our days, *simchah* will also be a crucial and fundamental contribution to lay the groundwork for the success and welfare of the future family.

Simchah, the Hebrew word for joy, is not only a very interesting concept, but is part of what makes the Jewish People a very spiritual nation. *Simchah* contains the idea of fullness, completion, contentment. Its opposite is *aveilus*, mourning, loss. The Jewish People live to attain the ultimate spiritual pleasure, the eternal bliss of the World to Come, which will bring the achievement of our fulfillment in this world. An unmarried man is considered to be without *simchah* because he is incomplete and unfulfilled.[4]

There are, however, specific requirements for achieving this eternal bliss.

Our Sages teach us, *"Ein simchah ela b'vasar v'yayin*—There is no *simchah* [for a man] without meat and wine."[5] Today, when there is no Beis Hamikdash, the meat is not as necessary. On the *Yamim Tovim*, festival days, therefore, when the Torah tells us that we must have *simchah*,[6] you need to serve meat and wine. In addition, a man is required to make his wife and family happy on Yom Tov because happiness on this special day is a mitzvah for everyone in the family.[7] It is the husband or father's responsibility to facilitate that joy. The preferred method for fulfilling this requirement as described in the halachah is to buy treats for his children and new clothing for his wife.[8]

We are a very spiritual nation, yet when we talk about the *simchah* of Yom Tov, as these various sources point out, we talk about treats, new clothes, good food, and good wine. Where does spirituality enter the picture?

---

4   *Yevamos* 62b.
5   *Pesachim* 109a.
6   *Devarim* 15:16.
7   *Kiddushin* 34b.
8   *Kitzur Shulchan Aruch* 103:4–6.

Living in this physical world precludes achieving the eternal bliss of total spirituality. We do not forget that the highest level of *simchah*, which is the maximum joy of spiritual connection and fulfillment, can be attained only in the next world. As long as we are attached to the physical world, however, we appreciate having good things here. We do experience joy with good food and wine when it is connected to a higher calling, but it is *never* a mitzvah to eat, drink, and be merry in order to be happy. When we have a real reason for happiness, i.e., spiritual connection such as a holiday or Shabbos, the first levels of joy are accessed through physical pleasure.

In terms of spiritual wealth, our Sages define a wealthy man as "one who is content with his lot."[9] Note that the Mishnah does not say "he who is happy," but one who is happy with that which is his, however much or little it may be. The happiness is generated by the appreciation of what he has, not by the amount of what he has. Sometimes we have more, sometimes less, but the ability to focus on the positive, on the many things in life that we *can* enjoy, is what can bring us *simchah*.

That is why a part of our *simchah* is engendered by the simplest things, like a well-cooked piece of meat, a cup of wine, or a new article of clothing. These small material things are not the essence of our life, but they can give us the opportunity to focus on something positive and to foster contentment. *Simchah* in a home means that the couple appreciates the fact that they have one another, a roof over their heads, and the basic possessions necessary for daily living.

If the husband and wife value one another, they can be thankful for the opportunity they now have to build a home. If they appreciate the fact that they were blessed with a child, they will be off to a good start in raising that child successfully by basing their approach to everything on bringing *simchah* into the home.

An overly solemn, gloomy, humorless home is a dangerous place to raise a family. Of course, life has its sobering moments. In addition, building a home, raising a family, making decisions, and accepting

---

9   *Pirkei Avos* 4:1.

responsibilities are serious business. Paradoxically, if our children are to understand the seriousness of life and take to heart the many messages we are going to give them, those ideas must be transmitted with joy.

In his very beautiful essay "Youthful Enthusiasm for Duty,"[10] Rabbi Samson Raphael Hirsch speaks about what happens to a person when Torah becomes merely burdensome and rote, and what will happen to his offspring and their descendants.

He explains that people seek to give up a Torah-based lifestyle when they no longer feel connected to it. *Simchah*, enthusiasm, and appreciation are tools that bring a positive association with Torah into a family. When a child thinks about his home, including his responsibilities there, it is positive encouragement and complimentary words that make the thoughts good ones. If preparing for Shabbos is filled with pressure and raised voices, if cleaning his room means anger and stress, then even though our motives are wonderful, our behavior is repellent.

A normal child will want to play, do homework, or spend time with a friend, but he heads home happily in time for supper. A child should enjoy being at home, and feel a connection to it. Why should a child want to be in an unhappy place? If the atmosphere in the home lacks *simchah*, the child will feel disconnected, associating his family, the Shabbos table, and even the mitzvos with gloom and tension. Almost any other place would be preferable.

As our children grow older and go off to yeshiva or seminary and then move on in life, we can be thankful if they are content wherever they are. Far from signifying that they do not love you, or dislike coming back home, they are thankfully learning well and growing in their new environment. If they are not homesick despite their love for us, we can be proud and grateful that they feel secure and confident, enjoying life, feeling fulfilled in their own ways.

No one wants to lose out on happiness or to miss being in a place that is joyful. Children want to be present when the family gets together, and they will feel the same way as adults. Even if they can't be there

---

10   *Collected Writings of Rabbi Samson Raphael Hirsch* (Rabbi Dr. Joseph Breuer Fdtn., 1997), ch. 7.

on a particular occasion, they will want to call and maintain that good connection.[11]

With a Smile and a Song

Consider this: How do you enter your home after a hard day at work, a long day teaching, an exhausting day of learning? What is it that you bring home to your spouse and children?

Distress? Tension? Anger? Worry? Frustration?

Or do you come home with a smile?

The attitude with which we come into our home is going to affect the attitude and responses of everyone else in it. Cheerfully greeting our family members shows that we appreciate them and makes a difference in the atmosphere of the home. The same is true if those in the home greet the one arriving with a smile and a cheerful word.

As we parents do, so will our children. It is worth investing time and thought in learning how to show appreciation and enjoyment in each other's company. It is easier to express love in a home that is full of joy than in one full of tension. If you are experiencing negative feelings, don't communicate them right off the bat when you or your family members enter the house, as these are all feelings of self-absorption which will quickly dampen a happy atmosphere.

Simchah, on the other hand, is expansive; it is outgoing and undeniably contagious. It is a form of *chessed*, giving to others, and a smile has the same power. There is a sagacious bit of anonymous prose that is sometimes put on magnets and posters:

> *A smile costs nothing but gives much. It enriches those who receive without making poorer those who give. It takes but a moment, but the memory of it sometimes lasts forever. None*

---

11 A child *never* wanting to be away is not necessarily proof that his home is a happy place. Children sometimes fear that the home might fall apart, or that something terrible will happen if they are not there all the time. This may be a signal for professional help, as it may be a symptom that either the child is emotionally off-balance or the home itself is dysfunctional.

is so rich or mighty that he can get along without it, and none
is so poor that he cannot be made rich by it. Yet a smile cannot
be bought, begged, borrowed, or stolen, for it is something that
is of no value to anyone until it is given away. A smile creates
happiness in the home, promotes good will in business, and is
the cornerstone of friendship. It can perk up the weary, bring
cheer to the discouraged, sunshine to the sad, and is man's
best antidote for trouble. Some people are too tired to give you
a smile. Give them one of yours, as none need a smile as much
as he who has no more to give.

An expression that transmits contentment, appreciation, and *simchah* is said to possess a light on the face, a spiritual smile that is a gift of Hashem. We ask in the blessing of *"Sim shalom—Grant peace,"*[12] that He may show us this light. Our benevolent Torah, the attribute of mercy, the gifts of life and peace, all the good things in life, came to us with one overarching, powerful tool: Hashem's smile.

When the home manifests this, a child is content. Should it be permeated with anger, frustration, and tension, the child, in self-defense, retreats within himself, self-absorbed and discontented.

When I was young, my father would sing a happy song when we walked hand in hand in the street. I would yank his arm and beg him to stop.

"Do you think anyone is listening?" he would ask.

"Yes, the whole world hears you!" I was so self-conscious about it that it drove me crazy. "Stop, stop," I said, and I remember saying to myself, "I am never going to do that when I'm a father."

Now, when I walk along the street with my own children, they are always yanking at my hand and pleading, "Ta, stop!" I sing because I enjoy it and I know that nobody pays any attention. And I know that my children are going to do the same thing with theirs because it creates a happy memory. I do not sing in order to embarrass them; I sing

---

12   Last berachah in *Shemoneh Esreh.*

from happiness, and they know it. I don't tell them that they will one day do the same, but I urge them to sing with me.

Not long ago, I was walking with one of my married sons as he held his own son's hand. Sure enough, he was singing.

Simchah in Doing Mitzvos

To better understand how our attitude toward the spiritual in our lives will most definitely impact our children, let us again refer to Rav Hirsch's essay about refreshing our *simchah* anew when we observe the commandments.

We want our children to follow in our footsteps, to accept our value system. Joy, excitement, and enthusiasm in the observance of Torah and mitzvos will carry us and them through the unavoidably difficult life challenges that will arise.

If they seem to be rejecting the very things we worked so hard to integrate into our own lives, it can be extraordinarily painful. When we see our children doing something that has overtones of rebellion or trouble, it is necessary to retain our sense of humor and thoughtfulness. More often than not, they are just feeling "grown up" or coming around to realizing that they have a *yetzer hara*. They are probably far from "going off the *derech*" or becoming troublemakers. Keep your relationship warm, loving, and happy, helping them to navigate the rough waters rather than pushing them over the brink. If you do not know how to handle the situation, seek assistance from someone with more experience.

> *A friend consulted me about his twelve-year-old daughter, who was very active and energetic. He was raising his children in the frum world that was so different from the world of his childhood, and he was concerned because she did not seem to fit into the conformist, constrictive system to which he now belonged. I suggested that he introduce her to someone who has had or knows how to handle children of that age, someone who could tell him if there was really anything to worry about.*

The meeting went well. The mechanech to whom he spoke reas-
sured him that his daughter was a delightful child, enthusiastic
and healthy, and he should just give her the space she needed
to grow. Little could either of those fine men imagine that
ten years later this young lady would marry a very successful
talmid chacham—the son of this mechanech.

Do not fear if your *frum*-from-birth children are not clones of you and
your family; it is necessary to retain a sense of balance if they choose
a slightly different path. We cannot let the fear that our children won't
be exactly like us overtake our common sense and impair the good relationship we've worked so hard to build. In general, we need to strive
for balance and understanding. Only rarely might a stronger reaction
be necessary, and then *only* with direction from people who are experienced and knowledgeable in what is to be expected with kids growing
up in today's religious communities.

Some of us have to deal with the other extreme, when our children
surpass us in observance of the mitzvos. We should be overjoyed, right?
After all, did we not change our lives in order to find a greater truth?
When we respond with angst to such a development, we need to question our motives carefully. Are we feeling inadequate in the face of their
greater piety? Are we, perhaps, trying to hold them back much as our
parents did with us? Might this be a time to reevaluate our own level
and degree of observance?

Mark and Sharon made their way to Yiddishkeit through
NCSY. After high school, they respectively went to yeshiva and
seminary in Yerushalayim, then on to college together. They
married and built their family in a large, beautiful Modern
Orthodox community in New Jersey. Mark, a computer pro-
grammer, was involved in the shul, participated in a Daf Yomi
shiur, and was an active member of Hatzolah. Sharon opened
a small, home-based business designing and selling jewelry so
that she could add to their joint income while taking care of
their four active children.

Shimon, their eldest son, went to a yeshiva in Yerushalayim for one year after high school, became inspired, and stayed for a second year. Staying a third year became a battle with his parents, in the midst of which Shimon turned to them and said, "Mom, Dad, what is the difference between what you did twenty-one years ago and what I am doing now? I want more of all the good things you taught me."

They were both silent for a moment; Sharon began explaining all the differences while Mark sat back and listened. That night Mark said to his wife, "I am surprised by how much of our fire has been lost. We need to help Shimon go as far as he can."

Sharon was not convinced. "We're frum Jews. Why is he having a problem with our Yiddishkeit? The next thing you know he won't want to eat in our house! I refuse to send him back for another year so he can become a black-hat yeshiva boy who will reject us and ask me to change my clothing."

Mark was taken aback by the vehemence of his wife's opposition. He realized that he had taken his home for granted while neglecting it spiritually. He had always seen himself as religious, even somewhat inspired. He sent his children to the local day school, reviewed their studies with them every Shabbos, and was involved in the community. Where had things gone wrong?

He called his rosh yeshiva in Eretz Yisrael whom he had not seen in ten years, but with whom he still felt somewhat of a connection.

"Rebbi, what am I doing wrong?"

As they spoke, he was questioned about where he davened, to which school he sent his children, and why.

"How do you speak about your shul's rabbi when you are at home?" his rosh yeshiva asked.

"Well, I am quite involved in the shul, I am on three committees."

"Yes, I understand," pressed the rosh yeshiva, "but I asked how you speak about the rabbi at home."

Mark was mortified by his own answer, "I guess I complain that he is so strict and sometimes call him our 'counterfeit Modern Orthodox rabbi' because he is always trying to be as frum as the Chareidi shul down the block. But I get along well with him. I really like him and help him in many ways."

In the ensuing silence, which spoke louder than words, Mark realized that he had traveled some distance from where he had been twenty years earlier. He had chosen a shul and school where he and his wife would be the more religious element. They were not interested in having people scrutinize their religious life and had decided to take the easier approach. They had always been among the more observant members of the shul, and they felt very comfortable with the lack of pressure from the community.

Little by little, their own resolve had faded, and with this came a slightly jaded attitude toward their rabbi, who was doing everything possible to strengthen his congregation. They were no longer comfortable in the shul. Sharon felt challenged because the rabbi's wife had commented that it was so nice to have another woman there who covered her hair properly. Sharon had been wearing a simple wig when the two had met, but it was neither her favorite hairpiece nor her standard head covering. From then on, she always felt judged, watched, and under pressure. Mark's response was to make jokes about their "counterfeit MO rabbi."

Now, their son was going in the way of their rabbi. They had sent him to what they considered a more modern yeshiva in Eretz Yisrael and now he was becoming "extreme." Mark actually didn't mind, but Sharon was petrified.

They spent a full three hours talking with Mark's former rosh yeshiva before they were able to understand what was really

happening. The couple decided that it was time to accept that
their son was inspired and help him live his dream. They also
decided that it was time to rejuvenate their own Yiddishkeit.

Children Cannot Live in Two Worlds

Now, we come to a key and sensitive point. Every person reading this book has an integrated system of thought. You came from one place, you have come to another place, and you have integrated your two worlds into a system that works for you. Some of you are comfortable with your system, others less so, but you are living with the combination. In order to achieve that comfort level, you most likely had to have incorporated some elements from your former world into your current one. While we want to be role models for our children, we have to understand that they are not always capable of achieving that integration.

We live in a clearly defined, labeled world. There are the Chassidic, Litvish, Yeshivish, and Modern Orthodox categories with variations on each, not to mention the varieties of Yeshivish and Chassidic. There are, perhaps, fifty different labels that define different types of Shabbos-observing religious people and their systems of belief.

When I once asked a young lady to describe her family, she said, "Well, they are *chassidish-frei*." I asked her what that meant.

"Well," she said, "my parents are basically not really religious. They look *chassidish*, and everyone thinks they are, but nothing we do at home has any meaning; it is all a facade. My mother likes to shop, my father likes to go to Atlantic City, but we are a *chassidish* family."[13]

Can you imagine having to find a label for this mixture and adding it to the list?

My father often joked that many of the young people he mentors should be called FFBWSI: "*Frum* from birth with some interruptions."

By the time you begin to raise a family, you have already integrated various values into your life. In choosing to join a community and select

---

13   Obviously, this is not meant to be suggesting that this scenario only relates to Chassidim.

a school for your children, you are also espousing a certain lifestyle. Children define themselves by their social surroundings and the schools they attend. You have no difficulty living with ideas and habits that may seem conflicting to your children, but they probably cannot live happily with them because they have to hear very clear messages.

Children need to feel confident in their present, uncomplicated situation. If there are certain elements of our own more complex world that we wish to retain, we can only introduce them into our children's lives when they are older, more intellectually mature, and secure in their way of life.

It is therefore necessary for us, as mentors and role models, to live in consonance with the values and behaviors of the people in whose community we have chosen to live. The message to our children needs to be that this is who we are, and this is our lifestyle.

While we should not label, we do need to fit into our chosen community.

Unfortunately, we can single out religiously observant Americans who have moved to Israel as a group with a disproportionate percentage of children who are going "off the *derech*." Another group with even a larger number of children at risk is that of the American *baalei teshuvah* in Israel, and after that come the children of traditional Sephardic Jews who were sent to strictly religious yeshivos.

The commonality among these groups is the transfer of the children from one cultural background to a very different one, with demands of behavior and observance in ways with which the parents themselves are not yet comfortable.

This kind of cultural conflict is extremely challenging. Our children need to see *us* conform to what we are demanding of *them*. We have to be comfortable with the values with which we are going to raise them. If we send our children to schools with a certain dress code, we have to dress that way, too. If we send them to a school that teaches certain values, we have to live with them, too. Sending conflicting messages to young children invariably confuses them.

If you are going out to do *kiruv*, outreach, in a community that is far from an ideal place to bring up your children, you will undoubtedly come up against a reverse challenge. Your girls will be the only ones wearing long skirts and stockings, and your boys will be the only ones with *peyos* and tzitzis.

It will have to be made very clear to your children that they can be proud and happy about the standards they are keeping because *you and they together* are role models, examples to educate the people in the community. It helps, of course, if indeed everybody in the new community is looking to you and your family as such. Then you can convey to your children that they are special, that they know things that the others do not, but want to learn from them. It is not easy, but it is possible, to give children the strength to be proud of the fact that they are different.

If you are able to send your children to yeshivos or Bais Yaakov schools, however, and they are being taught that it is *not* proper to do A, B, C, or D, and you *are* doing A, B, C, or D, how can you explain it? "We are better, smarter, or more sophisticated than our peers"?

This attitude is inconsistent and confusing, and your children do not have a clear path to follow. They do not know what is expected of them, as they have been placed in a lose-lose situation. If they respect you more than the school, they will rebel there. If the school has more weight in their eyes, they will not understand why you feel it is OK to go against the rules, and they will lose respect for you. Don't take that risk.

Setting Boundaries

Parents and educators are fighting a tremendous tidal wave of decadence today. Schools are scrambling to set up some kind of structure, a strong framework to hold onto during these difficult times.

When I was in *yeshiva gedolah*, for instance, it was fine to wear colored shirts during the week, and no one complained about sneakers. Today's standards are much stricter. It is not my purpose here to dissect, rationalize or criticize the stricter standards of our schools today, because we are not going to be able to change them.

I must accept that they have their reasons, such as they are, and if I choose to send my child to a school that has a stricter outlook, I had better be secure in that choice. Furthermore, I need to be comfortable defending and living up to it. If not, I repeat, my children are going to be conflicted and confused. We have to know the codes of the community in which we have chosen to live, and recognize which behaviors are and are not acceptable.

These behaviors are *not* determined by our comfort level. The decisions of where children are allowed to go in their leisure time, the way that they are supposed to dress, and the activities in which they may engage cannot be determined by what we personally deem to be appropriate and acceptable behavior. We cannot judge our children's conduct by some of the standards with which *we* grew up.

I have met with good mothers whose children were going through hard times and doing things that were wrong. They came to me after their children were already way, way off the *derech*.

"Listen, Rabbi," they would say, "to tell you the truth, I understand. I was the same. When I was fifteen, I had boyfriends and dressed very inappropriately."

You were the same? Wait just a minute. You did not know any better at that age, that is how you were raised, but your child has a very different orientation. She is rebelling.

Your empathy with where she is going and what she is doing is a result of projecting your own growing years onto those of your child. You cannot do this because she is growing up in a different world from yours. The boundaries need to be set in the world in which you and she are presently living.

Those wonderful mothers who came to me in despair are women who took a long journey to arrive in the world in which they now live. Unfortunately, they did not proscribe or limit behaviors that in this world are considered so highly inappropriate that their children were ostracized by all the schools in their present communities.

I have also had mothers who came to me in hysterics because their child was doing something that in their minds indicated a desire to stop being religious, when in fact the youngster was really coming of age, so to speak, and just testing the waters.

In both instances, parents were misreading their children's behavior based on their own lack of clarity as to what is normal and what is not, when to permit and when to say no due to their own inexperience.

Moreover, I can say with assurance that even parents who grew up in a *frum* home twenty-five years ago and are raising a family today are living in a different world from the one in which they grew up. The *frum* world, along with secular society, has greatly changed. The challenges and the problems differ from what they were twenty-five years ago.

We have no choice but to deal with the current challenges confronting our children. We have to comprehend what they are facing and know the limits we must place on them. We have to find ways to get through to them so that they can make their own peace with the system.

Even when we disagree with the system, recognizing its faults, we need to help our children understand that societal structures are not always perfect, but that overall, they work.

Assess your goals: What do you really want to achieve? Anything you perceive as wrong and would like to change for the better can only be accomplished if you are an integrated part of, and accepted by, the system you want to affect. You have to work from within it, whether it represents the school or your community.

If you want to become a doctor, you must go to medical school and conform to the basic rules in order to succeed. Everything that you or your children want to do in life will require conforming to some set of rules. This does not affect or reduce the importance of the absolute truth of Torah in your life, which requires you to be smart and aware while living in the real world. It is vital to know how to roll with the punches, understanding when to be flexible and when it is truly necessary to be firm.

It is not intelligent to be rigidly self-righteous and critical of faults found in the community, or to condemn the entire system because you perceive parts of it that could be improved. When we vociferously expound on how wrong and superficial *everything* is, we teach our children to rebel without realizing that we are encouraging this behavior.

Any system that deals with masses of people must be superficial in some ways in order to survive. While there is some superficiality in the school system as well, not all that it requires of our children is shallow. It is important to respect the school your child attends. When we can laugh off the petty, trivial things, they will learn to laugh as well. We need to keep a healthy sense of humor regarding those things we cannot change and take them in stride. Your children will pick up their cues from you.

Just as we sometimes need to be able to chuckle at ourselves, we sometimes need to laugh at the system. Not derisive laughter, the type that puts it down, but the kind that understands that sometimes things can become lopsided when you are trying to educate a hundred thousand children within necessary boundaries. There isn't an educational system in the world that does not have serious problems of one kind or another. A system that deals with thousands must have rules that apply to all and is, by its very nature, going to have faults. It is not possible to develop an educational or societal structure that is able to provide everything that all its constituents require.

Chapter 18

Large Families: What It Takes

The word "large" is necessarily a relative term. We refer to it here in relation to successfully managing a family blessed with many children. To some people five children is a lot, while to others this is on the small side. Then, too, our perception of size sometimes changes as our family evolves. In most cases, people who have made the kind of quantum changes in their lives that are the subject of this book find that there is a very clear difference in the size of the family they are building compared to the size of the family from which they came.

———————

My friend Rabbi Yaakov M. was working in the Israel Ministry of Education in 1991 on a project that was the brainchild of Rabbi Shlomo Zilberman. Reb Yaakov was sitting with some of the bigwigs in the Ministry when one of Rabbi Zilberman's older sons, also working on the project, came into the room. They spoke together for a few minutes, Reb Yaakov handed him some papers, and they finished their discussion. After he had left the room, Reb Yaakov turned to the visitors.

"My friends, what is your impression of that young man?"

"Very confident, very intelligent," was the general consensus.

"To what size family do you think he belongs?" asked Reb Yaakov.

Two of the men agreed that since he was so polished and self-confident, he must be an only child.

"Certainly, no more than two," said the third.

"Well," my friend said, anticipating their surprise, "he is one of eighteen children."

He was not disappointed. They were absolutely astounded.

People think that in order to raise healthy, happy, successful children, you need certain preliminary conditions. The only thing you really need, and this is the hardest thing to give whether you have one child or ten, is *yourself*—your love, care, and individual attention.

They don't need you with the same intensity around the clock. A few minutes a day can suffice if it is obvious to the children that those few minutes are meaningful to you, and that they have your full attention during that time. Being there when they need you is what counts. Children who feel that they can rely on parents who trust and love them, who know what behavior is expected of them and what they can expect in return, are happy and self-confident.

———————————

Building a family of upward of five children, as many couples in our community do today, requires a totally different foundation than that of a unit of three or four. The challenge is compounded by the fact that the society around us builds its families on the basis of relationships and commitments quite different from ours.

The responsibility of raising many children is a huge one, beyond anything most of us ever saw in our childhood homes. People I meet will tell me that their two children are "driving them crazy," and they don't understand how people with large families manage.

"Between the carpools and piano lessons," they clarify, "and gym and ballet sessions, I have no time for myself."

Time spent with your children and taking care of their needs is what "yourself" is all about during your child-raising years, I find myself wanting to shout.

The level of commitment and selflessness that is necessary for the task of parenting is something to think about ahead of time, before you set out to sea and find yourself being tossed about in a rowboat full of children without oars.

If you have taken on the task, I'm sure you must know what will be required to make it work. The model of a nonobservant home is usually not valid for you today, neither in relation to the luxuries nor the freedoms you might have enjoyed. Family life for a religious person is a world apart, with different requirements and expectations.

Perhaps it will be helpful to examine the relevance of the family unit in today's society to understand the difference between our goals and theirs.

The innate human desire for descendants to perpetuate one's existence obviously still impels people to marry and have families. In the world today, however, there are divergent households thought to legitimately comprise a family, which is another indicator of how the family unit has largely disintegrated.

Although the desire for self-perpetuation still exists, the average family in the United States consists of three members.[1]

Over the years, I have spoken with hundreds of young men and women about marriage. Many have an idyllic perception of family that has no connection to reality, built on an ideal of marriage based on what they see in the media, what they read in novels, or from meeting a family that looked perfect.

As with everything else in life, when this ideal is created from a false image, people feel inadequate when they are unable to live up to it. Their desire to build a family is built on superficiality, seen only from the outside instead of on a clear, meaningful actuality with rooted values and developed character traits. Without these, however, an ideal can have no meaning.

---

1   "Average number of people per family in the United States from 1960 to 2022," Statista, June 2, 2023, https://www.statista.com/statistics/183657/. The average family consisted of 3.13 persons in 2022, down from 3.7 in the 1960s, reflected in the decrease of children in family households overall.

The problem is so deep that there are couples today who prepare wedding albums with pictures taken beforehand, at a "rehearsal." The bride and groom will then appear perfect, in consonance with some preconceived, usually artistic, design.

When couples base their lives on a representation of reality instead of authenticity, their perspective is skewed, often resulting in an inability to create a true family. We need to add real values of sharing and responsibility, with behavior to match the picture, and that calls for hard work.

Working hard, in the Western world, is equated with earning money. Although some will disagree with me, I fear that many people in contemporary society are having children purely for the sake of having what everyone else has, and fitting into the generally accepted social image. We find a reference to this in the Midrash that without jealousy a man would not get married, build a house, or plant a vineyard, etc.[2]

The Jewish perception of family is solid and real, involving responsibilities and living up to ideals. It is not about having; it is about giving. We build a Torah family because it is our responsibility to contribute, share, build, and transmit. The whole concept of having a family is to allow us to give to the maximum.

Rav Itzele Volozhiner wrote, "My father [Rav Chaim] always used to say that the essence of a person's life is how much he can do for others."[3]

Life, then, is not about what we are going to have, acquire, or show off to others.

Living Up to an Ideal

Most of you grew up in a society where the picture of family differed from the new community that inspired change in your life, where you beheld a unique and beautiful scene. People were building large families, raising many happy children, and it looked very appealing. Perhaps, you did not think so carefully about what was needed to do to make this

---

2   *Midrash Tehillim* (*Shocher Tov*) 37.
3   Rav Itzele Volozhin, Introduction to *Nefesh Hachaim*, Rabbi Chaim Volozhin.

dream work, how you would pass on *your* values to *your* children, and put meaning into the entire picture.

Without fully investing in building your family, the internal relationships will have nothing to sustain them. In the society around us, families often break down because people are not aware of what it takes to make the "ideal family" function successfully. When a couple enters a community with a Torah lifestyle, the accepted picture is that of a large unit, and the couple sets out to build its own without proper preparation. Not every couple anticipates what having many children really means.

As a father of fifteen beloved children, I most certainly have no intent to be discouraging, but it is important to me that we go into life with open eyes. It isn't easy. It's going to require tremendous effort, plus an enormous amount of Hashem's grace and help to make it work. It takes a great deal of forethought and study just to achieve an understanding of what the job requires.

Preparing Yourself

I know that many people assume that having a large family is an absolute halachic requirement.[4] It *is* a mitzvah,[5] but it is *not* a requirement. People need to know themselves and what they are truly capable of before trying to fulfill it. They need to ask questions of halachic authorities, and they need to know their limitations as well as their capabilities. They should not feel embarrassed about asking when, how, and if they may or should use suitable methods of birth control.

As this is a handbook for adults, this is a topic that must be discussed.

Some young people seem to view this subject from two perspectives. They may take birth control for granted, not even realizing that its use requires the instruction of a halachic authority. Others, who understand why it is not an assumed and accepted practice in our

---

4   Please see "Important Note" in the Preface. All discussions with halachic consequences should be followed up with a rabbi to deal with your particular situation.

5   *Yeshayahu* 45:18, "לא תהו בראה לשבת יצרה"; *Chagigah* 2b: The world was created to be populated.

community, mistakenly presume that they are not even allowed to ask questions about it.

Both approaches are without basis. *Rabbanim* and *poskim*, halachic authorities, approach this serious dilemma with a balanced and responsible attitude. They will answer these questions *when the couple asks*. Please note that these questions need to be asked, and attention must be paid to the answers.

We need to choose halachic authorities who know and understand us and our circumstances, and also know what families and large families are all about. There are, assuredly, *poskim* who know how to deal with these questions, if not everywhere, then within easy reach of every community.

Having a large family means committing to sleepless nights for many, many years. Every additional family member adds to the burden. Many people find tremendous blessing and satisfaction in carrying this burden. They understand and appreciate that an investment in this undertaking is worthwhile, and they are capable of making it.

Individuals who have limitations of any kind, however, whether emotional, mental, or physical, should not automatically take on this kind of commitment without serious reflection beforehand. It is not wrong to weigh our choices earnestly, and to bring our questions to those who have great knowledge and understanding. It is preferable and appropriate that couples go to a *posek* together to discuss these matters when it is necessary.

In rare cases when *shalom bayis* is very challenging and there is no real dialogue between the couple, a woman can feel coerced and controlled. In these rare instances a woman may find it necessary to seek the advice of a *posek* on her own. In some of these cases a *posek* will speak to a woman without her husband's cooperation. He will give her instruction because bearing additional children can be a very challenging undertaking, requiring more than some women can handle.

It is unfortunate when a husband is nonchalant regarding the burden, fears, and challenges of pregnancy, childbirth, and running the home, which will fall for the most part on his wife. It may, therefore, be a necessity for some women to ask this type of question at different times in their lives.

Time Management

To successfully raise a large family, you need to know that a certain amount of what we call "control" has to be relinquished. Some people are by nature extremely orderly, others fastidiously clean, and many are very particular about the way they like things to be done in their homes. Although we see others who seem to be superwomen, capable of doing everything, we need to keep in mind that few are really able to do it all, and even they are relinquishing control in certain areas—just not where we can see it.

Raising children requires letting go of control, learning to become comfortable within an entirely new situation. The trick is to acknowledge our God-given strengths, accept our God-given weaknesses, and stay honestly within that framework before making the choice to take responsibility for bringing up and taking care of other human beings.

Learning to manage time efficiently is probably one of the most useful traits to develop whether you have two children or ten. This has also been influenced by constant access to the media, internet, email, and social networking, all of which take more of our time than we would like to admit to ourselves. We have also been impacted by easy access to many forms of supposedly time-saving luxuries and entertainment, but the bottom line is that they usurp a lot of our time.

I like the following story by Stephen Covey, a time management writer and consultant.

> An expert in time management was speaking to a class of business students and, to drive home a point, used an illustration that they will never forget.
>
> "Okay, time for a quiz," he said to the group of high-powered overachievers.

He pulled out a one-gallon, wide-mouthed Mason jar and set it on the table in front of him. Then he produced about a dozen fist-sized rocks and carefully placed them, one at a time, in the jar. When the jar was filled to the top and no more rocks would fit inside, he asked, "Is this jar full?"

Everyone in the class said, "Yes."

"Really?" he asked.

Reaching under the table, he pulled out a bucket of gravel and dumped some into the jar. He shook it, causing pieces of gravel to work themselves down into the spaces between the big rocks.

"Is the jar full?"

By this time the class was onto him. "Probably not," a student answered.

"Good!"

He reached under the table and brought out a bucket of sand, dumping it into the jar. It went into all of the spaces left between the rocks and the gravel.

"Is this jar full?"

"No!" the class shouted.

"Good!"

He took a pitcher of water and poured it in until the jar was filled to the brim.

"What is the point of this illustration?" he asked.

One eager beaver raised his hand. "The point is that no matter how full your schedule is, if you try really hard you can always fit some more things into it!"

"No," the speaker replied, "that's not the point. The truth that this illustration teaches us is that if you don't put the big rocks in first, you'll never get them in at all."[6]

---

6   Dr. Stephen R. Covey, "The 'Big Rocks' of Life," *First Things First*, http://www.appleseeds.org/big-rocks_covey.htm.

What are the "big rocks" in your life? Your children, loved ones, education, your dreams? A worthy cause, teaching or mentoring others? Doing things you love? Time for yourself, your health, your spouse?

Remember to put these big rocks in your schedule first, or you'll never get them in at all! If you sweat the small stuff (the gravel, the sand), then you'll fill your life with little worries that don't really matter in the long run, and you'll never have the real quality time you need to spend on the big, important things.

So, today, when you reflect on this short story, ask yourself, "What are the 'big rocks' in my life?" Then put those in your jar first.

Establishing Priorities

The anecdote that we just read is a useful lesson for anyone raising a large family, as it emphasizes the need to establish priorities. Commitments of lesser importance often catch our attention and pull us away from doing more significant things.

I am not such a great time manager myself, but I do use this lesson as a guide when I have to find time for marking tests that my seminary students take every year. Evaluating and marking over a hundred tests fairly can be enormously time consuming.

If I were to put aside all my other commitments, sit down and spend ten or fifteen minutes per test, I'd be at it for many hours of valuable time.

Marking these tests is less important than many of my other obligations, so the job kept getting pushed off. For many years I was returning my tests months after I gave them. I finally remembered the story about the stones and setting priorities, and arrived at a reasonable solution for my problem.

I often had ten- or twelve-minute intervals of free time between appointments. If I kept the tests on my desk, and marked even one or two during those intervals...

This is just a small, but I hope helpful, example for parents with an impossibly busy schedule. We need to weigh the various tasks we wish to accomplish and constantly ask ourselves which take priority. We know that our children are the "big stones" in our lives, so they come first, and we have to fit everything else around them.

Raising "Good" Children

Who doesn't want to rear good children? If we have already reached the stage of raising our families, we recognize that each child is different. We want them *all* to turn out well. Have you ever realized, though, that what makes our children good in our eyes is our attitude toward them?

If we have a predetermined picture of what we want our children to be like (or what we *think* they should be like), we attempt to fit them into that picture. Perhaps, we see how well-behaved our friends' children are, and expect ours to be just like theirs. In either case, we are comparing our children to our expectations and trying to fit them into preordained boxes.

We have to realize that when we observe other people's children, we never see the whole picture; we are seeing them when they know they are being watched. In addition, we are looking at *other* people's children who are going to resemble *their* parents. Our children are going to inherit our genes; to a certain extent, they will be and behave like *us*. We cannot compare them with others, nor can we expect more of them than what they receive from us.

Both our strong and weak points are reflected through our children, and to an extent, we see who we are. Our children mimic traits we may have ignored or been unaware of in ourselves, whether due to nature or nurture. The way we act toward them and our spouses is going to have a strong influence on their character development and the adults they will become.

We must see, accept, and live with the good they have within them. It begins, as we pointed out in the previous chapter, with having a positive, healthy atmosphere in the home that will help us to build happy children. When we are tired, frazzled, under financial strain, or feeling great pressure from work, we must nevertheless remember at all times that we brought these children into the world, and we are the ones who are ultimately responsible for them.

We raise them in the shadow of our actions, not our expectations. We do not create "good" children by sending them to certain schools and assuming that there they will learn how to behave. Our children are formed in our homes, where they inherit or learn our character traits and personalities.

If we expect to raise good children by ignoring our own behavior, hoping that they'll turn out well all by themselves, forget it! We are they and they are us. Whatever we invest in and bring to them is what they see and absorb. We cannot copy what we see in other homes; we are ourselves. It is neither sufficient nor advisable to say to a child, "Look at them."

Raising "Our" Children

Although we said earlier that we should be building and learning from role models, this is never just a copycat procedure. Learning from role models requires absorbing underlying values and studying acceptable behavior. I cannot count the number of times people who participated in my seminars or heard my talks on education came back to me later complaining.

"I said what you said, and it didn't work."

"I did exactly what you presented, and my son looked at me as if I were crazy."

"My daughter asked me who told me to do or say that."

The examples I give are taken from *my* life, given *my* character and the particular dynamics in play between me and *my* children. You cannot just repeat my words out of context. They will not be part of your nature or character, and your children will look at you in puzzlement and wonder what's going on.

Each couple needs to find their own way to raise children—learning from others, yes, but adapting the lessons to each individual's personal style. I can learn from others, for instance, to think before I respond. I can even learn that one should respond with respect, but I cannot use someone else's identical words. I can observe that a certain parent is very strict. It may be prudent to see if he is as strict with his own behavior as he is with his children's. In any case, what I see is just part of the picture, and we cannot copy the whole picture—even if we could see it—because *we* are not *they*.

> *I once spent Shabbos with a family in Givat Shaul, Yerushalayim, and was joined at the meals by my rebbi. The discussion came around to child-rearing and he told me to observe our host.*
>
> *"He can be stronger with his children than I because he demands so much more from himself than I do."*
>
> *I was obviously puzzled.*
>
> *"His children see how much he demands of himself. They see that he does not compromise when it comes to his own behavior, so when he is strict with them, they understand. Hopefully," Rav Wolbe added, "he will be successful even though he is so strict."*
>
> *My rebbi was clearly saying that differences in personalities require concomitant differences in behavior.*

Anyone reading this who takes it for granted that he can be strict with his children because he is strict with everyone else in his life will have seriously misunderstood the point. The reference here is to someone who demands of *himself* a great deal, whose relationship with his wife and children is impeccable, who relentlessly works on his *middos*, and whom no one in his family would call inconsistent or mean.

———————

Gaining from role models involves learning values, understanding the process of raising children in a Torah-observant household, and then figuring out how to internalize and adapt them to your own life. Just walking the walk and talking the talk does not work. You have to know and understand yourself and your capabilities. Look at that individual whom you admire, see what you can apply in your home, and tell yourself, "I hope that, perhaps, someday I will be able to respond to my child in that way."

Chinuch ha'banim, raising children properly, cannot be a gut reaction. It requires knowing what we want to achieve and forming a plan to attain it, rather than merely responding to our emotions. Going one step deeper, raising children cannot be just **re**active but must be **pro**active.

If we know in advance what we want to teach, we can find ways to make sure these things are accomplished. If we only react to situations as they crop up, our parenting will not be adequate. We do not even realize how emotional our reactions are. Even though we may have good instincts, acting emotionally will usually not benefit our children.

I have also gone through serious quantum changes in my life. Although I was raised in a very beautiful, *frum* home with parents who are wonderful role models, by nature I was a thinker and a rebel. In my early teens, I rejected essentially anything and everything I had ever heard and started from scratch. Although I never actually rebelled against the framework in which I was raised, I developed ulcers when I was fourteen due to the worry and trouble I experienced as I went through a very serious intellectual search over a number of years. I sought to find out who I was, how I needed to live my life, and identify what I wanted to keep of myself and what I wanted to change. The changes that I went through during those years were similar to those that one undergoes during the *teshuvah* process. *But those changes were mine, and do not belong to anyone else.*

Until the following incident took place, I thought I had thoroughly evaluated my life, personality, and environment, and that I was acting entirely in keeping with who I am and not as a result of my upbringing.

Until a few years ago (and intermittently since then), I was a world-class nosher. I was not ashamed of this habit, but I was also not interested in having my children know about it for reasons that you will understand. Keeping it under wraps became more difficult as the children grew and discovered empty Pringles boxes in the car and began to wonder about the origin of all those chocolate wrappers. My children figured me out very quickly, and it was no longer a secret.

So, there I was, the biggest nosher you can imagine, and when my children reached the age of nine or ten and prepared a cup of tea for themselves on Shabbos, I would grow tense as I watched them spooning in one teaspoon after another of sugar. After the third teaspoon,

I would say, "Stop it, sugar is poison." Afterward I would ask myself, "Who said that? Was it the same person who just bought four pounds of candies and ate a pound of them? Was I really the one who said that?"

Why was I reacting in that way? It was totally out of character and did not make sense. I could not understand my reaction. Today, I am embarrassed to think of my previous behavior. (I must qualify this story with the fact that when I was growing up there was no health food section in the local supermarket and whole wheat bread was not a regular item on the shelves.) At that time, I used to debunk the whole theory of eating whole wheat instead of white flour; I termed it "ridiculous" and "foolish," calling it "horse food."

I would tease my wife when she baked whole wheat bread or challah.

"Keep the horse food on the ladies' side of the table," I would joke, "we like the good things over here."

Humans are hedonistic. We eat cakes because they taste good. Why would anyone want to eat something made of whole wheat flour? I really believed this, so I could not comprehend why I was so opposed to the children adding a lot of sugar to their tea. Whence this reaction?

Then my mother spent a week with us. One day, one of my children made a cup of tea. One spoonful of sugar, another, and as he was about to put in the third my mother said, "Stop! That is poison."

"Ma, you just solved a very, very significant quandary of mine."

I realized that my mother has the right to say what she said about sugar because she usually avoids eating it. I do not have that right, so why did I do it? The answer is that my reaction was ingrained, a reflexive response made *without thinking*. When we react without thinking, our behavior can be inappropriate, inconsistent, senseless, and often hypocritical. It will not only confuse our children but disturb them. If our ingrained reactions are good and sensible because that is the way we were raised, we can count ourselves lucky. We cannot depend on this being true in all situations, however, because sometimes these emotional, reflexive responses do not match certain of our current beliefs, ideals, or actions.

How are we going to give our children values if we do not really believe in them?

"Do as I say, not as I do," does not work. You cannot *scream*, "Stop screaming," at your child. Our children see who we are, and that, to an extent, is what they become. It is not difficult to understand.

One of the basic laws of *chinuch* is that your children will usually observe and internalize your attitude: If you are a happy person, content with what you do, your children will want to be like you. If you are an unhappy person, they are not going to want to be like you. If you are a positive person, your children will usually be positive. If you are a negative person, unless you are blessed with a very strong, positive spouse, they will usually be the same way.

If we are going to have a large family, we need to prepare ourselves for the job. We have plenty of role models, but we need to know how to apply those concepts that we admire to the *chinuch* of our own children. We do not want to have a dysfunctional family, *chas v'shalom*, as a result of not having the tools with which to deal with the challenges that will definitely arise.

Acquiring the Tools

There are books, classes, and individuals from whom you can learn. Even if you are raising one or two children, you will encounter issues that must be resolved. Larger families will naturally give rise to more and different kinds of problems, for you will have to deal with a more diverse assortment of personalities.

Don't let this possibility cause you to feel inadequate.

If you have a child with an ear infection and you do not know how to treat it, do you feel inadequate? No, you go to a doctor who diagnoses the problem and gives you instructions. You do not think less of yourself because you did not know. You are not distraught that you did not attend medical school.

There is no school to teach us how to raise children. We learn about proper *chinuch* in the school of life, where there are teachers and experts whom we can ask for assistance in troublesome situations.

There is nothing wrong with asking for advice, going to classes, hearing new ideas, and reading books. The problem is that we need to be careful to find the right classes and the right books, and a direction that fits in with who we are. We cannot change our nature.

Some people prefer a doctor who studied at Harvard or Yale, others choose to see a homeopath, many rely on the doctor's reputation for success. Everyone finds a doctor with whom he feels comfortable. He will listen to what that doctor says because for whatever reason he relates to him and respects his advice. It is a similar process when we look for people to advise us in *chinuch*. There are those to whom we can relate, and others with whom we cannot. Knowing whom and how to ask is also a learning process.

Just as in seeking advice to resolve the personal questions that bewilder us as we tread this new path, asking questions of a *rav* in regard to the *chinuch* of our children also requires preparation. We have to know *how* to ask. Sometimes, in attempting to clarify our questions, we'll discuss them with our spouse or a friend and find that we can answer them ourselves.

In trying to articulate what the real question is when we disagree with our spouse, we need to pinpoint the problem. Through this process, we can either find a resolution through clarity or compromise, or better understand that the problematic situation may be the result of our disagreement. When our disagreements become such that we have been giving conflicting messages to our children, we might not have to ask a question, but rather agree on what point we wish to convey. Parenting should not be administered as a result of emotional entanglement. It requires understanding what is good for our child and the best way to communicate it. This does not ignore the fact that emotion plays a large role in our connection to our children. The intellectual and rational approaches require emotional balance, but we cannot allow this last response to lead.

A Mother's Intuition

The rational approach does not obviate another key factor in the job of parenting, however, and that is a mother's intuition. Fathers need to be aware of this gift that their wives possess and pay attention to it.

A mother can often intuit what is wrong with her child, or at least sense that something is disturbing him.

Relying on a mother's perception is not contradictory to what I feel is wrong with relying on emotional responses in general. In bringing up children, you cannot unthinkingly respond to a behavior, but when a mother has a very clear feeling about a child, you have to listen to her.

When the people around you are telling you to punish, discipline, or respond in a certain way to your child's behavior, yet deep down inside you, as a mother, feel strongly that they are wrong, don't do it. No one else knows your child as you do. There are times when you feel at a loss and do not know how to react because whatever you have tried does not work. If you feel strongly, however, that a particular response is not right, don't go against your nature and negate your knowledge of your child.

Hashem gave mothers a gift, an extremely refined ability to sense the feelings and needs of their children. He did not give them the infallible power to react the right way on every occasion, nor should they override how their children feel about themselves. Because although a mother has this sense, she should not assume that she "knows" how her children are really feeling. He did give them, however, an uncanny ability to sense certain things, and when they do, we have to stop and seriously consider their position.

If you, the mother, feel that the expert's advice you received will somehow be counterproductive for *your* child, go back to the *rav* or counselor and ask the question again. This time tell him about your intuition, explain what you are feeling. An intelligent *mechanech* will listen carefully, and very often, adapt his advice in consonance with a mother's clear instinct.

Chapter 19

Making Your Dream Come True

Your goal of building your personal Tabernacle, *Mishkan*—a Torah home—sounds wonderful. In the classes in seminary or lectures in yeshiva, in the stories the *rebbetzin* or *rav* told, it all seemed so beautiful.

The Shabbos Table

You pictured a large family of happy children sitting around your Shabbos table, all singing the *zemiros* together, listening quietly to or saying *divrei Torah*, talking about the parashah and telling you what happened in school.

The following typical Chelm story will illustrate something essential that is necessary to remember in order to be able to fulfill your dream.

> *The sexton of the shul in Chelm goes to Warsaw, and a man runs past him, frantically ringing a big brass bell. The sexton hears shouts, and sees people running with buckets, followed by teams of horses pulling wagons. He follows the crowd and sees that there is a fire. The wagons are carrying big vats of water, from which people are filling buckets, which they pass to others, until there is a long line of people filling, passing, and emptying them onto the fire to douse it. An hour later the fire is out.*
>
> *"This is amazing!" thinks the sexton. He goes back to Chelm and speaks at the next town council meeting.*

225

"Dear friends, I want to tell you about something I saw in Warsaw that we must bring to Chelm. You know that the last time we had a fire, half the town burned down. I found out that there is something we can do about it. I need fifteen rubles from the community coffers to solve the problem." The town councilors all agreed that it was worth fifteen rubles to implement his plan.

He returns to Warsaw and buys a big brass bell. He comes back to Chelm, puts it on the table, and says, "This is it."

The next time there is a fire in Chelm everyone says, "Call Yankel the sexton, call Yankel!"

Yankel dashes in and takes the bell. He runs over to the fire and frantically rings the bell, but the house burns down, and the next house catches fire, and the next…

He returns to the store and throws the bell at the owner.

"Liar, trickster, thief!"

"What are you talking about?" protests the store owner.

"I took this bell to the fire," says the sexton, "and I rang and rang and rang, and nothing happened."

The bell is part of a system. Something came before the bell, and something came after it. The people were trained, the horses and vats of water were ready, and everyone knew what to do and how it should be done.

It is the same with parenting. It is not enough just to make a Shabbos table by cooking the food, setting the table, and seating yourselves around it. The kids are not just automatically going to sit still, sing *zemiros*, and say *divrei Torah*.

There is a whole process of preparation involved—from building good relationships with your children to teaching them what it means to fulfill the mitzvos correctly. If you were invited to a Shabbos table where children said *divrei Torah*, then you know that someone was invested in teaching them how to do that. It did not happen by itself.

I have a friend who has a large family, and every child says a *d'var Torah* at every single Shabbos meal. I once asked him how he managed to have that happen.

"This was my father's dream," he said. "When my children were young, we used to spend Shabbos with my parents. On Friday afternoon, my father would sit down with each child, one after another, and prepare each of them individually. I did not have time to do that, but he did. He taught them how to look up the information and how to present it."

Their grandfather invested much time and energy into building a system to make the Shabbos table beautiful. The construction of your private sanctuary, your Mikdash, is not just setting the table, nor is the building of a Torah home merely sending the children off to school. It is the summation of all the things you do, and the ways in which you do them.

Singing should be enjoyed; it cannot be forced. Children need to be taught to sing. Some parents have a natural ability to do that, others do not. There are children who are musical, while others are tone deaf. The father's example and enthusiasm can carry the rest of the family, but sometimes, he needs to devote time and energy to teaching a song, to helping recognize a beat or rhythm.

There is a woman I know who loves to sing. Her husband cannot carry a tune and has no taste for music but doesn't at all mind her singing. She sang the *zemiros* alone at every Shabbos meal until her sons were able to learn the songs and accompany her. The husband still doesn't sing, but it is a joy to hear their children enthusiastically belt out the *zemiros*!

Sometimes, it is difficult to invest even though you know you must, so it is important to remember that your efforts ultimately become what you have.

Sibling Rivalry

This is another area where expectations versus reality cause much stress and dismay. We never expected to see this in *our* children. When they fight, we are disappointed in them and in ourselves as well.

Although in some families it seems as if the children get along and communicate effectively with each other, sibling rivalry is an issue in most homes. You must accept that it exists, is normal, and that children *will* fight. You have to understand the feelings that cause the fighting. Often a child will be hurt, and you have to empathize with the pain.

There is a serious strategy to alleviate some of the sibling rivalry that we see in our homes, and that is to become less involved yourself.

The reality is that it is rarely possible to get to the bottom of a fight between children. If you have ever tried to sort out a disagreement between siblings, you will be very aware of this. There is no end to it when we question them and listen to their confusing answers.

"Why did you hit him?"

"He hit me."

"Who hit first?"

"He hit first."

"No, you hit first."

"No, he hit first."

"I was here. I saw you hit first."

"Yes, but yesterday, he kicked me under the table."

"But last week…"

There is no way of knowing who started it.

"He was bothering me."

"That is not grounds for a fight."

What *are* grounds for a fight? The less we get involved, the better off we will be, unless, of course, a child is in danger.

When you know there is no danger and they are going at each other physically, take them both into a different room and say to them, "If you want to fight/argue, do it in here because you are really disrupting the whole house."

Close the door and walk out. Because I know that my children love each other and that the fighting is just part of growing up, I would sometimes say, before closing the door, that if at any point they need an ambulance they should notify me, and I will call one. The mere mention of that made them think five times about what they were doing.

Ninety percent of the time (this is an absolutely unsubstantiated statistic, but you get the point), children fight for one reason: to get *you* involved. We tend to blame the older children, while most of the time it is the younger ones who began the ruckus. Do you know why? Because they know you will always take their side.

The less you get involved, the better. I am almost willing to guarantee that if you follow this advice, by the time your children are fourteen, they will hardly fight any more. They may find something to fight about, but no one is going to get anywhere because there will be no winner.

There is no purpose in fighting if a parent is not going to take my side and settle it. If you refuse to do that, the fight is usually over. When children come to you and say, "He is starting up with me," respond by saying, "tell him that you do not really want to fight with him." The child answers with, "But he is…" Stand your ground and say, "Work it out."

You will be surprised how children can work it out themselves. I sometimes put my squabbling children into an extremely *small* room together, a room where they are crowded right up against each other. I tell them that they can come out when they are friends. Rarely will they continue screaming for even two minutes. The one who is really yelling is doing so because he thinks I'm going to come and "save" him soon. If you are sure that neither is in danger, it is safe to do this.

Let them cry, "It's your fault!" "It's not my fault…" After a couple of minutes, they feel like fools. They realize no one is going to do anything about their squabble. Each one realizes that he is not getting anywhere, and they come out smiling, if not friends, at least not enemies.

This is a proven method of minimizing fights. If you are going to be the judge because you feel that the fighting is really getting out of hand, go ahead, but this will only postpone their dealing with their differences and the inevitable consequences.

When and if you do say something, make sure it sounds more like, "You are both wrong. No one is right when he is hitting someone else. Fighting is not the way we deal with things. There are other ways to solve this problem. How? Talk it out!"

They are too young to talk it out on their own? Facilitate. Listen to both sides. But stop asking them what the other one did to him; ask instead what *he* did. Take child number one and say, "What did *you* do?" "He...," "No, no, no, what did *you* do?" Then ask the other one, "What did you do?" He will answer. Then you ask, "Is that OK? Is it OK to beat up your brother? Is hitting, kicking, and yelling OK? It is never OK, so let's stop right now."

This entire discussion does not relate to a bully who fights to hurt and to feel strong. It is the bully who needs to be compromised. The first thing to know about a bully is that he is either jealous or feeling very weak. His bullying is an attempt to feel worthy and powerful. Second, all bullies are scared, and when someone stands up to them, they back down.

Dealing with a bully, therefore, takes two steps. First, make it very clear that this behavior is unacceptable and that you will never stand for anyone in your home living in fear. This means that if he threatens or hurts anyone, he is the one who will be afraid of the consequences. Second, we have to take care of how he feels about himself, giving him real appreciation for the positive traits he possesses. We help him feel strong by allowing him to be a leader and helper, not by hurting and causing fear.

Each Child Is Unique

Our children are all different, and we want to raise them as individuals. Their distinctiveness, we have to understand, has to do with their personalities, not with the way they dress or with their acceptance or nonacceptance of rules. The way a child chooses to present himself may or may not be a part of his individuality, because some children are more conformist than others. Your role as a parent requires you to know your child's personality, to help him discover who he is as a unique person, developing his strengths and learning to deal with his weaknesses.

Children express their individuality in different ways. You want to understand each child's particular needs and decide when and where you need to encourage changes or adjustments, or be a bit more flexible.

In a family where there are a number of siblings, parents are often accused of not being "fair." There is no such attribute in this world. The only One Who can truly be fair to everyone is Hashem because He knows what every individual truly needs. Parents and teachers, although they may try, cannot always accomplish this. The closest we can come to a definition of the word in our world is helping every child according to his needs.

Is it fair that one child goes to a tutor and another does not, that one child earns a prize or is allowed something that nobody else may do or have? Is it fair that one child gets glasses and one does not or that one who is artistic gets paintbrushes and the other does not?

Since all of those examples may stem from necessity, we must respect each one's individuality, teaching the siblings that every person is unique. If we consistently instill this outlook in our children early on by actually treating each child according to his needs, they will grow up understanding and being comfortable with the differences in the way their parents interact with each of them.

In general, of course, when you buy a present or a treat for one, unless it is for an accepted reason, you buy for everybody. That is fair. We want our children to understand, however, that each of them will be accorded the attention, schooling, and the distinct elements that he or she requires.

In good parenting we say, "You do this well, and therefore, you can go to such-and-such a workshop or club, but your brother needs to improve in something else, so he will go to a special class because you each need something different."

When children ask, "How come he or she always…?" you can respond, "What is your name? What is his name? You are different people, who need and, therefore, receive different things. We love you all very, very much, and while we can't give you everything that you *want*, we try to give each of you what we think you *need*. You do not need a particular thing just because he has it, and he does not need it just because you have it." Of course, as we mentioned earlier, this is only effective if we are consistent in our methods and messages.

Obviously, if we single out one child, often giving him gifts unrelated to his needs, it will undermine anything of value that we are trying to achieve.

A Bed for Every Child

A number of years ago my wife and I were again blessed by Hashem, this time with twins, who became our baker's dozen, *bli ayin hara*. We were still living in a three-and-a-half-room apartment, and we decided that it was not right to have five or six children sleeping in one room, with some children sharing beds. We determined at that time that every child should have his own bed.

Adding additional rooms required obtaining municipal approval, a time-consuming and drawn-out procedure, and we also needed the consent of the other tenants in the building. As we had one neighbor who believed that adding rooms was too much luxury for our family, the process took a number of *years*. We had to plead our case in court, and we were fined for beginning the work in desperation before the final permission came through. I would not wish what we endured on an enemy.

Baruch Hashem, we were finally able to almost double the size of our house by adding a few rooms. When we ordered new beds, and every single child finally had his own, I was so proud. A few nights later, I came home very late, walked into one of the rooms, and saw six children in three beds.

Actually, they were not all in beds. Two were doubled up in one bed, and one was on the floor on a blanket.

"What is going on here?" I asked.

"I don't know," one child answered, "we like it this way."

Can you imagine? They *liked* it!

We sometimes project *our* needs onto our children, while those who grow up in a happy house are usually content with less. We imagine that we personally would or could not be happy under the same circumstances because we did not grow up that way. If every child in your family had his own room when you were growing up, you tend to think that it's terrible if each of your children doesn't, but this isn't necessarily true. Children can be happy with whatever they have if that is what they are used to. The exception to the rule is the child who really requires a private place of his own.

One of our children needed some private space when he was younger, so we made a little place in the storage room for him—not for sleeping, but where he could be alone when he felt the need and could keep his own things such as a drum set, which nobody could use without his permission. He had a key and could go down there when he needed his own quiet space. Fortunately, he was the only child who required that concession, and the others understood the necessity for it.

The Child Who Is Different

We cannot leave the subject of bringing up large families without touching on the subject of children with problems and challenges in behavior, religious observance, or learning. How do we deal with siblings when there is one child who has difficulties that none of the others have and who may require a different kind of school or special treatment?

Not only might his school be different, but he may need to engage in different activities, and he may be allowed to wear clothes that the other children may not wear. Sometimes, one child needs more space or freedom than the others. Do not fear that the other children will be jealous.

Let me share a secret: most children are not jealous of the child with special needs. They prefer to feel "normal."

When we love all our children, the one requiring special arrangements due to learning difficulties, emotional challenges, or behavioral problems must be allowed what he feels driven to do even though our other children are not granted the same liberties. This is imperative.

An older child who has already gone places and done things without our permission, for example, is going to need more freedom in certain areas. Restricting him too much when he is already acting behind our back may no longer be beneficial, as he has already experienced doing his thing while leaving us out of the picture. We should not be afraid of him or of his behavior, but we must be intelligent when predicting the realistic outcome.

We need to choose our battles and prioritize our actions. Children are not jealous of the child for whom we adopt a unique approach, as long as they see we are showing respect for their own needs as well. This is admittedly easier said than done.

The Fear of Patterns

When does a dangerous pattern begin to manifest itself in a family? What causes others to follow that one child who veered from the path and wants to move away from a life of Torah?

It can happen that when we fight with the child who is having a hard time, and life at home resembles a battlefield, the other children begin to feel that their parents have turned against them all.

The child in question automatically becomes the underdog, and a victim in his siblings' eyes. Once this occurs, the other children subconsciously fear that they may be next.

If my parents do not understand my sister or brother, what will keep them from misunderstanding me? Then another child follows the first misfit, and another and another. This almost always happens when the parents are not dealing with the first child properly because they do not understand her or recognize her needs. Fighting a child creates sides, with us in one position and the siblings lining up on the other side because they fear the same end for themselves.

When we support the wayward child, no matter how difficult the situation becomes, his siblings perceive our loyalty, see the efforts we are making to help, and how hard we are trying. They don't fully understand the extent of the suffering that child is giving us, but they see that we are warm and caring no matter what, so why would they want to go against that? There are no "sides" when the parents remain loving and supportive.

The exception to this rule is when a child has become abusive to the family, or involved with alcohol, drugs, or other really dangerous behavior. Then we need to show our love by standing up to him. There is no choice but to take drastic action, no matter what the consequences may be. Even in those extreme cases, we know that we are taking action to help, even if the child sees it differently. Let us hope and pray that by taking preemptive action and doing our best to raise our children in a happy, supportive, and loving home, we will never need to face these situations. If ever you find yourself dealing with extreme and challenging behaviors, please do not take your final advice from this book. It is time to find professionals with experience in whatever you are dealing with to get personal and exact advice for your child.

Chapter 20

Family Life:
A Closer Look

Throughout our lives, difficult times occur, many of which trigger powerful emotions. The birth of children, moving to a new community, suffering the loss of a loved one, illness, celebrating a *simchah*, and observing our many holidays all require extra personal effort to navigate properly. While these occasions may be challenging for everyone, there are factors that exacerbate the struggle for those who have changed their lives and moved away from familiar people and surroundings. It is all the more difficult when they have settled in a community where so many others seem connected to extended families.

Birth

No matter what our relationship may be with any particular family member, sharing the joy of bringing children into the world is an excellent time to attempt to build a better relationship. Grandparents are able to enjoy their grandchildren without having to take full responsibility for them.

I once heard a comedian describing the difference between fathers and grandfathers. "Sonny is setting the house on fire. His father yells, 'Sonny, give me those matches!' His grandfather says calmly, 'Leave him alone, boy, look how evenly the house is burning; it's a lovely fire.'"

Grandparents are usually filled with love and forgiveness when it comes to their grandchildren. Taking advantage of this kind of good feeling is an excellent idea.

Dassy Cohen, twenty-one years old, and her thirty-two-year-old neighbor Stephanie Kalon live in Passaic. They gave birth on the same day to beautiful baby boys, and even ended up as next-door neighbors in Beth Israel hospital. While Dassy's room was overflowing with her parents, nine siblings, in-laws, nieces, nephews, aunts, uncles, sisters-in-law, and grandparents, Stephanie received a phone call from her father in Dallas and an email from her mother who is in France for a year or three. Her older sister, Tammy, intermarried ten years earlier, just when Stephanie left Neve Yerushalayim; Stephanie did not go to her wedding and they have not spoken since. Her younger sister, Carol, is in college in Colorado. To the best of her knowledge, she has no other relatives.

At first, Stephanie was broken. Although David was a devoted and doting husband, her sense of loneliness was overwhelming. On the second day, Rebbetzin Weiss, the wife of a rosh yeshiva who had been a teacher for many years, walked in with chocolates and a big smile.

"It is so wonderfully quiet in here; you are so lucky. Take advantage of it and rest every moment that you can. Poor Dassy, I hope she can get some sleep with that hubbub going on over there!"

Stephanie smiled to herself. How sweet of the rebbetzin to try to make me feel better. She was feeling horrible, alone and lost. The thought of raising this baby in a foreign and sometimes confusing world washed over her again and again. No parents, no brothers, sisters, sisters-in-law. No aunts, uncles, and nieces. She had experienced these lonely, sad feelings since the day of her wedding. She knew that such thoughts would haunt her from time to time, but she accepted the rebbetzin's kind words and decided that from that moment on she would do her absolute best to try and focus on her blessings.

She emailed seven pictures of the baby to her parents and both sisters.

"Look closely," she wrote to Tammy, "because the baby resembles you, and I won't be able to handle not staying in touch when I have your face in front of me every day."

When her father unexpectedly called a second time, she asked him to come to the bris and almost fell out of the hospital bed when he said he would try.

Little Yaakov was named after his great-grandfather, who had been a rabbi and author of sefarim in Poland, a welcome fact that had taken her totally by surprise when she learned about it from her teacher in Neve.

Stephanie took a thousand pictures in the months to follow, and on Yaakov's first birthday the entire family came together for the first time in twenty-two years! Carol is slowly becoming observant, Mom is back in the US living in Hackensack, New Jersey, just twenty minutes away. She is in Passaic almost as often as she is home. Tammy and Stephanie have a date on Skype every Sunday. While Tammy defies statistics and is still happily married to her gentile husband who "feels" Jewish, they are considering sending their son, Justin, to the Jewish day school in Dallas, where they live.

There are choices to be made. With today's technologies you can send pictures, "visit" with family on any number of platforms, and communicate much more easily than in the past. You can involve your relatives with what is happening in your family. You can ensure that the grandparents, aunts, and uncles share in your joy from birth and on through the succeeding stages of childhood. Obviously, the excitement and participation you can offer may be quite different from that offered by your new neighbors who have relatives coming out of every nook and cranny, but the birth of a child offers the best opportunity to restart relationships, renew involvement, and rekindle interest, and you should utilize every tool you have to do so.

If you need help, and parents are unable to travel or too old to participate actively, or cannot afford to do so, and there is no one else in the family who can be helpful at this time, you should not hesitate to allow your community to assist you.

When a child is born, many people in the community are ready and willing to be of assistance. Families like yours need to stick together. In the Ramot neighborhood of Yerushalayim, a group that calls itself Tohar Rochel (named for Rochel Weiss who was killed with her three small children in a terrorist attack in October 1988) was established as a support system for new mothers and their families. Every family in the group gives a small monthly donation toward the communal fund. When a mother leaves the hospital with her baby, the fund allows her to stay in a recuperative facility for a few days. The organization provides meals and babysitting for the family.

It is a brilliant system. Many of the participants in this organization are *baalos teshuvah*, women who are themselves without family support. They recognized this opportunity when they saw that although their families were not there to help during their time of need, their friends and neighbors pitched in gladly and they could rely on one another.

There are other avenues for assistance, and additional means of building a support group, as we mentioned in chapters 8 and 9.

Moving

Moving to another location requires a great deal of thought, and taking this momentous step is definitely a time of need. Moving is an emotionally difficult time in the best of cases, but a family who has already made quantum changes has sometimes reached a certain comfort level and may find it harder to change its surroundings. There is safety in the familiar pattern. However, sometimes circumstances change, and despite their fears, the family must move. What should they look for in a new community? How will the change affect their lives? What is it going to involve?

One of the tests that Hashem gave to our Patriarch Avraham was the commandment, "*Lech lecha mei'artzecha*—Go from your land."[1] Many

---

1   *Bereishis* 12:1.

of us were similarly challenged when we moved away from our families to grow into what we have become. Our birthplace or hometown was our comfort zone. Leaving such a place is a very great challenge and can be one of the most significant decisions you make for your family's future. You have to make it carefully and thoughtfully. Wise planning is crucial.

Throughout it all, you must remember to keep Hashem in the picture, for, as the well-known Yiddish saying goes, "*Der mensch tracht, und Gott lacht*—Man plans, and God laughs." Since everything is in His Hands, can you really make plans? Nevertheless, you have to do your part, with the understanding that you have limitations in the prophecy department. You must do your best to try to make the transition as smooth as possible for every member of your family, because a move is often traumatic.

Moving changes the family dynamic. New jobs will have to be found and dealt with, and roles and responsibilities within the family will often shift. Your children will be going to new and probably different types of schools and have to make many adjustments. Their demands on you are likely to increase. These are all things you need to consider well. Hopefully, this move will have the positive outcome you seek, but you need to keep your eyes open wide in the planning stages, to define and prioritize that which you hope to find in this new community.

One thing that you should certainly not do is jump to quick conclusions. Try to make a pilot trip, and, if possible, spend more than just a Shabbos there. Speak to people in the schools and shuls. Get more than one opinion and perspective. If you can get to know some people in the community before you move, you can hopefully build a fledgling support group. Even a few friends or acquaintances can help make the move more pleasant.

Illness

Serious illness is a most trying time for any family, and is even more grueling for those who have already made significant changes in their lives. When facing the specter of illness in the immediate family, and extended family is not nearby, we must turn to the community for assistance.

Becoming a burden on others is a tricky business. When relying on the help of others, our attitude toward their aid is crucial, and will color the way potential benefactors will respond. While it is difficult to be in this position, we must learn to accept *chessed*, kindness, in the same way that we must know how to show it for others. Being on the receiving end helps us to understand and appreciate it even more.

Perhaps, a note here on the nature of challenges would be in place. One of the greatest difficulties in the management of suffering is the unbidden thought, *Why me?* Those who have traveled the long road of altering their lives in order to fit into Hashem's will, who have "given up" so much in order to keep the mitzvos, may sometimes feel that this question is justified.

I have done so much for Hashem's sake; why is He doing this to me?

Entire books have been written on the subject of suffering.[2] I do not feel that I can add anything new, nor is this the place to address the full gamut of issues involved.

I would like to point out, however, the erroneous basis for this question. When you made the decision to change your life, the foundation on which it was based was and remains submission to the will of Hashem. You made the choice of right over wrong, good over evil, light over darkness. In doing this, you brought meaning, purpose, direction, and eternity into your life. You gave up nothing for Hashem, but immeasurably added to your life. All that we learn and achieve when we change only adds to the integrity of our existence. When we begin to feel as if we are doing favors for Hashem, we lose this essential value.

Suffering, however, is a part of the human experience. The *teshuvah* process allows us to access and be a part of that experience. As we cannot, and indeed should not, assume that suffering is retribution for our decisions, we are now capable of dealing with whatever it is meant to

---

2   Rabbi Ezriel Tauber, *Darkness before Dawn* (Shalheves, 1992); Rabbi Samson Raphael Hirsch, "*Edoth*—Training through Suffering," 7th ed. (Soncino Press Ltd, 2002).

achieve on a new level. The process of change did not cause the suffering; the process allows us to access that which can be achieved through that suffering.

Death

The loss of a loved one and the terrible pain it creates are not challenges to be dealt with here, as there are many helpful books available. Nevertheless, we will point out that people who have made major changes in order to adopt a Torah-true life tend to suffer from feelings of guilt more than others in this situation. When parents are taken from children who left home to grow in a different direction, having second thoughts is common.

Was I there enough for them? Did I take proper care of them? I moved away and the many changes I made brought about so much distress, so much worry. Did I give them any nachas, any pleasure at all?

An overwhelming sense of guilt seems to attach itself to the already difficult experience of loss.

One possible response to loss is preparing for it in advance. We know that one day we will lose our parents. While we are busy building families, they are not getting younger. It would be wise to internalize two things: the fact that we are building something really special, and that we must consider how our parents and siblings can be part of our new lives.

We have discussed the idea of exerting maximum effort to maintain a good, healthy relationship with your parents that will ensure you do not suffer from regret when something sad does happen. When experiencing a loss of this magnitude and feeling guilty for whatever reason, it is necessary to talk to someone, perhaps a mentor or professional, because guilt can turn into a very dangerous form of negativity.

Those who have made major changes often feel that reduced contact with their parents and siblings is a result of their choices. If we did not have the kind of contact we once enjoyed, our guilt is doubled and tripled when that person is no longer there. Such feelings are real and disturbing and have to be dealt with rather than allowed to linger.

Bringing Simchah into Your Lives

The *Yamim Tovim*, the Jewish holidays, can be the stuff of wonderful memories for families. If you were fortunate to grow up in a strongly traditional home, you and your parents and siblings might still be getting together at these special times. If that is not the case, and you are in a different situation altogether because you have no extended family, it becomes necessary to take a different approach.

Lacking an extended family with a similar background, you can create one to the extent and depth that you invite others into your home and make them a part of it. Yom Tov should be a time when you make it your business to include others in your celebration.

Many young, unattached people who have just started out on their journey are looking for families from whom to learn. Take those young people in and make them feel welcome in your household. When you become close to students in their late teens and early twenties who are going through their process of learning, they become family. You will have great *nachas* when they include you in their future *semachos*.

On Yom Tov, your home can become a place of *simchah* and joy. If you do not have biological brothers and sisters who can be with you at these times, you can join together with other families. Sharing your celebrations goes back to the heart of the meaning of *simchah* that we talked about earlier: appreciating what we have, giving, and sharing. This is a basis upon which you can build.

If, however, you only look through the lens of negativity and focus on what you are missing—at what seems to be a lack of opportunities—it is easy to become discouraged. You have a great deal going for you because everything you have learned and developed is a tool for further growth. Having a loving spouse and a family is a responsibility and a challenge to be sure, but it is a berachah. It is a blessing that most of the world today unfortunately does not have, and its lack is sorely felt.

We and our families can serve as an inspiration to others because this is really what life is meant to be. It is about sharing, giving, and perpetuating, and that is exactly what we do. Others will look at us with admiration and envy, but only if they sense that we appreciate what we have. If we value our blessings, we will be able to share, give, and continue to grow, even in the face of the many challenges that family life presents.

These people whom you have made welcome in your home may not be your "real" family, and perhaps, your children might miss having that. I can tell you with certainty, however, that as with everything else in life, 10 percent of every situation is circumstance and 90 percent is attitude. Your attitude can create the desired atmosphere, and with the right approach to "family," your children will learn to appreciate the extended unit you are building.

Chapter 21

Your Children and Their Grandparents

W hen your parents are normal, healthy people, even though they may be angry or upset with your new way of life, you must try your best to maintain a close relationship, repairing anything that has been damaged. Recognize that you probably were not respectful enough when you set out on your own, and continue to reach out and accept responsibility for whatever may have driven a wedge between you. Actively try to rebuild the relationship, convey the fact that you really love them, and stay in frequent touch by phone and email.

Unfortunately, this is impossible to do in the case of unhealthy, controlling parents who cause their grown children and family great suffering. Worse still is the situation when parents just about declare war to get control over their grandchildren, actually feeling that they have the right to do so.

"If my children won't listen to me, at least let me try to talk some sense into my grandchildren!"

The Golds, both baalei teshuvah, came to consult with me a number of years ago. They have nine children, the oldest of whom is sixteen. Mrs. Gold's mother, they told me, will stop at nothing to get her grandchildren back to "normal," i.e., secularism. The grandparents invest time and money in sending them inappropriate gifts, and consistently convey manipulative messages to the younger children. They call to say hello or happy birthday, but make sure to get another message across as well.

"Did you get the gift I sent or did your parents not give it to you?"

"I really don't know why you can't watch the movie I sent."

"Why can't you wear the beautiful outfit we sent for you? Well, when you are eighteen, you'll be able to come and visit, and then we can do whatever we want together."

As unbelievable as this scenario may sound, there are people reading this book who know only too well how real this situation can be. I know parents who cannot allow their children to be alone with their grandmother who lives nearby. During her frequent visits, she brings up subjects she knows are inappropriate with the intention of planting seeds of rebellion. Such people are only doing what they think is right for their grandchildren, but it can destroy the family.

As discussed at the end of chapter 11, if parents are emotionally unhealthy or have malevolent intent, it is important to explore the possibility of breaking away. The mitzvah of honoring one's father and mother changes in such a situation. The Gemara deals with this challenging issue, advising us to separate ourselves both physically and emotionally.[1]

Taking Control

In the aforementioned story of the Golds, where the grandparents are literally fighting to reclaim their grandchildren to their secularism, there was one serious complication. These grandparents were providing a significant amount of money to support the family.

I told the couple that they must make a very difficult decision. They are either going to allow the grandparents to wreak havoc in their lives and those of their children for the sake of financial security, or cut all

---

1   *Kiddushin* 31b. Please see "Important Note" in the Preface. All discussions that have halachic consequences should be followed up with a rabbi to deal with your particular situation.

ties with them. Cutting ties meant that this family would likely live in poverty.

This is a very grave challenge. It is unfortunate that as young parents, they allowed such a critical situation to develop. They accepted the funds knowing that their children would pay the price.

Late as it is, however, it is necessary for this couple to face up to the difficult decision and insist that the wife's parents respect their guidelines even if it means that the cash flow will stop. If her parents wish to continue the relationship, the rules will have to change. The couple must take that next step in assuming responsibility even though it seems impossible.

The *pasuk* says, "And he who listens to Me dwells in confidence, unworried from fear of evil."[2] The Midrash quotes this *pasuk* when it explains the concept that Hashem says that those who listen to Him will not lose out.[3] While this is not a guarantee for any specific reimbursement of funds or continued financial security, it can give us the confidence that in the long run, we will not lose out in life when we do what is right.

Building the Relationship

If our parents oppose us ideologically because they are sincerely convinced that we are ruining our lives and making seriously wrong decisions, how should we respond? How do we answer when our parents are deeply worried about us, believing that we are going to end up becoming "depressed" or a "baby factory"? Having read a book about the terrible situation of the religious Jewish woman, they are certain that we have been brainwashed by an "old-fashioned rabbi" who is "not living in today's world."

We have to know how and where to draw lines.

---

2   *Mishlei* 1:33.

3   *Devarim Rabbah* 4:5.

When do you allow your parents to intervene and when do you not? What should you do when they send a hopefully well-intentioned but nonetheless inappropriate present?

It is necessary to draw firm lines right from the beginning, so you will not be afraid to tell your parents later on when something is inappropriate. At the same time, work on developing a close connection despite your ideological differences so you will have the acceptance, understanding, and respect on which to maintain a solid relationship now. It is always better to make clear boundaries before your parents spend the money and give the gifts rather than afterward. Even if you have not yet done so, however, it is not too late to begin to learn to draw clear lines.

"Mom, if you want to send a birthday present, thank you so much, but let me just tell you what the kids need (or like)."

It is a very simple way to be proactive. It is much harder when you have to say, "Thank you very much, but I have to send it back; he can't use it."

This is an important lesson that can apply to all relationships. It often happens that we have something we feel we should convey, but we are afraid of hurting someone. What will be the result, though, if we decide *not* to say anything? Will the outcome be better? We are almost always better off dealing with it as soon as possible and not delaying because the situation will only worsen.

I see this happen so often among teenagers.

A young woman feels that a friend is using her. She doesn't want to ruin the friendship or hurt the girl, so she is at a loss to know what to do. It becomes a potentially unhealthy situation as the friend turns into a leech that she really wants to shake off but doesn't know how.

"What can I do?" the young lady asks me, "If I say anything, my friend will be devastated."

My answer consists of several questions.

"If you do not say anything, how long are you going to be able to sustain this situation? Will you be able to go on like this for three months, six months, a year, two years? How long is it going to take until you just want to explode? When you do explode, how messy is it going to be?"

The answer is, "If you let it go and don't deal with the situation right now, it will be many times messier."

When relationships are allowed to deteriorate, the outcome will be much worse than if we take a firm grip on the situation from the beginning. We can say, "Listen, these are the differences between us. How are we going to hash it out? What would you like? What do I want? How can we handle this? I don't want it to reach the point where we are fighting, or either of us is hurt. I want to discuss our relationship now because even though it may be uncomfortable, it will be much worse if we allow things to deteriorate."

This rule applies to all relationships. If your parents have sent an inappropriate present to your child for the third time, and they find out he did not receive any of them, they are justified in saying, "Why didn't you say anything to us about this earlier? Are you trying to cut us out of your children's lives?"

"We didn't want to hurt you," we sheepishly reply.

How many times do we say those words?

"Why didn't you say something?"

"I didn't want to hurt you."

"Now, I am ten times more hurt because I found out by accident. Whenever I called the kids and they didn't say anything about their presents, I thought they were being rude and ungrateful. I began having hard feelings toward them, and I was angry at you for not teaching them better manners. Now, after so much time has gone by, I finally understand."

It snowballs.

The way to draw boundaries is by respectfully but firmly saying what works and what does not, what you can accept in your home and what is unacceptable. This has nothing to do with how you feel about your parents; it has to do with how you are building your home.

"When I was a child, you said that certain things were not acceptable whether I liked it or not because those were the rules of our house. Now, I am running my own home, and these are the rules of my house. This is the way my wife and I are going to be raising our children. We want you to be a part of our lives and to come to visit. I want them to think of you as the best grandparents in the world, just as you want to *be* the best grandparents in the world, so please let's work together."

You can respectfully but firmly define boundaries. If you find yourself unable to do that, or if no matter what or how hard you try it doesn't work, I strongly urge professional consultation. There may be something untenable in the situation.

Normal, emotionally healthy grandparents want very much to fill their roles, and you want to give them that ability, but they cannot be the parents in your home. If they cannot or do not want to accept this reality, you must determine if there is an unhealthy element in their approach.

Unless you informed them of your boundaries in an angry or disrespectful manner, or if you made conditions in a way that made them feel rejected, you should be able to enjoy a great deal of cooperation.

Perhaps, you have treated your parents with respect, maintaining good communication and properly fulfilling your responsibilities toward them, and they still cannot accept your boundaries. Recognize that there is a problem and find out what it is.

"Am I not accepting my role as a child properly, or is there something wrong with my parents?"

You must then determine if you are dealing with emotionally healthy people, and you should consult with a professional to figure out what to do.

When Grandparents Are Not Observant

How do we speak to our children about grandparents who are not observant? What do we tell them about our parents who are blatantly not performing the mitzvos, who very clearly are not willing to buy into the new values that we have chosen? We may not denigrate, belittle, or paint grandparents as wicked people.

"When I come to visit, are you going to tell your children that I am a gentile?" a nonobservant friend once asked me.

"I suppose you mean that you are not going to wear a *kippah*," I replied. "That's OK. You can come to my house without one. I will just tell the children that you were not fortunate enough to have received a good education."

"But I did get a good education," he said.

"No, you didn't. If you had received a good education, you would still be wearing a *kippah*. Yes, it's true you went to the same yeshiva I went to, and we are friends even though now you're in a different place, but you did not get a good education. I don't know if it's because the teachers weren't good enough, because you didn't accept what they taught, or any of the myriad reasons that people lose their way. Whatever the reason, I can still tell my children you did not get a good education."

There is nothing wrong with telling children that some people, even those we love, were brought up without Torah and mitzvos and that it is unfortunate. At the same time, we can also say that we hope that someday they will learn about Torah and mitzvos, and then they'll do all the special mitzvos that we do. It is not disrespectful to say that Grandma and Grandpa do not know.

"But why don't we teach them?" the children might ask.

We can reassure them that it is not so easy to teach older people new things but that they are learning, and someday, if we set a good example, maybe they will want to learn and do more. This seems agreeable and understandable, and no one can argue with it, including the people themselves.

By the time children are old enough to realize that *someday* might never materialize, they will also be old enough to integrate the understanding that there are people who are religious and others who are not.

Very young children need crystal-clear messages. We cannot tell them that some people do and others do not, leaving an opening for them to respond, "So maybe I'll be one of those who don't."

We do not teach children universality and humanism: whatever everybody does is OK because everyone is convinced that he is doing the right thing. Besides the fact that it is blatantly untrue, it will only confuse them. As clarity is essential, they need to know the difference between right and wrong, good and bad. Gray is not something a child's mind can integrate; everything has to be black or white. When you try to teach them that things seem acceptable for others but not for them, they don't understand.

"If it's OK for them, why not for me? If it isn't OK for me, it shouldn't be all right for them, either."

We teach our children that Daddy can drive the car and Mommy can light matches, but they may not.

"When you are older you will also be able to do these things, but they are dangerous for you at your age."

Our mitzvos and *aveiros*, sins, on the other hand, are inherently good and evil actions. That is why we must tell young children that there are good people who just never learned Torah properly, and we all hope that, someday, they, too, will learn, and be able to differentiate between right and wrong.

I remember that during my childhood, whenever a particular relative would come to our home without a *kippah*, it would bother me until my mother said something like, "He thinks he has so much hair on his head that he doesn't need a *kippah*." Her comment quieted me down as a child; it was sufficient. That was the best explanation she could give me at that time.

Of course, there will always be the little kid who goes over to Grandpa and asks, "Are you going to go to *cheder* someday and wear a *kippah*?" Or, "Grandpa, when you get older you will wear tzitzis like me, right?" Children can say such things, which may cause a momentary embarrassment, but the odds are that Grandpa will laugh and understand why the child said it.

The point is that we should never say derogatory things to our children about family members whom we want them to love and respect. We want to give our children room to grasp that people grow and develop just as we have done, and allow them to hope that their relatives will do so as well. If we teach them to see that change is part of a positive process, then no one is bad.

I have friends, *frum* from birth, who became Chassidic as they grew older. This decision is not exactly quantum, but it is nevertheless a major change in lifestyle with the potential to cause a disruption in the parent-child-grandchild relationship. One friend became a Belzer Chassid and one a Gerrer. They are raising their children with *peyos*, long jackets, and all the other distinctive customs.

The grandparents are religious Jews, God fearing and devoted, good people, full-fledged FFBs, and the father learns *Daf Yomi*. The children of these two newly Chassidic Jews have to be taught understanding just as do the children of *baalei teshuvah*. To a Chassidic child, the grandparent who does not have *peyos* could be considered an outsider, as in his world a child who cuts off his *peyos* is a youth in trouble.

What does this Chassidic father say to his son? It is not who is right or wrong. He must know how to speak about grandparents, relatives, and friends who are not living as his family is without putting them down. We give our kids grounds to respect them as people because we say good things about them.

Children might ask, "Why don't you tell them to do things our way?"

The answer is, of course, that we are children too, and as such are not allowed to tell our parents what to do. Parents tell children what to do, and that is a clear enough answer.

In the loving family I described in Chapter 11, in which the grandparents were not ready to keep an Orthodox Shabbos, both sides preserved a warm, healthy, respectful relationship despite their differences. The grandparents belonged to a Conservative synagogue and took part in all of its social events, but as they were not ready to stop driving on Shabbos or take on any mitzvos, they visited the children and shared meals only during the week.

They all felt comfortable being together because it was clear that the parents were not going to keep Shabbos and no one ever told them they had to. They were able to accept that their grandchildren were being raised in a certain way, so *out of respect*, they remained home or went somewhere else on Shabbos. They were able to do this happily because it was obvious that they were respected by their children.

We must be able to speak with confidence to our parents, and they to us. Fear of communication about necessary things is an indication that something is wrong with the relationship. It might be that we lack self-confidence, or even that our level of commitment is shaky. We need to gather our thoughts, speak to a *rav*, and figure out what we need to do to improve the situation. Children should not fear their parents in this way.

Outgrowing Childhood Perceptions

One of the great challenges of parent/child relationships is relinquishing prior expectations. Young children view their parents as almost perfect beings. It is not rare to hear children boasting, "My father can lift this car." "My mother knows everything." A normal, healthy child believes that his parents are the biggest and the best. Parents represent something very, very great in their eyes.

The *Ramban* explains the mitzvah of respecting one's father and mother in a most fascinating fashion.[4] He says that we learn how to respect our parents from the very rules of how to respect Hashem Himself. Hashem is our primary Father, and our biological parents are secondary parents, as it were. Nonetheless, since our parents were partners in our creation, we must respect them as we do Hashem.

If we delve a bit deeper, we will understand that our parents stand in as God until we grow up and can build a relationship with Him. This explains why we see our parents as God-like figures, expecting the world of them.

Our first steps toward maturity bring the realization that our parents are only human, with corresponding strengths and limitations. Our reluctance to accept those limitations stems from our disinclination to accept complete responsibility for our lives. The ambivalence that follows us for many years is the result of knowing that our parents are far from perfect, yet not wanting to let go of the illusion that they are.

While we are aware, and at times may even be disrespectfully vocal, about their deficiencies, *accepting* those shortcomings remains difficult for us even into our twenties and thirties. Mature people must go

---

4   *Ramban, Shemos* 20:12.

through the process of understanding and valuing their parents for whom they are in order to take responsibility for their own lives.

Growing up without the ramifications of the Ten Commandments, you never felt it necessary to respect your parents regardless of your love for or disappointment in them. In the natural process of growth, when you realized that your parents were human, you still wanted them to be constantly available. If you have made changes in your life and they are not always there for you, it is not unusual to become angry or resentful, wondering why they are not acting as expected.

In a sense, you remain the small child who knows he can approach Mommy or Daddy and say, "This is what I need," with the understanding that his parents are supposed to be there emotionally and financially and lend moral support. Subconsciously, you expect your parents to be there just as they have always been, even though you have made major changes.

We are now building our own families and must ask ourselves if we have shed our childish expectations of our parents. Are we ready to take on accountability for our lives, or do we still secretly want our parents to be responsible for us? Admittedly, it is difficult to relinquish illusions even if the relationship is not ideal. We may fear losing their support. Sometimes, we are afraid of not having anyone on whom our failures can be blamed!

In order to move on, we need to take responsibility for all those things ourselves: *I don't know how I'm going to take on financial responsibility, but it's time for me to do so, especially if my parents are going to use their help to control me. I need to ask myself if the money is important enough to me to surrender the values I cherish. Am I afraid to take responsibility for my own life?*

Defining Our Choices

In 1998, I consulted Rav Aharon Leib Shteinman about a challenging financial predicament confronting me. I believe that his opinion is relevant to all of us at some point in our lives. I had to make a decision: either take a loan I did not know how I would repay, or close down an urgent project. It was my opinion that I had no choice but to borrow money.

"In your position, you are not allowed to borrow money," he said.

"But I must," I answered.

"That is a decision you must make. If you decide that you do not have to borrow, then you will manage without borrowing."

"I cannot manage," I said. "I know the situation."

"Go raise the money," he said.

"I can't, which is why I have to borrow. I am not able to do it on time, and I need it by a certain date."

Then he said something to me that I will always remember.

"Look, you are right in that you have made that decision. Once you made the decision that borrowing the money is an option, it became one. But if you decide that it is not an option in your life, you can't do it; if you borrow, you will turn into a 'pumpkin'—you will go further into debt.

"Would you let yourself turn into a pumpkin? You don't think that will happen; you think you will be fine. Because you think that, it becomes an option, and then it is almost inevitable.

"You have to turn this option into an ultimatum for yourself: if you borrow, you are finished. Once you make the decision that borrowing the money is not a possibility, you live in a different realm, one in which you are saying that you know that there is a Ribbono shel Olam. You are going to function and do whatever you have to do in the best way you can, but you do not have other options. When you do not have other means of dealing with the situation, He will be there for you, but if you create unsuitable options, you are going to need them as long as you live."

Rav Shteinman's advice was extremely difficult for me to hear. We do not tell people to have *bitachon*, trust in Hashem. It is an inappropriate thing to do. Rav Aharon Leib Shteinman did not and would not tell me to have *bitachon*. He was telling me that what I see and accept as options become my reality. He was saying, "I am not going to tell you not to go and borrow money. I am telling you that you are *not allowed* to borrow money. What you do from here on is up to you."

At the time, I was running a yeshiva that had put me in serious debt. It had reached the point where our financial situation threatened my family's ability to function. Yet, the Gadol had said to me, "You are not allowed to take one step further."

His point was not, "Just have *bitachon*; everything is going to be fine." His point was that robbing a bank is not an option, and neither is taking a loan you have no way to pay back. Now, you need to define your priorities.

No one else can have *bitachon* for you, nor can anyone else tell you to have it. Perhaps, at this point, we should discuss its real meaning.

Chapter 22

Bitachon

For people who were raised in a secular world, *bitachon* is a very new concept. The cause and effect of taking "responsibility" and "action" is embedded in our society's DNA. The idea that our actions and our interpretation of what we see can be less important and distorted is a very challenging concept. When introduced to the idea that our actions are necessary but not definitive, there is often misunderstanding. Many people think that having *bitachon* means that if I believe in Hashem and pray for something, it will happen. If I pray that someone who is sick will get better, that person will recover. If I trust that everything will work out for the best, it will work out for the best—whatever *I* believe is best. That is not what having *bitachon* means.

The Chazon Ish[1] elucidates the Torah perspective taught to us by the *Chovos Halevavos*,[2] who goes to extraordinary lengths to explain this crucial concept.

Bitachon is not being certain that my situation will become better in the way I envision "better," but knowing that my circumstances have been decreed by Hashem, Who alone determines what is better for me. Whether I am sick or well, rich, or poor, it is all from Hashem and is for the best.

---

1   Rabbi Avraham Yeshayah Karelitz, *Emunah U'Bitachon*.
2   Rabbeinu Bachya ben Yoseph ibn Paquda, *Chovos Halevavos, Shaar Habitachon*, ch. 1. He was the author of the first Jewish system of ethics, written in Arabic in 1040 under the title *Al Hidayah ila Faraid al-Qulub* [Guide to the Duties of the Heart] and translated into Hebrew by Judah ibn Tibbon in the years 1161–1180 under the title *Chovos Halevavos* [The Duties of the Heart].

Bitachon means knowing that my current situation is exactly what it is supposed to be. I am calm knowing that after I did that which I was supposed to, Hashem is the One taking care of me and the outcomes of those actions I have taken. I am allowed, in any way I can—bounded by the strictures of right and wrong—to act to change it. I cannot steal in order to acquire *parnassah*, but why not? It works! *If I steal, I will have enough money to get through the month.* The obvious answer is that Torah, which defines absolute right and wrong, prohibits it. I will have to seek other means, those permitted by the Torah. Disregarding its laws would be tantamount to changing the rules of the world to, "I can kill, steal, or do whatever is necessary in order to be more comfortable, to better my situation, to have what I feel I need."

Furthermore, one with *bitachon* is calm and relaxed, as the *Chovos Halevavos* emphasizes.

> When Rav Aharon Leib Shteinman answered my question about borrowing money, he was saying that in my situation at that time, it would be prohibited. We are not allowed to borrow if we have no plan or method to repay the loan. We are also not allowed to lend money to someone who does not return loans, which includes someone whom we know does not have a way to pay back,[3] unless we mean to forgo its repayment at the end of the stipulated time.
>
> "If the bank ends up repossessing whatever the yeshiva has, and therefore, it has to close," Rav Shteinman told me, "it is not under your control. You put in your best efforts, did what you could, and Hashem has His plan."

Borrowing money when you cannot return it is just pushing off the eventual accounting for a little longer. You tell yourself and the lender that it is only temporary, but the truth is that you are doing something that is equivalent to stealing.

---

3   *Shulchan Aruch, Choshen Mishpat* 97:4.

Having *bitachon* demands accepting that whatever the circumstances, Hashem always has your best interest in mind. My father would ask me every week, when I called to wish him a good Shabbos, "So, everything under control?"

"Yes, absolutely, but not my control!" I would always answer.

I think he enjoyed hearing me say it, as he repeated his question almost every time we spoke.

Bitachon means saying, "I accept my situation for what it is. I accept my ability to change things for the better *within the bounds of what is permissible*." I can daven. If I am sick, I may go to a doctor; if I need income, I'll look for a job, and so on.

Many people have heightened their level of contentment with life by having a set time for learning one of the many books regarding *bitachon*.[4]

Practical Aspects of Bitachon

Once we establish the values and guidelines we want to follow in raising our children, there are important decisions to be made. What are we going to allow into our homes, and how far will we allow others to undermine this bastion of safety?

When that young couple consulted me about their problems with Grandma, saying that they couldn't manage without her help, I said, "But you cannot function *with* Grandma's help because she is going to destroy your home. You will end up with nothing because Grandma is not an emotionally healthy person. By allowing her to control what enters your home because you need the money, you are basically deciding that your life is no longer going to go in the direction that you know it should take. Due to a lack of *bitachon*, you are choosing to

---

4   I will list just a few very good books on the subject: *Becoming a Baal Bitachon* by Rabbi Yechezkel Abramov, *Rav Asher Weiss on Emunah and Bitachon*, *Rav Avigdor Miller on Emunah and Bitachon*, *The Six Steps Of Bitachon* by Rabbi Chaim Goldberger, *Faith Over Fear* (adapted from Harav Yechiel Perr's *vaadim* on *Sefer Madreigas Ha'adam*) by Rabbi Yehuda Keilson, and many more.

lose the battle by not being steadfast to your values of what is right and wrong."

No one can tell you that if you don't take a job that causes you to work on Shabbos you don't have to worry because everything will work out well. That is not *bitachon* either. If you do not have a job because you are *shomer Shabbos* and you are now living in great penury, your *bitachon* tells you that this is the difficulty you are supposed to experience right now. Can you try to get another job? Absolutely! But in the same way that stealing and killing are not options, working on Shabbos is just not an option for you.

When we define the priorities in our lives, we discover what our options really are. Once we ascertain them, we are better prepared to raise our children despite challenges from parents or extended family with deviating ideas. We are able, with great dedication to our values and sensitivity to the lifestyles of others, to disallow anyone to interfere with the proper upbringing of our children.

If we are bitter, upset, or angry on Shabbos because we are losing business, our children will likely not feel that keeping it is a good option. We must feel and exude thankfulness for the gift of Shabbos, confident that we are gaining far more than we can possibly lose by making this day sanctified and special.

With this understanding comes a willingness to be ready to make some level of sacrifice. Forgoing support because we are true to our values is a sacrifice of great significance.

I once had a student in the yeshiva for a couple of years who was not an easy young man, to say the least. Despite his difficulties with learning, we were very close, maintaining the relationship even after he left.

One day, I needed some help to put together some closets for new students in the yeshiva, and I called him to ask if he would be of assistance. My wife and I had just bought our apartment in Har Nof, and when he came to the yeshiva, he wished me mazel tov.

"I almost had an apartment in Har Nof," he surprisingly added.

"Really?" I asked incredulously, as he was only nineteen years old at the time.

"Yes, my grandmother said that if I leave yeshiva and go to a secular university, she would give me an apartment in Har Nof. But I am not going to do that because I want to stay *frum*."

Remembering that just two years ago, he had finished *yeshiva ketanah*[5] with some difficulty, I realized for the first time what an extraordinarily committed individual he must be. His grandmother, behind his parents' backs, had in essence said, "Leave yeshiva and everything you're striving for, go to college, live my kind of life, and I will reward you with an apartment in Har Nof."

Grandma, knowing that her grandson was not the greatest student in yeshiva, was being subversive—betraying her own child—but this young man did not fall for her lure. The boy knew that if he left, he would have no chance of maintaining his commitment to Yiddishkeit, and he refused to go. He made what for many would seem a sacrifice, but to him it wasn't even an option. It seemed an obvious choice.

We are not willing to sell cocaine in order to make money, nor are we willing to steal. We are not going to sell our souls just because we are suffering economically. This will mean being willing to live within the bounds of what is a clearly defined value system, to raise ourselves to a higher moral level and conduct our lives accordingly.

Simchah through Sacrifice

If you must make a sacrifice, do not be disheartened, for something valuable often comes along with the effort. Finding happiness in recognizing what you have and seeing all that you have acquired is a source of *simchah*, a vital element that you want to include in your home. It isn't always easy to recognize what you have gained by having made those initial decisions and sacrifices. Being able to raise your children with *simchah*, no matter what your situation, is a tremendous plus.

Simchah allows you to be happy with what you have and with your place, whatever and wherever it may be. It comes from having *bitachon* that your present situation, for better or for worse, is good because

---

5   In Israel, a yeshiva for high school–aged boys is referred to as *yeshiva ketanah*.

although you may have hoped for something different, you understand that the ultimate wisdom regarding your destiny rests with the Ribbono shel Olam.

Rav Wolbe told us many years ago that the secret to *simchah* lies in one berachah we say every day. Every morning, every Jew, wherever he is and no matter what his status in health, wealth, or anything else, says, "Blessed are you Hashem, Who has provided me with all I need."[6]

"Is this not a blessing said in vain?" my *rebbi* asked. "How can I say that Hashem has provided all my needs when I *need* health, I *need* a livelihood? How can I possibly say these words as a blessing? I could make a list of twenty-five things that I'm missing, so how can I make that berachah every day?

"A starving Jew in Auschwitz, who had just lost his family and did not know whether he would still be alive in another three hours, also had to recite that berachah when he woke up in the morning. What were Chazal thinking? How can you tell someone to make a berachah that does not accurately describe his true situation?

"The answer is that this berachah is never said in vain. The Sages had the perception that what we need is what we have, yet we may strive, within permissible bounds, to obtain what we require to live our lives properly."

We need that which is necessary to do all that Hashem expects of us, and nothing more.

Simchah is a natural result of that perception of *bitachon*: *If this is my situation, if this is what I have, then this is what is supposed to be.* I, therefore, have to appreciate it, not because it could have been worse, but because it could not have been otherwise.

If I am missing an arm and cannot put on tefillin, if I do not have money to give to charity, then those mitzvos are not required of me, so I do not *need* them.

"Thank you, Hashem, for giving me everything I need in order to achieve all that You require of me in this world."

---

6   Siddur, *Shacharis*, morning blessings.

This attitude may be hard to acquire, and it certainly is challenging, but I have to thank Hashem for *now*, for this moment. That is *bitachon*, and with this solid understanding will come happiness.

Although disappointed when we pray for something and do not get it, we should never feel that Hashem let us down. He gives us exactly what we need, at the right time, in the exact way, and in the order that we need it. We only see a very small part of the whole picture, as our perception of reality is acquired from our limited human perspective, and our eyes see a lot of things we mistakenly think we need. Our prayers are never lost, however, and never ignored; they are applied to Hashem's full perception of our needs rather than our narrow view.[7]

Defining our needs in light of what our relatives think might have given us a false estimation of our situation. The size of our family may mean we need to adjust our definition of an acceptable level of comfort, and we have to be able to do it with *simchah*. We must ensure that our children feel joy in our home so that they will not look elsewhere with envy. To an unenlightened person, having *more* means having it *better*. In the eyes of a Torah Jew, having *Hashem* means having it better.

How do we live with that? Do we appreciate the quality of our life because we are doing what is right, living well in the eyes of Hakadosh Baruch Hu? If we can transmit that degree of satisfaction to our children, we will not have to be worried that they will feel envious of others. We have something much more valuable.

———————

My wife and I have a dear friend who is a very successful entrepreneur. We have done some business together with fruitful results, which has been very helpful in purchasing our home and marrying off a few of our children.

A number of years ago, one of my children asked me, "Why don't you just go and work with him full time, and then you can buy or build

———————

7   Rabbi Moshe Rosenstein, *Yesodei Hadaas* (Warsaw, 1935), essay 46.

houses, and then we, too, could be wealthy?" I answered my son by explaining to him that we were already very wealthy, but in a different kind of way.

"Maybe we are not wealthy with money, but our family is constructing palaces in a more significant place, in the World to Come. If we were to decide to change the way we live, it would mean giving up Torah learning and teaching to build houses and make money in this world. I think that would be a poor investment in both worlds, and would not be worth it to me, not one little drop."

So, while I have used and continue to use some of my precious time to make additional income to provide for our "needs," I am constantly evaluating how to remain committed to my highest value of remaining in the world of Torah and Torah education.

When you feel absolutely secure in your choice of direction, your children can be taught this with joy and confidence. To achieve that certainty, you have to constantly be learning and growing, in touch with the Source of your strength and making sure to utilize your support systems.[8] Defining your priorities and living them with *simchah* is really the mainstay of your home!

My *rebbi* once told of a young man who approached him with a dilemma regarding taking a second job.

"I am not sure if I am disinclined to take the job because I have *bitachon* or because I am lazy."

"If you are not certain, then it is most certainly laziness," my *rebbi* replied, "because the nature of *bitachon* is that you would be confident and sure."[9]

---

8   See chapters 9 and 10.
9   Rabbi Y. M. Homnick, *Avnei Shlomo* (Daas Shlomo Kollel, 2006), p. 34.

Chapter 23

Self-Esteem
and Success

The greatest educational challenge in our community today is raising children to have positive self-esteem, especially in a family blessed with more than two or three children. This is a central topic that I propose to address somewhat at length here. Developing a healthy sense of self and individuality is one of the greatest challenges to our generation, and most certainly so in a large family. In this chapter, we hope to gain a deeper understanding of the dynamics of self-esteem, as well as an answer to the question of why, in our generation, it is so difficult to attain.

We will try to develop a new depth in understanding topics already discussed to see how we can better cultivate individuality in both our children and ourselves.

It Begins with You

It is very difficult for a parent to teach self-esteem when he or she is suffering from a lack of it. As we mentioned earlier, anyone coming into a new society with new values and priorities will be challenged. A young man of twenty-four was sitting at our Shabbos table. He had been in yeshiva for a few months and was very interested in his Judaism. After the meal, he asked if we could speak, and with tears in his eyes told me that watching the interaction regarding the parashah with my children made him feel hopeless. "That eight-year-old child knows more Torah than me and everyone in my class combined!"

Even years later, if you find yourself comparing and measuring your-self with the yardstick of others you will have a hard time giving over the message of self-worth not being dependent on others. Every human being has his journey, and comparative knowledge or achievement is the guaranteed path to low self-esteem or false self-esteem. When we compare our children to others, when we want our children to "be bet-ter" than their peers, to have more and achieve more, we are the cause of that low self-esteem.

Rav Wolbe, in *Planting and Building in Chinuch*, in the chapter regard-ing unrealistic goals, speaks about an even more problematic process of parents living/achieving vicariously through their children, which goes against the essence of *chinuch*. He explains how *chinuch* is **only** about your child and their life, with their abilities and limitations. He explains that a child will not be successful when the goals of his parents—as noble as they are trying to be—undermine the needs and abilities of the child they so want to make successful. "The child's abilities are not encouraged and that which the parents are providing is not what the child wants. It only follows that the child will not be successful."

Achievement

Every human being needs to feel that he is important, that he is a unique person possessing a special something that makes him worth-while. We live in a society, however, that uses achievements as the measure of worth. This per se is a very dangerous concept because it defines a person by the outcome of his efforts.

If you try to explain to Grandpa why your son has been learning in yeshiva for seven years, he will invariably ask you what he will have to show for it. Will he earn a degree? What will it be worth in dollars and cents? What is the bottom line?

His successes must be quantifiable in something that society values. There is no regard, in his world, in accomplishment for its own sake, no understanding that something should be done just because it is the right or good thing to do. Effort alone is not sufficient if there is nothing tangible as a result.

The Midrash tells us that even if we learn Torah, forget it, learn, and forget it again, we will nonetheless be rewarded for the time and effort of studying.[1] However long we sit and learn, our achievement is not how much we know, but what we have attempted with all of our heart and soul to acquire. We are assured and believe that every word will bring us immeasurable reward in the eternal world of goodness. In a superficial society, no one can understand that what we are trying to achieve in yeshiva has nothing to do with getting a degree. We are involved with what we are supposed to be doing with our lives. Every day we need to have a set time for learning because the process is what counts. In our world of ethics and morality, we recognize that the final outcome of our efforts is not up to us.

This attitude does not make sense to modern Western people, focused as they are on achievement. Unfortunately, this outlook has encroached on our own community's value system.

Success

Given that the world's definition of success is having achieved something tangible, and that everyone wants to feel successful, our self-esteem is placed at risk.

A successful person is represented by a business card that he proudly presents to others. The letters that follow his name on the card—CEO, CPA, DDS, PhD, etc.—show that he has reached a certain status. This is who I am, which is defined by what I am good at, what I have achieved.

In my calling as an educator, I have had the great privilege of working in a number of schools. One of them was the Darchei Shalom Educational Center, a high school for bright students who needed alternative motivational devices, as they were not prepared to sit and learn for eight to ten hours a day. They were extremely intelligent, capable young men,

---

1   *Tanna D'bei Eliyahu Rabbah*, ch. 13.

but for a hundred and one reasons they did not have the learning habits or skills necessary to succeed in the average yeshiva.

Many students showed signs of what was once known as "ants in the pants," and is now generally labeled as ADD. Their self-esteem, as you can imagine, was not high, and nobody wanted them. They had been rejected or expelled from several other schools. Several boys had been told that they were never going to get into a yeshiva high school, or indeed any high school at all. Some had not learned anything from fifth, sixth, or seventh grade on. Most of them had not been able to become dedicated, motivated, or studious in their former schools.

In our school, they found several alternative areas of endeavor wherein they could easily succeed. In the afternoons, they had a choice of learning carpentry, electronics, photography, or computers. There was a garden where they planted different kinds of crops, and they ate the food it produced. We had an apiary and an aviary on our campus in addition to some farm animals, all of which were cared for by the boys.

It was a very interesting school. Many of our students had no history of even attempting to learn Gemara because they knew from past experience that they would not be successful. Our goal was to help these children find areas in which they could shine, and perhaps, transfer this newly earned self-confidence to their learning ability as well. *Baruch Hashem*, by utilizing this approach, over the years, we saw many former students become respectable members of their respective communities and even *talmidei chachamim*.

In 1999, I became involved with a teachers' seminary for highly successful young women who had just graduated from high school. With tremendous kindness from Hashem, the seminary has flourished.

The first day I walked into the classroom, I wasn't sure what to do. As I began to speak, all I saw was twenty-four heads of hair as the girls looked down to begin taking notes. The second day I came into class, I was really distressed. They were all looking at me, listening with their mouths agape in rapt interest.

"This is not for me," I said to my wife after the second day.

"Why not?" she asked.

"There is nothing for me to do," I answered. "They are angels, they are all perfect. Why do they need *chinuch*? I can give them more information, but what can I add to their lives?"

"I know girls," she said. "Give it three weeks and get to know them a little bit better. You will soon find out whether or not you have your work cut out for you."

Fortunately, I listened to my wife, and did not quit that day, but gave myself some more time before making a judgment.

Little by little, I did get to know the students, who were determined to project an image of achievement and accomplishment. Anything less on their part would have meant vulnerability and weakness.

It took me a little bit longer to realize something surprising, yet very central, about the task I had accepted. In terms of the objectives, there was no difference between being a *mechanech* in a school and being a parent.

More to the point, there was a great similarity between the boys in Darchei Shalom who were erroneously viewed as losers, and these students at the seminary who were the cream of the crop. The only difference between them was that the girls in the seminary all had "business cards" that they could present with pride, while the young men in the boys' school had never found anything to write on theirs that would impress their communities.

Possessing self-esteem means, *I know there is purpose in my existence. I am a valuable person whose life is meaningful; I can and want to achieve its goal.*

The challenge is that if I can identify and present my life's value, and **other people accept it as well**, then I can be comfortable with myself. But if I can find nothing to present, it seems that my actual worth makes no difference. When that happens, I don't even have to know very much about my mind and emotions; there is no value to myself at all.

The only thing I need to succeed today is to have something that I can put on that business card.

There are kids who are great at academics. Their business cards read, "I am a successful student."

There are girls who are beautiful, talented, or socially gifted. Some can sing and others can dance very well. Having talent allows individuals to feel good and present themselves as special. It follows that they can and will do their best at everything else. More often than not, these abilities are gifts with which they were born, or talents that were easily acquired.

Self-esteem that is based on such gifts, however, is not authentic. It says that my whole life, my entire self, is really not valuable, and the only thing that makes me worthwhile is the one thing of which I am especially capable. Having an A-plus average, or being prettier, more talented, or more seemingly religious than the other girls in my school makes me feel successful, makes me who I am.

You cannot speak sharply to young people who live with this perspective. If you were to voice serious constructive criticism regarding the need for self-improvement, most "successful" young people today would have great difficulty hearing it. If they have to accept that something in their character requires serious work, they become distressed. They do not want to think about all the other parts of them that may not be A-plus. Doing so throws them into a tailspin, and they get sucked into a totally negative state. If something about them needs to be changed, they feel they are worthless.

Criticism is difficult to accept because it hints at something that is imperfect within themselves. Are they not special? Well, yes, they are, but that is because they are better at something than others around them. Hearing that they may be less than flawless in other areas is difficult for them.

On the other hand, the students who attended Darchei Shalom felt worthless to begin with. If they were neither brilliant nor hardworking, neither popular nor *tzaddikim*, they had no way to present themselves as winners.

They did not do well in school for a hundred reasons that had nothing to do with their brains or their worth, but nevertheless impacted on their success.

There is nothing about any human being that makes him a loser except that he thinks he is one. The essence of man is that he was created for a purpose, Hashem wants us to be here and no one else will ever be able to live our lives, which means that we are all winners, all purposeful and valuable.

The Perfection Syndrome

I perceive the greatest challenge to successful growth and development to be what I call the "perfection syndrome," which creates the facade called success.

Every year, *Forbes* publishes a list of the hundred richest men in the world; if you are the 101st, you did not make it. Today, there is a hierarchy of everything, the top-ten musicians, movies, best-dressed people, books, singers, etc. People endeavor throughout their entire lives for recognition, an award, or to break a record, resulting in a world of depressed losers. We only accept the Emmy or Grammy winner, the champion prize fighter, as being successful. People buy the magazines that write about those people, and dream about the lives they think those people live.

In at least a hundred of my lectures, when participants were asked to name a successful businessman, approximately 80 percent chose Bill Gates because he had "made it."

In the area of competitive sports, the most highly valued global ideal of success is winning a medal in the Olympics.

> *Danny, among the ten fastest runners in the United States, trained for the two-hundred-meter sprint event in the Olympics for fifteen years. Then he met over a hundred runners, who in their respective countries were seeded to run just in the Olympic preliminaries; only the eight fastest would actually race for gold. These eight fastest runners in the world would then compete for some twenty-odd seconds. The first to cross the finish line would win gold; the second, silver; and the third, bronze.*
>
> *Danny came in fourth. Although he was the fourth fastest sprinter in the world that year, five minutes after the race no one remembered he existed.*

In Iran, they would have tortured him,[2] but in the more civilized United States of America he is just a loser.

I've told this story to thousands of students, yeshiva boys, high school and seminary girls, and secular college students. Not one person ever protested or even blinked an eye when I called Danny a loser. The fourth-fastest man on the planet is a "loser."

It is sad to say that this perception has infiltrated our special world of Yiddishkeit. We have adopted similar themes.

From the perspective of an educator or parent, there is really not much difference between the successful young person and one at risk of falling out of the system. Our collective responsibility is to make all our children understand that they are of utmost importance in the world because they have intrinsic worth as human beings.

Their value does not depend on what they can sell or what they can achieve that makes them better than others, nor do they lose their worth when they are not as successful as the next person. Children evaluate themselves in school by their marks, friends, and popularity, as those are the factors by which everybody else is making judgments. This module warps our children's self-esteem.

There is only one way to truly evaluate people, and that is by accepting them for who they are regardless of all of the above. We, as parents and educators, need to provide our children with the absolute confidence that their value is dependent on nothing other than the fact that Hashem created them with purpose, meaning, and importance.

Sibling Competition

It is often difficult to figure out what is bothering a child until you meet his brother who is a year younger and more talented, or her sister who is a year older and is Superwoman. The problem then becomes clear. The child herself is talented and capable but is constantly measuring herself against a sibling she thinks outshines her. Even when the

2   John F. Burns, "Aftereffects: Reign of Terror; Soccer Players Describe Torture by Hussein's Son," *New York Times*, May 6, 2003.

parents lean over backward not to compare them, he still feels inferior. His self-esteem is nonexistent because of these invidious comparisons.

In many cases, two siblings feel threatened by the perceived superiority of the other, not realizing that each feels the same way. Without authentic self-esteem, neither will be able to grow and develop in areas that really need improvement.

True Success

Let us redefine the idea of success by deriving some vital lessons from our Sages. Ben Zoma in the fourth chapter of *Pirkei Avos* defines it in ways that run strongly counter to everything that secular society tells us.[3]

A wise person learns from everyone, a strong person is one who has self-control, a rich person is happy with his lot, and one who is respected is he who accords respect to others. Achievement that is dependent on anyone else's lack of it is not real.

The achievement of *chochmah*, wisdom, is in the *process* of obtaining it. Defining a *chacham* relative to others is not a valid definition. Develop yourself into a person who is constantly in search of *chochmah*.

When students come to a seminary from schools where they have been at the top of their class, they arrive feeling bright and capable. Suddenly, they are surrounded by eighty others just like them. They begin to question themselves, their worth, and their abilities. All of this grief is due to the definition of self being determined and defined by the people around them. Chazal teach us not to look at ourselves in contrast with anybody else.

The world defines strength and power as relative concepts: ruling over others, being stronger than someone else. The Sages teach us, however, that our ability to achieve power or control is not dependent on others. He who possesses real power, real strength, is the person who controls and dominates his own life, inclinations, and instincts.

Chazal's perception puts everything into perspective. We think we know what respect signifies, assuming that it should be shown to the

---

3   *Pirkei Avos* 4:1.

person whom others honor. Not so, say Chazal, as the person who sits in the front row is not always respected. People will stand up for someone merely out of fear or need.

Being worthy of respect depends on how we value people, not on the way they look at us. If we look down at others, not seeking the good in them, all the achievements in the world will not have earned us respect. The way we treat others is the only thing that will determine whether we are persons of *kavod*, value, or essence.

The constant need to achieve, overachieve, and outdo others is a malady of the greater society in which we live that has lamentably filtered down to our community. We have many very poor rich people among us, as whoever thinks he lacks what someone else has is needy. Being content with one's lot means that wealth is determined by its *inherent* value, which is subjective. If I appreciate what I have, then I am wealthy. I do not need anything more.

You Are Alive

This is the chief lesson needed to live happy lives, and we must share it with our children so that they can begin to understand their own value as human beings.

A poster in the office of an organization devoted to children with special needs depicts a smiling child with Down syndrome. Under his picture it says, "I know I'm OK because Hashem don't make junk!"

Your value as a person is that you exist. If you are alive, you are here for a reason and you have a job to do. Herein lies self-esteem. You were born the way that you are because Hashem wanted you to be like this. Your life is now a process of progression, work, and attempts to become a better you.

The Vilna Gaon shares an extraordinary insight in this respect. He says, "Man lives to fix that which he has not yet fixed. If not, for what purpose is he still alive?"[4]

---

4   Vilna Gaon on *Mishlei* 4:13.

I am alive today because there is something on which I still need to work. Hmmm...

Man was born incomplete. The reason we exist is to fix our imperfections. It is brought down that the reason man has to be circumcised instead of being born that way is to teach us that we are created imperfect in many areas, and it is incumbent upon us to finish the job.[5]

"It is impossible for a man to be born with a sublime character without deficiency," says the *Rambam*. "It is, however, possible for one to have in his nature a proclivity to certain sublime characteristics."[6] The *Rambam* clearly speaks about man's need to work in order to achieve true greatness.

This is difficult to understand when looking at the world superficially. People constantly try to project just the opposite impression.

"Look at me! I'm the perfect businessman, singer, surgeon...this is who I am."

"No, that is *not* who you are," says the Torah Jew.

We do not earn great reward for doing what comes naturally to us, but for working toward a goal and overcoming challenges. We tell our children that this is the way the world of *emes* works. It is the only way to build true self-esteem.

---

5   *Sefer Hachinuch*, mitzvah 2, regarding circumcision.
6   *Rambam*, commentary on *Mishnah Sanhedrin*, introduction to *Perek Chelek*, eighth of "The Eight Segments."

Chapter 24

Competition and True Growth

E mphasis on competition has created a sad society. As the "People of the Book," we unfortunately also study, read, and learn from the society around us. Many, sadly, have integrated the Western value system in which "making it" means nothing more than being on top of the heap.

Our children must be accepted into *the* best yeshiva, be *the* most popular, smartest, best-looking, get *the* best *shidduch*, and so on, in this false existence that we have adopted. They, unfortunately, become part of this sad society because they must spend their lives living up to expectations that have nothing to do with their abilities.

This is not the Torah perspective, which maintains that you have to be the best that *you* can be.[1] There should not be any element of competition in your world or in that of your child's.

"Jealousy, desire, and honor remove a person from this world," says the Mishnah.[2]

Competition comprises at least two of those!

You are an individual. You are who *you* are, deal with what *you* have, and become what *you* can become. Others are brought into your life so that you can learn from them, but they are not your competition. That is the unconditional basis of *chinuch* and the absolute foundation of *avodas Hashem*, serving Hashem.

---

1   *Sanhedrin* 37a, "Every man must say, "The world was created for me."

2   *Pirkei Avos* 4:21.

Because our society has become so materially achievement-oriented, the secret of our being able to raise our children to be well-balanced adults is first learning to accept ourselves for who we are and stop competing. This does not mean stagnation, but self-acceptance along with continued personal growth and development. There is nothing wrong with being a work in progress. Every man who walks the face of this earth is just that because, once we "arrive," we are no longer in this world.

A young man with whom I had spent some time learning once told me of his frustration. He had participated in NCSY[3] for a year or two and entered yeshiva later than his peers.

"I can't handle it," he said. "You guys are so far ahead of me that I don't even have a chance!"

I still remember the words Hashem put into my mouth.

"Your problem is that you are looking at the world as a race, which it is not. If you can't accept that, and you can only see that I am twenty-five miles ahead of you, you're correct—you will never catch up. Let's look at the racetrack from Hashem's point of view, so to speak.

You are looking down from heaven. The racetrack is a million miles long. I am twenty-five miles ahead. Who cares? If it were a thirty-mile track, I'd be way ahead of you, but it's a million-mile track and *no one is expected to finish*. Anyone can pull ahead at any time, and no one knows how long anyone else will be in the running.

"On this racetrack, you are moving forward at your own pace, and there is no competition. You don't have to catch up with me. Actually, you may even be ahead because we don't really know where you, I, or anyone else is on this track. Looking at it from a different perspective, I just see a bunch of dots on a very, very long road."

Self-acceptance means accepting where you are, how far you've come, and being aware that getting where you want to go is a long process that only you can achieve. Comparisons are valueless because it makes

---

3   National Conference of Synagogue Youth, a movement sponsored by the Orthodox Union.

no difference what someone else thinks of you. By accepting yourself, you have a place in the world and so do your children. Aiming to arrive at a specific point is very good, but knowing where you are at any given time is an extraordinarily important prerequisite.

When I was fifteen years old, I studied in a prestigious yeshiva high school. I was taking in too much, too seriously, too quickly. There was an older fellow in the yeshiva named Avraham Ackerman, who taught me one of the most essential lessons I ever learned.

One evening, he saw me looking a bit down. He called me over and asked if everything was OK. Everything was not OK, and I told him about it. I had been listening carefully to the *mussar* speeches and in general approaching my learning seriously.

"Here I am learning about all these lofty concepts of love of God, fear of God, etc., and to tell you the truth," I told him, "I don't know what they are talking about. If I die tomorrow, I'll be going straight to the lowest place in Gehinnom."

Avraham sat me down. "Why do you think people generally live to eighty or ninety?" he asked. "Why doesn't everyone die at fifteen?"

I shrugged.

"I guess it generally takes about eighty to ninety years," he continued, "to reach where a person needs to get to in this world. If we all could be finished with our jobs here within two years of becoming bar mitzvah, we would all die at fifteen."

Now, I was listening carefully.

"Zecharya, do you think Hashem doesn't know how you grew up, with which challenges and hardships? Do you think He doesn't know that you had and have battles with your *yetzer hara*? Do you think He expects you to reach the level described in the *mashgiach's mussar* speech in the ten months since you started really thinking and trying?"

I was feeling better already; it made so much sense.

"Take it step by step, start moving in the direction you know is right, and don't let yourself become frustrated. Hashem knows and understands your battles and challenges, and He will help you get to where you need to go as long as you are trying."

I believe that with those words he saved my life.

Everyone, especially those who have made great changes in their lives, needs to understand this concept as a basis for continued growth. We cannot feel discouraged because we still have battles. We may not look at others and think, "See where they are, and where am I?"

More than forty years later, I still need to remember the lesson I learned that day, as I continue to fight to move forward, at times with greater success and sometimes with less.

The light at the end of the tunnel is not a place I need to reach, but the direction toward which I need to keep moving. That is the movement for which I will ultimately be judged.

Lot, the nephew of our forefather Avraham, was not someone you would call a good person. Why was he saved from the cataclysmic destruction of Sodom if he chose to be a resident there?

Chazal tell us that when Lot went with Avraham and Sarah to Egypt, and Avraham said to Sarah, "Please tell them you are my sister in order to...keep me alive,"[4] Lot did not reveal the truth. He obeyed his uncle and kept his mouth shut. To appreciate how difficult this was for him, let us take a moment to see it from the historical perspective.

Lot lost his father when he was a child, and Avraham and Sarah took him into their home. They took him along wherever they traveled, and he built his wealth on theirs. When they arrived in Egypt, he did not snitch and get them killed. Is this why he was rewarded and his life saved? We also know that he took in the two angels, which was a selfless act that endangered his life. Why wasn't he rewarded for that?

Chazal infer a valuable lesson from this incident. Lot loved wealth more than anything else. When they arrived in Egypt, and Avraham

---

4   *Bereishis* 12:13.

said, "She is my sister," Lot's eyelids started fluttering; he saw gold coins raining down. This was the jackpot!

All he had to do was send a little piece of papyrus that said, "Hey, fellows, it's not true. She is that man's wife." He didn't need to say a word; he only had to pass them a note while his lips remained sealed.

In Egypt, when a man wanted a wife, he purchased one. Lot, as Avraham's next of kin, stood to inherit not only great wealth, but Sarah as well. Pharaoh would have immediately had Avraham killed so as to be able to respectfully ask for her hand in marriage by paying a queen's sum for her, and there would be only one man from whom to make that acquisition: Lot, her nephew.

Double lotto! He was on the verge of winning everything. One tiny piece of papyrus...This was the biggest test of his life, and he passed it.

He did not suddenly become righteous, however. When he later had a dispute with Avraham over his cattle eating from other people's fields, he made the decision to live in Sodom, a city of greed and sin. He did not become a *tzaddik*, but there was one time in his life when he overcame a great challenge, and his reward was being saved from the destruction of his city. On the other hand, having grown up in the house of Avraham, leaving guests outside was never an option. Welcoming travelers was so ingrained in him that it was perfectly natural to take them in even at great risk. Reward is given for that which is difficult, not for that which is natural.

Teaching Our Children about Rewards

Children need to know this story, to know that they are cherished not because they give us *nachas*, but because of who they are. Their battles are their path to growth and are what make them even more valuable. They will win some and lose others, but personal setbacks and failures do not in any way lower a child's worth.

Our value lies in trying to overcome obstacles, in being ready to do our best. That is what Hashem expects of us in this world. We want our children to know that their success in school, as in life, does not depend on whether or not they get a better mark than anyone else in their class. Their parents need to make it clear that they are not interested in anyone else's marks. "What could *you* do, and what did *you* do? How are you doing compared *to yourself?*"

We use the same benchmark in the matter of their success in relationships. "The way you treat your friends," they must hear, "will determine whether or not you are going to have a successful life. Never mind how they act toward you. Your success has to do with how *you* treat *them.*"

Our goal is to teach our children responsibility for their actions in terms of themselves and their own abilities. If they see we don't measure them against others, they will learn to trust themselves.

Mental Health in Our Society

Eating disorders, which have become so common, are fed by the images promoted in the media. People feel that they must resemble those in the magazines, not realizing that the models and celebrities are so professionally made up and dressed that they would be unrecognizable walking down the street on an ordinary day. Depression, anxiety, and obsessive-compulsive disorders are so common, they are almost expected. The civilization in which we live has created an extremely unhealthy, distorted, depressed world.

"An estimated 26.2 percent of Americans ages eighteen and older—about one in four adults—suffer from a diagnosable mental disorder in a given year. When applied to the 2004 US Census residential population estimate for ages eighteen and older, this figure translates to 57.7 million people.… In addition, mental disorders are the leading cause of disability in the US and Canada for ages fifteen to forty-four."[5]

My friend Dr. Ron Hizami, a psychiatrist of note from Monsey, New York, told me that 50 percent of American adults will have a psychotic event in their lives. I thought that he was exaggerating until I saw the resource statistics available at the National Institute for Mental Health.[6]

---

5   R. C. Kessler, W. T. Chiu, O. Demler, E. E. Walters, "Prevalence, Severity, and Comorbidity of Twelve-Month DSM-IV Disorders," National Comorbidity Survey Replication (NCS-R), *Archives of General Psychiatry* 62, no. 6 (June, 2005):617–27.

6   Kessler 6 (K6) Behavioral Risk Factor Surveillance System. For 2007 K6 data, based on

I questioned that statistic as being inaccurate in the Torah community of which I believe I have an intimate awareness. Although we do not have accurate statistics, he agreed that my assumption could be correct but added, "The professionals are aware of more than even you know among those around us."

Indeed, Torah life provides a healthier environment *when applied as prescribed*; among those who do so, there certainly is a lower percentage of disorders. There are many serious issues that have infiltrated our community, however, and we are not immune to the ills of Western culture and their consequences. It is vital to know to whom to turn and how to get help when these issues surface.

Eating disorders in our community in the United States, especially among women, are on the rise, with a higher level of prevalence than in the secular community.[7] This may well be attributed to the fact that we have become obsessive in regard to our daughters' achievements. The pressure of *shidduchim* does not make the problem any easier to solve and can unfortunately wreak havoc in the mind of the most normal young lady. I am too embarrassed to cite some of the ridiculous questions that parents have asked me about my seminary students. What are people thinking? Serious, devoted parents, who seem to live normal lives, can force their children into bad eating habits.

Being thin and beautiful has been elevated by society to value status and has inevitably osmosed into our own merit system. When we become motivated to do something, we do it better. As a community of hard-working, highly self-disciplined, and capable individuals, we are more perfect perfectionists than anyone else. We have fallen prey to unparalleled peer pressure, which creates enormous insecurity in our youth and often adults as well, I am sorry to say.

---

a period of "in the past 30 days." Approximately 40 percent of persons in thirty-five states had serious psychological distress (SPD, defined as a score of 10 or more on the K6). Of respondents indicating they had SPD, 37.7 percent received mental health services in the preceding year.

7   Rebbetzin Feige Twerski, "Body and Soul," in *Heaven on Earth* (Michigan: Targum Press, 2002), p. 203.

Our children can only appreciate themselves if they have felt secure about their true worth from the time they were little because we've been communicating how much we love and accept them, whatever they look like. They don't have to be the prettiest or most handsome on the block, or have to contrast themselves to others.

Of course, we are not the only people in our children's lives, and there can be teachers, other adults, or peers who might make them feel disappointed in themselves and their abilities. As their parents, however, we can still have a greater effect on them than others, as they are at home more than they are anywhere else. We are their primary authority and first responder to most of their needs. In addition to the emotional basis of our relationship, which developed from birth, we play a role that creates anticipation, desire, and a need for our support. As long as they feel our respect and love, we will be the most significant influence in building them up.

The messages we transmit to our children from infancy until they go to school have the tremendous power of setting the foundations for their self-esteem. When children do something wrong, the way we react, whether we understand or not, will make a huge difference in their view of themselves.

How do we accept them in spite of their incorrect acts or decisions? One thing we can do is to teach them to fix their mistakes because everyone makes them. In most cases, they do not create the havoc that justifies the kind of exaggerated reaction that parents often have.

Living with Our Mistakes

A number of years ago, I spoke to a young lady who had made a very foolish, terrible mistake. A few weeks after the other girls discussed marriage in class, she came dejectedly into my office.

"Why should I even think of looking to marry someone who is special? I don't deserve it. Why should anyone marry me?"

"Why not?" I asked.

"Because look how stupid and irresponsible I am," she said.

"You are? You mean you *were*! Stop for a minute and think about what happened. You made one mistake, and the rest of your life is nothing?"

The young woman had always been responsible, a good girl who always did the right thing. She made one really imprudent mistake, and in her eyes, her life was over because very often in our society, you get to mess up only once. We as parents, however, do not have to buy into such a false notion. We can allow our children to make the inevitable mistakes and to understand that they can usually reverse them.

Being Comfortable with Themselves

Young teenagers enter a world that expects a great deal of them. By the time they are fourteen—before he can get into yeshiva; before she can get into a high school—they are scrutinized by scores of critical eyes. If they are comfortable with themselves, it is because we taught them to be so. If they can laugh at themselves when they err, it is a good sign that they can be happy and well-adjusted despite their mistakes.

Our children need to accept that they, along with everyone else, have imperfections. If they cannot accept whatever limitations they have, even those that may be extreme, they will never be able to improve in those areas.

We cannot allow our shortcomings to make us feel worthless. Healthy people are aware that they can always advance, as they know what they have to do in order to improve. Those who have never accepted the fact that they, like all human beings, have some degree of inadequacy, cannot grow beyond their present self.

Becoming depressed or going into denial when you recognize that you are not perfect will leave you with no choice but to live with your business card. You will acknowledge only the things at which you excel, and everything else will disappear. When children don't have or have lost that business card, it does not take long for them to feel that they are no good at all. This attitude becomes a self-fulfilling prophecy.

We Believe in You

Children must be pointed in the right direction. If a child has a flaw or is weak in one or two areas, some schools are ready to give up on him. If a child steps over one of the many red lines, some schools are so afraid of outside influences that they can write him or her off for life. We have a parental obligation to show our children that we believe in them *anyway*, while letting them know that schools have limitations, too, and cannot always deal with situations in the best way possible.

But we can. We can help our children get up, brush themselves off, and either get back into class or learn somewhere else. We are the ones who give them their self-respect and self-esteem.

We do not have to agree with everything our children do, but we have to understand them. If we do not, they begin to think that their feelings are not valid, at which point they either suppress their natural emotions, which is unhealthy, or they rebel because they feel totally misunderstood. The only choices they can see are to either give up or fight!

Not Giving Up

Children learn how we define growth. If they know we value the fact that they are good at something, they become motivated to get better at it and then try to improve in something else.

A child does not have to become The Best, but he can learn that he is able to grow.

"Last week, you got a seventy, and now you got a seventy-five, which is really good! That shows growth."

"Yeah, but everyone else in the class got a ninety."

"I'm not interested in what marks the other children in your class received," you must respond with conviction. "It is you, and only you, whose growth and progress I care about right now."

Report cards must be private. Unless a child feels sufficiently comfortable to show his report card to someone else, no one but you should see it. Your children appreciate your respect for their privacy and their feelings. We want them to be proud of their achievements, no matter how modest. A healthy child should be able to say with pride, "Look, I didn't do so well in this subject, but I did better at that one."

If he is adamant that nobody sees his report card, you have to respect that sensitivity. If he is embarrassed because he didn't do well this semester, and he knows he flunked out because he really didn't try, that is fine. It is good that he is embarrassed because there is a chance that next time he will do better. A child who doesn't feel good about herself never wants anyone to see her marks, and should not be coerced to display them. I would let her see that she is respected despite a poor report card.

> *One of my children wasn't doing too well in school. He was a hard worker but had some learning disabilities and various other problems. My mother is one of those loving parents who almost never discarded anything associated with her children. This was fortunate because she gave me a file containing all my report cards from first grade on. I would not show them to everybody, but I did call this particular child over to show him my first-, second-, and third-grade report cards. They were not so good. I wasn't very much of a student myself, I told him.*
>
> *I was not trying to demonstrate that he doesn't have to do well in school. I was giving him the important message that even if you don't do well when you are younger, as you get older and try to work harder, you can still achieve. I did not want him to give up on himself just because he couldn't do so well at present, nor did I want him to think that all was lost just because he had done poorly in some areas. If he sees that even though I didn't always do so well in school, I did not give up and did well later, he won't look at me and think, How can I ever make it?*
>
> *He does not know what I went through to achieve whatever I did. It was not always easy. When children know that their parents have also undergone hardships, perhaps also got into trouble in school, it reassures them. It is important for a child to see the bigger picture.*

Parents are sometimes reluctant to be open with their children about their own weaknesses or past difficulties in school because they are afraid their children will think it is OK to make trouble or do poorly. I doubt this is true.

They can be shown that you regret misbehaving, but that you learned from your mistakes. They can see that you understand your child, and you can share, talk, and communicate with each other because you are all valuable human beings who can grow and develop despite the difficulties.

It is common knowledge that to develop a muscle, you have to exercise and work at it. When the muscle you want to work on begins to hurt, you know you have targeted correctly.

I once went to a local men's gym for help with back pain and followed the trainer's instructions. There was another man there who told me to stop doing a particular exercise and do something else. After three minutes, I told the trainer I was going to listen to the other fellow because I saw I had not been using the muscles in my back, but rather those in my arms. I understood that because my arms were sore, and my back felt the same.

When we know what hurts, we know what is being challenged, and we can only meet that demand by growing. In other words, if it's not hard, we are not going to become better at it.

If we can successfully teach our children this lesson, they will learn about handling life's challenges by not giving up. We give up when we think our efforts are worthless, that trying won't make a difference.

One Step at a Time

When your children overcome a challenge or improve even a little in some area, they should be praised. Show your appreciation, especially for that first, important small step. I cannot tell you how many times I have heard children whose parents are overly demanding in their Yiddishkeit say, "It doesn't make any difference what I do because I will never be good enough. My parents don't know how hard I am trying; they just want to see results *now*."

The child is not there, yet. It is very hard for him to make the attempt, and if his parents seem to not even notice his efforts, he might very well give up.

"My parents want me to look like everybody else. They didn't even notice that I *am* wearing the shirt Mommy wanted me to wear."

For this child this was a step that went unnoticed because we are more interested in the final result. *Does she look like everybody else or not? Yes, she wore that blouse, but the skirt is…Does he look the way I want him to? Does he say what I want him to say, is he learning what I want him to learn?*

When we reprimand him for not doing well in school, something that has been going on for some time, the child is confused, "What do you mean? I *did* learn well this week…four times, and I was sent out of class only twice."

The *rebbi* does not appreciate that he is progressing. After having been sent out nine times, twice is a very big step and should be noticed. If we appreciate the small steps, we are teaching him that there is great value to growth. If we do not, we are just causing further erosion of his self-esteem. We cannot always be critical, regarding whatever he does as not good enough. When he is trying to do better and is reprimanded for one mistake, it discourages all future attempts. He is sure that he is worthless in his parents' eyes, and he may even begin to rebel.

How many times do we make the grave mistake of saying, "*You never…*"? You *never* help. You *never* speak nicely, you *never* give. The child reminds you that she just helped for five minutes or took her little brother for a walk and bought gum for him. When we react by saying, "Yeah, thanks a lot, but do you know what you should have been doing?" we destroy the child's belief that his life and what he does has value.

If we are willing to look inside his head and see that he is trying, and show him that we *appreciate* that fact, then we can encourage him to do more. We, who the child respects, have to recognize the significance of what he is trying to do, focusing on his efforts, not his accomplishments. When we negate his efforts and put him down, we are basically demonstrating that success is all that matters to us. It is the wrong lesson.

Entering New Stages

When it comes to stepping stones, such as getting into yeshiva, *shidduchim*, or various other issues, your children are likely to think, *How would you know? You are a baal teshuvah who cannot understand how we feel. You grew up in a different world.*

After having been considered a fool for becoming *frum* by secular relatives and friends, your children now think you don't know anything! It can be disconcerting, to say the least.

Before you become insulted, ask yourself some questions: When Pesach comes around, do I still not feel one hundred percent confident that the cleaning is going right because I lack previous experience to base it upon? What is the proper way to prepare for a *vort*? I never actually helped prepare for a bris, or a bar mitzvah.

All these occasions may have been a first for you, and that feeling of lacking knowledge and experience may still haunt you. Your children don't know about your travails and challenges. They don't know what you went through to get to where you are, and what you have had to overcome in order to bring them up properly. They don't have a clue, and they feel entitled to say those hurtful words because they don't know anything about the process.

First of all, ask yourself, *Am I really out of it? Am I not tracking what's going on around me?*

Can it be that you have separated yourself somewhat from your community? If so, maybe your children are right. You can wake up and express a desire to learn, but don't become nervous, because this has very little to do with experience.

Everyone confronts new situations. If you have to solve a problem that arises, you can even do it together *with* your children. Let them know that you are willing to solve whatever you need to in order to help them.

Yes, you are a *baal teshuvah*, and yes, it is true that you grew up differently.

Perhaps, you are living in Israel and they say, "You're American, what do you know?"

It is fine to answer, "You are right, society in the United States is different from how it is here."

Where you were raised doesn't matter. You may presently live in a type of American community different from the one where you grew up, and you might hear, "You grew up in Denver, but we're growing up in Brooklyn."

"You are correct in saying that your environment is challenging in some ways," you can tell them, "but you are not the first one to encounter problems. My setting was problematic in other ways, but I live in your environment now, too. There are things here that are challenging for me, but we can figure it out together."

You cannot allow your own insecurities or uncertainties to affect how you are guiding and teaching your children. If you need help, you may certainly seek it, but your children are your responsibility. Sometimes, you may indeed feel out of the loop.

Your parents made a different kind of Pesach from the one you make. This is the first real bar mitzvah in your family in three generations. What are the rules for giving out honors at a bris or under the chuppah? You do not have to know! Even those who are born into religious families don't always know this information first time round and need to verify it.

There is nothing wrong with asking. You can easily sit down with a neighbor or friend who is knowledgeable about these things and get the lowdown. You may make an appointment with your *rav* and ask him how and where to draw the lines. You might be embarrassed because you think you should know the answers by now, and you are afraid that your friend or *rav* will find out how clueless you are. Well, you are welcome *not* to ask—and then everyone will *see* how clueless you are.

I grew up in the United States, and leaned heavily on my older children when it came to knowing the protocol of *chassan* and *kallah* gifts in Eretz Yisrael. I let them help me decide when to send flowers and which gifts to buy and when. They do not make the decisions, but they keep me up to date with what is currently considered acceptable, and then I can use my own common sense to determine where to go from there.

A Final Thought

Before summing up this chapter, I want to share a story that ought to be helpful in emphasizing the importance of using the ideas presented here in raising your children successfully. The story is about a young American woman studying in Israel who suffered as a result of the heavy load of unhealthy expectations that she carried around with her.

> *Malky was doing well in school, but at one point, she suddenly notified one of the teachers at her seminary that she needed to talk to someone. They made an appointment with me, during which Malky opened up and admitted that she was being very self-destructive. It was an unusual and challenging situation, and the teacher, who is a friend of mine, worked with her for a while, trying to convince her to see a professional.*

> *Having finally agreed to speak to a rabbi, Malky walked into my office and asked me to read some pages of her journal. She was not yet able to discuss what she had finally figured out, but wanted to show it to someone who could help her get direction.*

> *In short, Malky wrote that her older sister, Chanie, had serious problems. She was physically sick and emotionally unwell, which caused a great deal of distress in the family. Both her mother and father, preoccupied with Chanie, expected great things of Malky. Between her parents' and her own self-expectations, she was assigned the role of the perfect child of the family, able to do everything well.*

> *She was never allowed to show negative emotions, nor did she permit herself to show any sign of weakness or imperfection. Malky feared that if she ever indicated she was not one hundred percent in control, the rest of the family would not be able to function. The mother had her hands full dealing with the older sister, and the father felt he could not handle any further problems. But Malky was not a perfect child. There is no such creature.*

Over the years, this poor girl built up an inner knot of feeling neglected, hated, and rejected. No one understood this. She initiated self-destructive behavior at the age of fourteen and it continued until she was almost nineteen, when she realized she needed help. I hope the person Malky eventually saw was able to help her; I will probably never know.

We cannot and would never want to put that kind of pressure on our children—the cost is too great.

I recounted this story to show that there are things going on inside the minds and hearts of children of which we must try to be aware. We can create their self-esteem, or Heaven forbid, destroy it. It is really up to us. If we demand that our children be perfect, they will either comply and present as flawless on the outside but have very low confidence inside, or will rebel by purposely become very *im*perfect—with the bravado that often comes with that rebellious state. In both instances the outer presentation of self-esteem is false.

As good parents, we do not want either of these options. We prepare our children for successful lives by giving them the essential ingredients of appreciation and acceptance of whatever strengths and weaknesses they possess. This will give them the self-assurance to face the hardships and challenges that will inevitably arise. We love and respect them for themselves and want to help them continue to achieve and go beyond what they thought possible. This is our goal whether we have one child, two children, or fifteen.

Children need to hear the following message: "When we talk to you, it is only about you. Not your sister or your brother, or anyone except you."

Believing this, your children can trust the confidence that you have in them as individuals so that they can become truly distinctive personalities no matter how many children there are in the family. Their self-esteem is not dependent on any kind of comparisons. It has to do only with them, with who they are, and with whatever they have achieved.

Probably the greatest challenge of raising a large family, besides the extraordinary physical toll and the exceptional dedication that is required, is the thought and energy it takes to give whatever is needed to help each child develop self-esteem. This does not mean we need to provide every child with nine different kinds of private lessons. It means we have to clearly let our children know that they are appreciated, and that we are always available to help them to become even better.

Chapter 25

Adapting
to a New Life

In this chapter, we will examine how and why we choose the way we want to live in our present community. All over the world, in Eretz Yisrael, the United States, or Europe, there is a broad variety of religious communities, each with its own flavor, nature, social and religious standards, and sometimes expectations. Some are a mixture, while others are smaller and more religiously homogeneous with economic diversity. After having made serious changes in your life, you may be further challenged with deciding how the steps you have chosen until now are going to affect those that remain to be taken. These decisions will be even more difficult to implement if you made the initial changes when you are older.

Decisions in the Formative Years

Young men and women who turned their lives upside down by becoming religious between the ages of fifteen and twenty-one have usually not yet invested too much in their plans for the future. Subsequent decisions will be less challenging, therefore, as the transition to a yeshiva and religious life at that stage entirely transforms their thought processes, directing thinking toward new commitments. The process of change initiated at this stage thus takes root quite deeply, usually in a structured religious framework. The young person will have had easily accessible direction from *rabbanim* or teachers for guidance through the next level of decisions.

Sometimes, it is more complicated, as there are issues of honoring parents and continuing with a secular education or career, but in general it is less difficult when the *baal teshuvah* is young.

> *Sheila was a student at Neve Yerushalayim. Her rabbi there had promised her parents that she would finish college after two years of uninterrupted studies learning Torah in Yerushalayim. After two years, Rabbi Yosef Shalom Elyashiv was asked if she should keep that promise. Her father had already paid for one year of university and was worried that Sheila would drop out. Rav Elyashiv ruled that she had to go back to college because of the mitzvah of honoring one's parents. This was very difficult for Sheila, as there was not one religious female student for her to befriend for the next two years at the University of Oklahoma.*

While no ruling can be used in all situations, it is clear that making great changes in one's religious devotion can seriously challenge a person's plans and commitments.

Decisions at a Later Stage in Life

Those who have taken the giant leap when they were between the ages of twenty-five and thirty-five or above have already made important decisions regarding lifestyle and present and future goals. They be married or in a long-term relationship. They may already be professionals, have responsible jobs or established businesses, and have bought homes. Those investments may be profoundly affected by the quantum changes with which they are already living. This can cause confusion and doubts. What should they do about what has already been achieved until now? Stay in the same job, remain in the community, and continue in their careers? Enroll in yeshiva or seminary, and attempt to catch up? Take a year off from work? Perhaps the job or career itself challenges an individual's new values; it may be that the place in which a couple lives is not appropriate for bringing up their children as they now wish to raise them.

These new decisions are much weightier because the individuals have already invested so much in their livelihood, relationships, and lifestyle. They have developed mature expectations and formed a picture of what life was going to look like. When a younger person makes crucial, life-changing decisions, it is easier for those decisions to be absorbed later on. The older one is, the more difficult it will be to make major changes.

Decisions: The Process

When values have evolved and ideals have undergone serious intro-spection and change, it is of the utmost necessity to keep a balanced perspective to facilitate healthy growth. It is not uncommon for mature and intelligent people to make impulsive decisions.

Simcha and Judy, both well-integrated baalei teshuvah, had four young children. Simcha worked as a computer programmer, and Judy taught English in the religious girls' high school near their home. They were doing well and enjoying their new lives. Raising their children as observant Jews was exciting. The children were in kindergarten, first, third, and fifth grades. All were happy and doing well until one day, Judy was watching her students interact, listening carefully to their dialogue and becoming increasingly frustrated. Was it for this that she had become observant? These girls presented as superficial, self-centered, and utterly preoccupied with clothing and fashion.

That evening, she told Simcha how she felt, and he, in turn, shared with her his disillusionment with the shul where he davened. The talking during davening, disrespect for the rabbi, and the often-inappropriate intermingling that went on at the Shabbos kiddushim bothered him greatly. Together they reminisced about their years in Israel, the institutions where they'd studied, their spiritual growth, the inspiration they'd felt, and the friendships they'd made. Their first year of marriage had been blissful. Simcha studied in kollel, and Judy, who was due to give birth ten months after the wedding, stayed home and prepared for her firstborn. Money was not an issue, as that first year in Israel they lived off their wedding money. With a child to care for and the wedding money running low, however, they needed livelihood and decided to go back to the States. They both found jobs in their respective professions, but that first year was a beacon of light that gave them fortitude and the aspiration to continue to feel alive and dynamic.

As they discussed the challenges of raising children in what they felt was a dry and sterile environment, they came back time and again to their memories of Eretz Yisrael and the year they had spent there. They went to their local rabbi, with whom they had a very good relationship, and told him about their desire to return. It was clear that he was very nervous about such a move for them, raising questions regarding their children's education, job availability, and their own integration into Israeli society. Simcha heard the rabbi's questions and began having second thoughts, but Judy insisted that they go to a Gadol, a great person, for advice. A friend from the community helped them to obtain an appointment. Fearing that he would pose the question inadequately, Simcha allowed his wife to take the lead.

Judy told the rav of their disappointments, of their aspirations and goals, and how constricted they felt in the States in regard to religion. The rav asked Simcha about his feelings. Simcha answered that he agreed with Judy, but that their rabbi had tried to scare them off, so he was not so sure anymore. The rav asked if they were taking the rabbi's questions seriously.

"Of course, we know it will not be easy," Judy answered, "but we are Jews, and we have bitachon!"

"You have my berachah," said the rav, "but be very careful. Take it slowly and make sure you know what you are doing. I must tell you that many have tried what you want to do, but only some have been successful."

They left perplexed but were afraid to go back for more clarification. After reviewing the conversation again and again, they came to the conclusion that the Gadol had given them a berachah and simply warned them to take it slowly and be careful. Two years later, after extensive research and two exploratory trips, they moved.

Yerushalayim was too expensive, and the job market was not very good at the time, so they went to Ashdod, where Simcha found a job. They decided that Judy would wait six months before seeking work so she could help her children acclimate.

With two of the children now aged ten and twelve, the move proved to be far more challenging than their worst fears. The sad saga took seven years, ending with two children off the path, and debts that would take five more years to repay.

My intention in recounting this story is not to frighten anyone about making important decisions, nor to discourage people from moving to Israel at any point in their lives. I would, however, like to review the decision-making process and point out the inherent problems that were not taken into account.

- Looking back at "better days," says *Koheles*, is not wise.[1] Every day is different, and thinking that *now* can be *then* is ignoring the myriad situational changes in our lives, needs, and emotional states.

- We must ask advice from people who know us well and understand our situation. Their rabbi was the right address, answering their questions honestly and accurately. Going to the Gadol without giving him a very full picture was a way of getting the answer they wanted to hear, but not getting advice suited to them. We go to a Gadol when the information we have does not seem to be enough on which to base a decision, or when our rabbi says he

---

1   *Koheles* 7:10, "Do not say, 'What was in earlier days was better than these days'; it is not from wisdom that you ask yourself this question…"

cannot answer the question as it is too difficult. A Gadol cannot be assumed to have *ruach hakodesh*, Heaven-inspired knowledge; he will only be answering the question that is presented.

- Simcha was afraid to voice his opinion because he did not want to appear to be against the idea of growing religiously. In his mind, moving back to Israel was equated with becoming better. It is necessary to understand, however, that there are very few questions that are religious in nature. Halachah is paramount, and exploring religious implications is crucial, but advice is dependent on where you are at a given time. What represents religious growth for one person can be religious annihilation for another. We cannot divorce growth from our present position; we can only move forward from where we are. By refraining from voicing his fears, and including himself in his wife's comment on *bitachon*, Simcha was overlooking vital and overriding points.

- Ashdod is not Yerushalayim, and looking for a connection to what transpired in the past would have meant putting themselves in a position that was similar to the original one and staying close to those who guided them in those years.

- By moving away from their entire support system and leaving their rabbi of thirteen years behind without having listened to his advice, this couple was sailing their family's ship without a navigator. The many random rabbis to whom they posed diverse questions in Eretz Yisrael did not have enough understanding of their situation to advise them to go back.

We need to be so careful when making important and life-changing decisions to follow all the steps of responsible resolution and seek methods with honest and open self-evaluation.

Disregarding the Opinions of Those Close to You

When your siblings are violently opposed to or resentful of your new lifestyle, it is critical to weigh up reaching out to them versus disregarding their opinions. Siblings are often important figures in our lives. Some are close in age and/or in spirit, and others are twelve to twenty years older or younger. Emotional connection is a greater defining factor than age. The closer we are emotionally to a sibling, the more difficult it is to deal with such opposition.

Often, the amazing thing about the attitude of family members is their assumption that they have the right to determine and control the way in which we should conduct our lives. It is true that we might want the input of those closest to us regarding some of our decisions, as bonds with blood relations are difficult to break. There is no greater love than that which exists among family members, and therefore, there is no greater animosity than that which can be aroused with them. It is not rational but blood-deep, and blood is our lifeline; when our lifelines are connected, everyone has an opinion.

As we mature, we need to learn to separate the emotions involved in family opinions from the sincere concern that comes from respect and appreciation of who we are and what we need. While maintaining the peace in a family is of inestimable importance, the laws of mutual respect precede that. When family becomes vehemently opposed to our decisions without demonstrating the respect necessary to understand our position, we must acknowledge that their emotions and passion are speaking, and not their minds or intelligence. If this is the case, it is time to be assertive. We have the absolute right to demand mutual respect.

When siblings voice concerns that we would rather not consider, however, or when they ask questions to which we cannot reply, it is time to look inside ourselves and find the answers, because people who care about us are voicing genuine concerns that we may have overlooked. It doesn't hurt to look again.

Decisions within Families

In every decision that parents make in which their children are involved, it is their responsibility to take the interests of the young ones into account. Not only because they are essential, which is obvious, but it is possible that the outcome of the decision and its effect on them will totally subsume the parents' own situation if it is not the right thing for the whole family. I have seen parents make colossal mistakes, thinking that their children would benefit if only they were better off financially. One of my students told me how her parents were not happy with the size of their home in Chicago. They felt that the children needed more space and a larger backyard with a higher standard of living. When the father, a physician, was offered a very lucrative position in a wealthy community in Indiana, they jumped at the "opportunity." This was the beginning of many challenges that were not fruitful for my student or her siblings. School was a problem from day one, involving extensive traveling and eventually having to go away from home for high school. Yes, they were very well-off and could afford many perks, but some of her siblings did not survive the challenges and ended up in public school.

> *In 1972, Caspar Weinberger, politician and later US Secretary of Defense, offered my father the position of Director of the US Department of Health, Education, and Welfare in Washington, D.C. The outgoing secretary of that agency, he wanted my father to take his place. It was the kind of once-in-a-lifetime opportunity that most people would grab. My father thought about it for a few days, and then said no. Weinberger was surprised. So was I. When we questioned his decision he said simply, "I looked into the opportunities for you children, and I do not feel that you would have the same chance for as good an education in Washington as you have here."*

That decision not only taught me the value of setting firm priorities in life but also to respect my father's enormous self-sacrifice for the Jewish schooling we received. I know that when he looked at his children and their later accomplishments, he knew he had made the right decision.

Chapter 26

Choosing a Lifestyle

I n Eretz Yisrael it is almost taken for granted that if you are Chareidi and want to raise a Torah-oriented family, a young man will learn in *kollel* for a good few years after marriage. Serving in the armed forces is obligatory, but until recently, *kollel* men were allowed to postpone their service, often indefinitely.[1] If you were not in *kollel*, you had to serve in the armed forces or forfeit obtaining a regular job unless you were approximately twenty-eight years old with two children. This state of affairs influenced the religious community to develop with less diversity than Orthodox communities in other countries.

While there are populations in North America and elsewhere outside of Eretz Yisrael where a young married man is expected to begin his married life studying Torah, there are many who do not regard this as the only way to retain a commitment to keeping the mitzvos. In those communities, a young man who studied in yeshiva for a year or two during or after high school can continue his secular education and go to work.

One's decision to study Torah and keep mitzvos will not be seen as an indication that he will automatically change his educational or professional goals. It might mean that he has to fit those aspirations into a new framework, or make some compromises. The decision to keep the mitzvos is not always accompanied by the decision to take on the

---

1   Current political changes in Eretz Yisrael are reforming the laws of army exemption. At the time of this writing, the changes are still in flux.

high level of devotion to the inspiring and beautiful *kollel* life as the yeshiva world presents it.

Though learning Torah all day is a lofty goal that can dictate a beautiful and special way of living when done properly, not everyone is ready to make that kind of commitment. Someone who grew up with it or who was exposed to it at a younger age finds learning in *kollel* to be a natural progression, the next stage of his process. For an individual who comes to it at a later stage, however, it can be unnatural and sometimes even undesirable.

About thirty-two years ago, I had planned with a group of friends to consult with Rav Elazar Shach.[2] Our goal was to discuss the introduction of a then-groundbreaking organization in Eretz Yisrael to provide job training for *kollel* men when it became necessary for them to support a family. Unfortunately, I fell ill and was not able to participate in the visit, but the following is an accurate synopsis of the dialogue.

The discussion focused on various questions, for example: Is job training for *kollel* men a good thing? For whom and at what age can this be introduced without causing upheaval in the Torah community?

Before Rav Shach gave them his berachah, he shared a little historical background with my friends.

He told them that when the Ponevezher Rav[3] decided to open a *kollel* in Bnei Brak some sixty years earlier for his married students to continue studying, there were almost no yeshivos in Eretz Yisrael—no more than a couple of hundred boys sitting and learning in the whole country. *Kollelim* were even rarer. The Ponevezher Rav, a brilliant visionary, didn't do anything in a small way. To those who scoffed at

---

2   Rav Elazar Menachem Man Shach (1899–2001), Rosh Yeshiva of the Ponevezh Yeshiva and seen by many as the most influential leader of the yeshiva world in Israel for the last twenty years of his life.

3   Rabbi Yosef Shlomo Kahaneman (1888–1969), visionary founder of the Ponevezh Yeshiva in Bnei Brak.

his aspirations he would say, "The difference between my dreams and those of other people is that I dream while I am awake."

He knew what he was dreaming about. He was making very serious decisions for Klal Yisrael and the rebuilding of Torah after the horrific destruction of the European Torah community in World War II. When he wanted to open his *kollel*, the *rosh yeshiva* at the time, Rav Shmuel Rozovsky, said it should only be for those elite, brilliant young men who would be the future leaders of Klal Yisrael.

The Ponevezher Rav demurred. "No, the *kollel* must be open to everyone. We need to make this for the general public."

The discussion between these two Torah giants went back and forth, but the consensus of opinion among the Gedolim at the time supported the position of the Ponevezher Rav. Torah learning had to be reestablished after the terrible destruction of European Jewry. After Yiddishkeit had been uprooted and destroyed in Europe, there remained only several yeshivos in Eretz Yisrael, some in America, and even fewer in various places in Europe.

Rav Shach explained that there had been a time when a religious Jew *knew* that the Torah was his life. "*Ki heim chayeinu v'orech yameinu, u'vahem nehegeh yomam va'lailah*—For they [the words of Torah] are our life and the length of our days, and in them we will toil day and night."[4]

Of course, people went to work and did what was necessary to earn their livelihood, but it was taken for granted that every spare moment was reserved for studying Torah. It was not unusual for working men in Europe to be knowledgeable in the entire Talmud. Young and older children alike knew much more than their counterparts today. Every *rav* in every village in Europe was a monumental *talmid chacham*. There were hundreds of communities in which Jews knew the entire Torah because they all spent much of their time learning. They arose in the morning, learned a little bit before going to work, worked a full day, and went back to the *beis midrash*, study hall, and learned some more. That was life.

---

4   *Siddur, Maariv, Birchos K'rias Shema.*

After the destruction of European Jewry and the further dispersion of Klal Yisrael, the need to rebuild became essential. Yeshiva students were no longer looked up to as the elite of a community. The prestigious students of Mir, for example, often did not marry until they were in their forties and fifties, not for ideological reasons, but because no one wanted to marry a yeshiva man. How would he make a living?

In the Diaspora you had to work. Immigrants in America, the *Goldene Medinah*, where the streets were "paved with gold," were told, "Here, you do not have to keep Shabbos; here, you have to make money. Forget about what you did in Europe."

In Eretz Yisrael, the spirited energy of the Zionist founders lauded the image of the "New Jew," hardworking and secular, tearing down the old image of the studious yeshiva boy. Youths were taught to despise and disdain Torah scholars. There was very little appreciation or understanding of Torah anywhere in the world at that time.

The Ponevezher Rav saw the need to rebuild Torah, and the Gedolim agreed with him. He wanted to make the *talmid chacham* the central figure of Klal Yisrael as he had been before the war, and raise the Gedolei Torah once again as its leaders. The religious community, in order to be rebuilt, would have to have Torah learning as the accepted norm.

From those roots, said Rav Shach, would sprout a renewed version of the Yiddishkeit of old. Some would be able to learn full time and some would have to work, but they would learn as much as they could. There would be no question, however, that Torah is the cornerstone of life. Eventually and naturally, men would leave the yeshiva in order to earn a living.

What was important to remember, he said, was that the basic perception of this new generation of yeshiva students would see Torah as its default understanding, and the underlying stratum of its responsibility would always be Torah, Torah, and Torah.

This, in brief, is the way the *kollel* movement began. When the Ponevezher Rav ruled that *all* yeshiva students after marriage could and should continue to learn Torah in *kollel*, it was a move that changed the structure of Klal Yisrael. *Baruch Hashem*, we see today a rebuilding of the Torah community to the extent that it is unusual *not* to sit and learn in *kollel* for some years after marriage.

This being so, it is now essential for the creation of the spin-off phenomenon of the many new institutions that offer vocational or professional training for *kollel* men so they can support their families. As a result of the surge of Torah learning, however, it is almost a given that they will continue to learn in their spare time.

Torah and Earning a Living

In the course of my work as head of a boys' high school that required professionals to teach varied vocational courses, I found it necessary to send five men, *baalei teshuvah* with professional certification in their respective fields, to seek the advice of Rav Shach to help them decide their direction for the future.

At the time it was very hard to find observant role models to teach the higher levels of vocational studies because most religious people in Eretz Yisrael were *kollel* men, *talmidei chachamim*, or businessmen. The *baal teshuvah* community quickly became the only pool of human resources from which we could draw. We found the people we needed for our school among those who had become religious only after they had achieved expertise in their fields.

As I finally identified a trained individual, I would bring him down to the school and his eyes would light up.

"Oh, this would be so great," he'd say. "I'd love to be a part of it, and the salary would make my life much easier."

A brief pause, and then he would suddenly exclaim, "No, no, no, I can't do it! This is my evil inclination speaking! I have to stay in *kollel*."

At that point, I was sending one individual after another to Rav Shach. He would ask what they were doing, what they had done previously, and what their lives were like at present. Then he'd tell these men, "You should teach. You should work."

"What? And stop learning?" they would ask in shock.

Rav Shach—always honest, always clear, and always focused—told them that he thought that they needed to go to work. Some of those men listened and others did not. These were *baalei teshuvah* who had become *frum* when they were over twenty-five years old and had families and professions. They had left everything and entered *kollel*. Rav Shach advised them to continue learning part of the time, but to work as well. This, he told them, was for their own continued spiritual growth and intellectual development as well as for the good of their families.

I would like to share a *Meshech Chochmah* that I discovered when I was still in yeshiva.[5] I brought it to my *rebbi*, who was very excited about it. Please note that when the *Meshech Chochmah* speaks of a *baal teshuvah*, he is referring to a *frum* person who sinned during his lifetime and came back to mitzvos, not someone who grew up secular and found his way to Hashem, as is the case with most of our present-day returnees. The following is a synopsis in English of what he says.

The verse in *Parashas Ki Savo* states, "Hashem will provide you with an overabundance with all the fruits of your labor..."[6] In *Parashas Nitzavim* the same verse appears without the words, "with all the fruits of your labor."[7] To explain this difference, the *Meshech Chochmah* cites the Gemara that describes the two ways of living.[8]

Rav Shimon bar Yochai says you must learn Torah, and others will come and take care of your sheep, plow, plant, and reap your fields. On the other hand, Rav Yishmael says every man needs to do these things for himself. The Gemara is summarized by Abaye, who says that many followed Rav Yishmael and were successful, and many who followed Rav Shimon Bar Yochai were not.[9] This seems to make it clear that only a great *tzaddik* can learn Torah and be confident that others will take care of his physical well-being.

The *Meshech Chochmah* explains the variance in the verses as follows: It is proper for a total *tzaddik* to do as Rav Shimon bar Yochai says

---

5   *Meshech Chochmah*, "V'hosirecha," *Devarim* 30:9 (Feldheim, 2006), p. 609.
6   *Devarim* 28:11.
7   Ibid., 30:9.
8   *Berachos* 35b.
9   Ibid.

because he can depend on the fact that his needs will be provided by others. It is not healthy, however, for a *baal teshuvah*, one whose life was formerly steeped in transgression, to be totally immersed in spiritual pursuits, as it might result in his regretting his decision (to repent). Hence it is better for him to follow Rav Yishmael by pursuing both Torah and *parnassah*.

Therefore, the verse in *Parashas Ki Savo*, which refers to a time before the sin of the Golden Calf, does not mention the words "with all the fruits of your labor," because the Jewish People were still on a high spiritual level and did not require involvement in the physical world. The verse in *Parashas Nitzavim*, however, refers to a time after the sin of the Golden Calf, and, therefore, includes the words "in all the fruits of your labor."

One who was formerly steeped in transgression and has now done *teshuvah* and wants to live a spiritual life would be more suited for a lifestyle of Torah and working. The transition to full-time Torah learning with no source of reasonable income could later cause regret and dissatisfaction.

Rav Wolbe became excited upon seeing this commentary, saying that this was precisely the advice he had been giving for many years to people who had made substantial changes in their lives when they were adults. Although he knew this was the proper direction, he was pleased to see it in the *Meshech Chochmah*, as he had been looking for a source for a long time.

This does not necessarily apply to young people who became *frum* while they were still very young and less involved in the physical transgressions of established secular life, but to those who already had established secular lives that usually included some involvement in sin and professions or jobs where material achievement played a central role in their lives.

When I was looking for religious teachers for the school I ran from 1979 to 1990 to teach electronics, carpentry, agriculture, and other subjects, I turned to many *baalei teshuvah* who were professionals in those areas. Many of them had decided to go to *kollel* and stop working when they became *frum*. They were enthusiastic about this opportunity but felt guilty about leaving *kollel* life. Rav Shach—I believe, in consonance with the *Meshech Chochmah*—instructed each of them to take the opportunity and to learn only part time.

Most people have certain expectations and hopes as to how their lives will look in the future. Those expectations are often seen as needs. It is not my place to tell people what they do or do not need, as it is the responsibility of intelligent people to perceive this for themselves. Having made the decision to strengthen your religious commitment does not always mean the immediate full transition to acceptance of every value that can and, perhaps, should govern your life. It does not mean that in one fell swoop you begin to live on a totally different standard and level. Trying to do so can not only be challenging, but at times even counterproductive.

A happy home is one in which people live within their comfort level. If you have changed your life and that of your family, and everyone is content to live on a different material standard than the one that you were used to, your comfort level is doing well *if* it is still possible to have a happy atmosphere at home. When making these decisions, you must be absolutely confident that you will be able both to raise your children properly and be at ease with your economic status.

Spending six years of schooling as a lawyer, doctor, or professional of any kind was a long-term commitment, and you certainly pictured a certain standard of living in your future. Now that you are sitting in yeshiva or *kollel* with a much-reduced income, you may see yourself as a failure. Your wife may feel that you are not providing what she perceives as her needs, and these feelings will trickle down to the children.

It is not a question of right or wrong; if that is the way you feel, you will be unhappy and so will your family. Unhappy parents who are feeling negative about themselves cannot give to their children in a full and positive way. Families can become "at risk" if they do not understand that their commitment to do the will of Hashem does not necessarily mean taking on the loftiest spiritual, but most frugal, lifestyle if it is not completely in harmony with who they are.

If life becomes harrowing and depressing, it is neither lofty nor truly a life of Torah, which should be one with potential for growth with joy. For those in this category, it might be best to choose a job (or make changes in the one they have) that will enable them to continue practicing their profession and still have time both to learn and be together with the family.

It is important to acknowledge that we need *simchah* and satisfaction in our lives, in addition to keeping the mitzvos. If you find fulfillment in learning and can inspire your children, live well with your wife, and build a beautiful home life similar to those who inspired you years earlier, that is wonderful. But if you still constantly think back, wondering what you might have achieved had you kept your job, it is time to reconsider some earlier decisions that have resulted in a life too spartan to be happy.

Another aspect of the work versus study question is how it affects maintaining *shalom bayis* in large families. A husband remaining in *kollel* while the wife is taking care of many children at home, while simultaneously carrying the financial burden, can often appear to be an imbalance of responsibility, and as such, a cause of serious hard feelings. Dealing with this appropriately takes some introspection and planning.

Such a situation necessitates an inversion in the roles of husband and wife. There is only so much a woman can be willing to accomplish, and it is linked to what she is capable of doing.

It is not proper to say, "Well, if you aspired to more, you could do more," because a person's aspirations have to come from within. We cannot make someone else's goals into ours. We can try to help someone else be more appreciative of a certain objective by teaching them its value, and perhaps their desire to grow in that respect will increase.

If a woman takes on the task of being the mother of a large or growing family while her husband is studying or going out to work, it must be a joint decision. Leaving *kollel* out of the equation for a minute, we can, perhaps, understand the issue. Before a man works in any business that requires dedication of time and resources, it is necessary to define an arrangement between husband and wife.

Two people have committed themselves to raising and taking care of their family. What is of value to them? What is each willing to give, capable of giving, and what are the boundaries? How much of a burden is each of them prepared to carry to supply the family's needs?

There is no imbalance if it is understood that the couple decides *together* what kind of life they are going to live and how they are going to implement it. Sometimes, of course, they do not have the luxury of making this decision, but even then, they need to accept that they are in it together. They must decide as one how they are going to deal with their situation and clarify their choices. A family unit is built of a husband and a wife working jointly to make decisions and deciding together on the *chinuch* of their children.

Mutual Concern

A couple grappling with the challenge of maintaining and raising a family, with all the responsibilities entailed, must consider how the load can best be shared. The mechanics of this include the husband recognizing his wife's responsibilities and how much she is doing, appreciating her efforts, and showing his gratitude. The wife must understand the pressures involved in her husband's life, whether in the *kollel* or at work, and acknowledge his commitment and the difficulties he may be encountering.

When couples debate who had the harder day, you know their *shalom bayis* is not being well maintained. When there is competition over who is more tired, or who has the greater challenge, it is obvious that there is already something wrong in their connection.

A good wife should worry about her husband assuming too great a burden. A good husband ought to be concerned about his wife wearing herself to a frazzle. They will help one another as much as possible, as a shared load is a lighter burden. When one of the two is unusually exhausted, the other one takes on a little bit more to help out until the crisis passes.

The Gemara tells of a time when people were so poor that "six students had to share one blanket."[10]

"When it is cold, one person can hardly keep warm with one blanket, how could six people possibly do so?"[11] asks Rav Chaim Shmuelevitz. He answers that when each individual is concerned for himself, one blanket is not enough. When each is concerned for the others, worried about the warmth of his friends, then the blanket will be sufficient.

Coping with challenges is a mindset. Parents who have made the decision to have a family, and are indeed blessed with one, must adopt an attitude of "we are in this together." If not, the burden will be too heavy to bear. A couple who live their lives with each looking out for the other will always manage to carry the burden.

Some Practical Hints

Life can be difficult. Husband and wife may both be tired and not know how they are going to cope. Some people verbalize their pain while others do not. *Shalom bayis* issues very often arise when one or both partners do not know how to express the fact that they need the spouse's help. Arguing over our spouse's input or lack of it is rarely successful, as the one who feels attacked becomes defensive.

"Why don't you realize what a hard day *I've* had? Give me a break. Why can't you…?" or, "I don't understand. How could you *not* notice that I am totally…so why can't you…?" are antagonistic approaches that will not work.

Husbands and wives can learn how to speak to each other in more effective ways.

---

10   *Sanhedrin* 20a.

11   *Sichos Mussar* (1980), p. 23. Rav Chaim Shmuelevitz (1902–1979) was a disciple of Rav Yerucham Levovitz, the legendary *mashgiach* of the Mir Yeshiva in Belarus. After the yeshiva was reestablished in Eretz Yisrael in 1948, he became Rosh Yeshiva, guiding the yeshiva until his passing.

First of all, inquire about your spouse's day. If it has not been very difficult, explain what you happen to be experiencing, without making demands. Good communication is an indispensable necessity for achieving *shalom bayis*, and all the more so when each spouse is carrying a big load.

If the husband can be involved in learning, and his wife supports this decision, they are a blessed and fortunate couple. Together they have the opportunity to build a family in the best Torah environment possible.

However, should the wife reach a point where she feels that there are just too many demands on her, and she can no longer cope, something has to change. Although she may respect her husband's desire to continue learning full time, she cannot continue functioning in the same way as before and needs assistance. This problem can be solved either by the husband taking on more responsibilities at home, or increasing his income to take on additional help so she can function. A man's responsibility is foremost to his wife and to *shalom bayis* in his home. This entails both husband and wife knowing their limits in terms of their commitments. If you cannot meet these obligations together, then you are not doing it at all.

A home cannot be considered based on Torah if there is no peace and tranquility. Attempting to build a home on the foundations of Torah knowledge and the stringent observance of mitzvos when discord, fighting, and disrespect reign is self-defeating and does not work. Such a home does not offer children the environment we so dearly wish to create. We are studying Torah all day in order to give our family a more elevated and spiritual life, but what are its members actually experiencing?

If they see that dedication to learning brings unpleasantness, they lose respect for us, for Torah, and, most frighteningly, for Hashem as well. We will not achieve what we wanted with all our hearts to accomplish. Learning in *kollel* is an awesome responsibility because it has the potential to show our children the beauty and love that can result from that kind of life. If what results is not a positive, healthy, happy existence, then they are receiving the absolute opposite of the message we wish to convey, resulting in a situation fraught with danger.

Rav Shach advised many, many *kollel* men **individually** to begin to work part time because he knew that otherwise their families would be lacking the necessities of life. Not many people can be perfectly content living below their comfort level. Barely making ends meet may be especially difficult for those who were brought up in a world of plenty and comfort before making quantum changes in their lives.

It is not embarrassing to acknowledge your responsibility to provide for your family. Besides your interest in maintaining a high level of commitment to Torah learning, you are aware that it is also your responsibility as parents to provide for your family. Making the decision of how much income you need and at what point it may have to be increased is a personal decision that every couple must make.

What are your goals for your children, and what would you like to provide for them? They will need help to get married, and if you are living in the Torah community you will be expected to help them get settled after the wedding as well.

Do not fool yourself about your position in the community. Let's face it: you are not the *rav* or *rosh yeshiva* whose children are considered desirable catches for *shidduchim* regardless of income because of your status. Your ability to support your children through yeshiva day schools, high schools, yeshivos, and seminaries will affect your standing among your peers.

If you are hardly making it in the *beis midrash*, you question yourself every few days as to why things are so hard, and your wife and family are kvetching about their unsatisfied needs, then you need to recognize that this is not the way to raise a well-adjusted, happy Jewish family.

I have seen many people who could be successful and happy but are trying to live someone else's ideals of greatness. Do not be a *nebach*! Do not sit in the *beis midrash* wishing you could be productive. Be a builder, a doer! If you are capable of being a productive, happy, reliable person, but find yourself becoming needy, unsuccessful, and unhappy, you are not fulfilling the aspirations of Judaism. Do what you must to find your place in the community. Join the builders, and your home will not know sadness, depression, or feelings of dependence.

At the time that you feel the necessity to work in order to take care of your family, you cannot look at the people around you and assume that their level of *bitachon* is greater than yours. You have to believe that yours is just as high. Real *bitachon*, as discussed in chapter 22, means that you know you have responsibilities and are confident Hashem will show you the way to fulfill them. You will use the resources of your community and be an active and contributing member within it. You chose a neighborhood in which you could be comfortable while being challenged to grow, but that does not include trying to live up to other people's expectations. You can be a contributing member of your community, at peace with who you are there, while making sure that your family's needs will continue to be satisfied.

Couples often come to live in Eretz Yisrael because it is a place of unequaled opportunities in spiritual growth, yet not everyone's expectations can be met there. The communities in the Holy Land make certain demands of their residents, and you have to know whether or not you can live up to their standards. Differences in lifestyle must be addressed. Couples have to be honest, anticipating whether they are going to be misfits or fit in. *Parnassah* has to be recognized as a real necessity and consideration.

Similar situations have also occurred in New York and New Jersey communities in the last twenty-five years. Young religious people wanted to live in an inspiring learning environment, and they came from all over. The men, and sometimes the women, now travel from Lakewood two or more hours every day to and from their jobs in New York; they've changed their lives in order to bring their children up in what they considered to be the best surroundings.

Now they have "better" schools for their children and a stronger community. They have little or no time, however, to parent their children in a society that will judge and expect certain things from them. They cannot give them what they need to receive the most from their parents: time, love, and self-esteem.

The Job Market

The workplace itself has many challenges, from availability to retaining the values of our lives in contrary environments. For someone who is keeping Shabbos, Yom Tov, and halachah, finding a job can be more difficult than for others even though it is somewhat easier than it was forty or fifty years ago.

My grandfather, *zt"l*, came to America in the 1930s and worked at a different job from Monday to Friday every week. On Friday, he would come to work and say that he had to leave early because of Shabbos. The employers would say, "If you leave early today, don't come back." On Monday, he would have to search for a new job. He was a professional baker yet suffered the indignity of being fired weekly. Although physically weak, he finally secured a five-day-a-week job working with the New York City street-repair crews.

My father-in-law came to Eretz Yisrael in the early 1960s and found a similar challenge. Here was a man who had been the principal of a school in his native country, yet in Eretz Yisrael, he was not able to find a job because he was not willing to work on Shabbos. He was forced to do physical labor for months until a relative found him a government job. Although this job was somewhat easier, he went from being an educator to a menial laborer in order to keep Shabbos.

Today, in most countries where *frum* Jews live, the laws are more accommodating. For the most part, people today respect individuals who adhere to their values, but there are still many companies that, without saying it outright, will not hire those who are *shomer Shabbos*.

Another challenging aspect of the job market has to do with a person's commitment to his or her family. In most cases, a commitment to Yiddishkeit means that your family comes first. This often forces a change in profession for one growing in observance and values, as the demands of the workplace often require religiously committed people to make adjustments in their goals and at times even in lifestyle. This is especially true for those who were already working in a particular field or held a certain position before raising their levels of observance.

Religious commitment also demands adjustments in terms of the way we conduct ourselves with coworkers. New questions will arise in connection with our professions, and some jobs will even be challenged because they bring us into contact with prohibitions we do not want to transgress.

> *A friend in the discount food industry thought he had made a great deal when he bought a sizable closeout of a major brand-name dog food. He was very excited, as he had purchased half a million dollars' worth of the stuff at ten cents to the dollar. He paid the entire amount in cash, some of which he had to borrow, thinking it was an excellent opportunity. He already had connections at some large food stores and could pass this great sale price directly onward.*
>
> *What he did not know until after the deal had been finalized was that this brand, as is most dog food, was basar b'chalav, meat and milk that are cooked together, an item in the category of asur b'hanaah, from which a person is not allowed to derive any personal pleasure or gain. This man, who carefully observes halachah, asked his rabbi what he was required to do, and did it—choosing not only to forfeit all his profit on the deal, but losing his entire investment.*

That is just one little story. Imagine someone who built up a business and is the owner of a major food company. He has become observant and finds that he has this problem with many of his products. Then there is the owner of a large firm that derives most of its profit on Shabbos. He has begun keeping the mitzvos and suddenly finds that there is a question as to whether or not he is allowed to continue owning the firm.

Maintaining Standards

There are hundreds of stories of people who had close relationships with others that cannot continue, as their associations now have to be viewed through the lens of halachah. Men and women in the workplace have to review their relationships: no more touching or handshakes, and no more just hanging out together. Interactions that were formerly comfortable have suddenly become awkward. It takes thought and consideration to implement changes in relationships, as well as good humor and some self-deprecation to back out of sticky situations. Take the blame, smile at yourself, and continue to be very nice to everyone around you.

Become more focused on and more involved with other things in your personal life so that there is less time for the things that used to be part of your routine.

As a man who traveled the world for humanitarian causes, my father had dozens of stories regarding his many escapades to save and assist Jews in various parts of the world. He found that almost everywhere he went, people respected the fact that he kept to a set of laws and did not lower his standards when it was inconvenient. He had some very moving and often funny stories. He taught us that when you don't violate halachah, choosing to be hungry rather than eating something that is not kosher, the world at large generally respects you.

If you are employed by a business known to be antisemitic, you have to question if you really want to work in that kind of environment.

Twelve years ago I had a student who went to work for an advertising company that fired her because she wanted to leave early on Fridays. She took them to court. I believe it was the Agudath Israel of America that backed her fight. The company was forced to rehire her. She has worked there for many years since, and they are very happy with her. She has a great personality and is a successful person, but she had to fight for her rights.

The challenging part of the workplace is its general immorality. I go to business meetings with a friend every once in a while to help support my family. I have found a way to avoid shaking hands with women at those meetings. This may seem rather uncouth, but I find that a hearty sneeze into my palm as I enter the room works every time. No one wants to shake my hand after that!

A preferred safety tactic I use is to carry things with me. I keep many things in my hands during all the formal introductions, and then I remember to sit down and rest everything on the table. I suppose some people think that I'm a little absent-minded, but it solves the problem of avoiding physical contact with women and, *baruch Hashem*, I have been able to retain my standards. I often end up not being able to shake the men's hands as well. I don't wish to sound overconfident, but as far as I know, no one has ever said they can't do business with us because we haven't yet shaken their hands. In any case, I usually pick up all my odds and ends again as we are leaving and hold them while everyone is saying goodbye.

I don't really know what they think of me, but after one meeting, a woman walked us out to the car. As we were speaking, I mistakenly placed everything I had in my hands into the trunk. Then, right before the lady left, she put out her hand to be shaken. I was trapped.

"I am sorry," I said to her, "but I travel a lot, and I made a promise to my wife: I will never touch another woman besides her."

The woman looked as if she was going to faint. The next time I came to a meeting she was attending, I heard her say to her friends, "Oh, oh, wait—do you see this guy? Well, he and his wife...and he really keeps to it!"

All the women there were green with envy.

I am not a *posek*, and therefore, I am not telling you whether or not you may shake hands with the opposite gender; I am simply sharing my limited, but with great thanks to Hashem, successful experience.

I do not think that we need to always describe or explain our religious values to people who do not and cannot understand. It is, in my opinion, advisable to avoid getting into philosophical discussions about religion. The shorter and the less complicated such conversations, the better.

At the end of the day, people who retain their standards are of the opinion that you can do so in any way that is comfortable for you. Most people are not offended if you keep to what you believe, and they will even respect you as long as you are not being judgmental of *them* in any way. I try to avoid the need for explanations by avoiding the situation technically, but if necessary, I would minimally clarify the situation.

Every person has to ask his *rav* about the job environments in which he is allowed to work. There are actually many dangerous and problematic situations out there in the workplace, challenges you may have to overcome, and some things you must avoid at all costs.

You need first and foremost to know yourself in addition to knowing halachah. At times, something is allowed, but you know it would be best for you not to do it. Sometimes, halachah does not allow a certain thing, and although you think that you can do it without repercussions, you choose not to do it anyway because you know that it is best to keep to the laws.

> *Miriam had a job in a small software development company. The office was on the seventh floor of a building with doors that locked automatically. On Tuesdays, she was alone with a male colleague for about three hours. Her rav said that leaving the door open slightly would be sufficient, but her boss was a real stickler for security and refused to allow it. Miriam had to find another job; the prohibition of yichud[12] could not be resolved in that particular situation.*

These decisions are not something that can be discussed in a general way, but it is clear that people need to know who they are, what they want to accomplish, and what they are allowed and not allowed to do regarding employment. It is of utmost urgency, therefore, to have access to your *rav*.

Career versus Livelihood

Torah life trains us to be family oriented; we are a people who have purpose and meaning in every single part of our lives. The society in which we live has trained us to have a career rather than Torah as

---

12   *Shulchan Aruch, Even Ha'ezer* 24:1

our main focus, and we may therefore need to rearrange our priorities. A career should be seen as just a livelihood. The way I support myself becomes a necessity to provide for my family, as that is my responsibility.

This changes the perspective with regard to our work. A career is a self-fulfilling project, but a livelihood is a responsibility-fulfilling project, and that definition changes our imperative to achieve and to move ahead for its own sake. For us, the idea of advancement is to get a raise in order to support our family and pay for things like tuition. There is clearly a difference in perspective here.

Whatever the impetus for getting that raise, we in the Torah world view our responsibility to the workplace as a secondary responsibility. This relates to how much of a commitment we should make to our job. In any case, we should attempt to turn every job into serving Hashem. By doing everything with integrity, according to halachah, we can make a *kiddush Hashem* every day at work or in business.

> *I have a cousin who is a very special talmid chacham, who spends many hours a day learning Torah. I admire him for his ability to keep his priorities intact, even though he was tempted to do otherwise. He became an actuary while he was in yeshiva, without ever having attended actuarial school. Not too many people could achieve that, and his capabilities showed up in his workplace as well. He reached level two or three and was working for one of the larger insurance companies in the United States. A brilliant man, he did his job and still kept up with his learning. The company kept on pushing him, though. "You have to go to level four," and he did. "Now, we need you to go to level five."*
>
> *At some point, he felt that the demands of his job were going to compromise his commitment to his family and learning. He made a career change, going into computer work instead. The company kept him on, but he did not get the serious increases he would have received had he continued to advance. These*

are my priorities, he felt. I only need this amount of money to live; I don't need more than that.

This decision showed that he is working for a purpose; he is working to live and not living to work.

Definitely, a concept worth considering.

Chapter 27

Repairing
the Broken Chain

U nlike any other race or belief system, Judaism has an unbroken chain of *mesorah*, the transmission of our heritage. It is a seamless continuity of integrity, honesty, and intellectual inquisitiveness, revealed to us at Sinai and transmitted from one generation to the next. We know the names of every single person on that chain. We know where and how they lived, what they did, whom they married, and what they wrote and said.

No other group in the world can claim that a cataclysmic event occurred in the presence of three million people and that they know precisely what was said there because they heard it from their fathers, who heard it from their fathers, all the way back to Har Sinai. Within this transmission lies the tremendous force of the truth of the Torah. The *mesorah*, unique in history, is the power that enables us to make such an extraordinary claim.

We who have studied in yeshivos and seminaries have learned of the clear impossibility of a community remembering the details surrounding an event of that magnitude for such an extended period of time if that event were false. Our *mesorah* is a powerful truth that we received with absolute confidence and give over with that same conviction to our children.

What happens, however, when the chain has been broken, and your parents are not part of that *mesorah*? Does that mean that you too can no longer be a part of it?

"Just be careful and take exceeding care of yourself lest you remove from your heart at any point in your life *the day you stood before Hashem at Chorev* [Sinai]."[1] That day, when we all, three million strong, heard the voice of Hashem speaking from the fire on the mountain, is when we first became a nation.

The *Ramban*[2] makes a very powerful statement about this.

> "*[A]t Har Sinai*" *(Shemos 19:9)—[Hashem says to Moshe Rabbeinu,] "In you, as well, they shall have faith forever," for when...we transmit the true replica of that event to our children, they will know that the event is true without doubt, as if all generations had seen it, for we do not bear false testimony to our children nor bequeath to them nonsense...and they will not at all doubt our testimony that we relay to them, but they will have absolute faith that all of us had seen it with our eyes, as well as all that we have related to them.*[3]

And this is precisely where the answer to our question lies.

Even if your great-grandparents dropped the chain, you can pick it up and give it intact to your children. Quite clearly, however, you have to find a teacher, a *rebbi*, or a mentor whose integrity you do not question who is a part of this chain, whose own life is such that what he says can be depended upon without one iota of doubt. It may take time to find the right person or persons, but it will be a worthy investment. Learn from them, implementing their teachings in your home with complete and total confidence so that you can then pass them on to your children.

---

1   *Devarim* 4:10.
2   Rabbi Moshe ben Nachman (1192–1270), commonly known as Nachmanides or *Ramban*, was the foremost halachic and Kabbalistic authority of his time and a prolific writer in all areas of Torah, best known for his commentary on the Chumash and *Rashi*.
3   *Ramban* on *Devarim* 4:9.

You must have confidence in what you are doing. Sometimes, having made major changes, you are not sure of yourselves and want to take a little bit from here and a little bit from there, just to be certain about what to do. You'll ask what one person has to say about this, what this neighbor feels about that, and what a teacher mandates about something else, hoping to patch it all together and know that what you're doing is right. Eventually your children will begin to feel a lack of consistency in what you're doing, that there's nothing they can depend on, and they are not really sure that what Mom and Dad are teaching them is really the truth.

When someone can say, "This is what my father, my grandfather, my great-grandfather, and my great-great-grandfather did through all the generations," you are offering a clear tradition. Lacking that, you must have a firm and consistent alternative, a clear direction to give to your children so that they can feel part of a concrete and integral system.

"This is the way we do it."

Many *baalei teshuvah* have found out about a distant forefather or relative who was a rabbi or scholar. Share that with your children! Let them know they are part of something bigger than you and them together.

If you cannot say "It is this way," because of my father, grandfather and prior generations, the answer will need to be "because we have a rabbi to trust and follow." That rabbi is your link in the *mesorah*.

What is the relationship of this rabbi to your family? He is a vital part of your lives. You respect and trust him because his integrity is unquestioned. What he says has the same veracity as if you had seen it yourself. You know the way he lives his life, what he does, what he says, and that he always thinks before he speaks.

Children need to know that there is something called "halachah," the laws by which their parents live. "Our family has a *rav*, and we listen to him when he tells us what the law says."

Although you may be searching for personal growth and continuing development, which is fine, your children need the clarity of feeling part of something larger than themselves in which they can have confidence. They do not want to be different, nor do they want their parents to be seen as such. If you are unique as an individual for being successful, special, or a parent whom others respect, they can be OK with it. If they view a parent as different in terms of being confused or lacking direction and confidence, however, they will feel extremely insecure.

Insecurity can gnaw at them until they are distinctly uncomfortable, at which point they may conclude that they don't want to be a part of this way of life.

Mesorah will give them that confidence and comfort.

There is also something called *"minhag,"* custom, which also imparts security to children. When two or three generations of a family have not kept the halachah, family customs are lost. A family can originate in one part of the world and end up living in a place where customs are totally different. Those who do not have customs handed down from generations past are permitted to take on the *minhagim* of the community in which they live.

Familiarize yourself either with your own customs or those of the community that you are going to adopt. When a child asks, "What do we do?" you can answer with confidence, sure that the way you daven, dress, shake the lulav, and wear a tallis is because you are a part of something great.

Now, let us return to the *Ramban's* important statement about passing on tradition. Children have to be confident of their father's integrity before they can accept what is being passed on. They have to know that he is not going to sell them a counterfeit bill of goods; that he will give over only what is honest and true.

Parents can develop that confidence from their children by relying on a *rav* or a *rebbi*, and knowing without a doubt that this is the way we live our lives. Parents should not come across to the child as lacking in direction and knowledge by fishing around for *minhagim*. Searching for nice customs in different communities may work for parents. It does not work for children, who want and deserve the confidence of a *mesorah*.

Schools and Responsibility

"*V'shinantam le'vanecha*—And you shall teach it [the words of Torah] to your sons."[4] It is a father's responsibility to teach his children Torah. Since we cannot do all that is required on our own, we have schools to complete the job.

Schools are our agents, one of the means through which we give our children the *mesorah* they so desperately need. We ask the *rebbeim* and the teachers to be our messengers to teach our children the Torah we have the responsibility to transmit.

We cannot rely entirely on the schools, however. They have to deal with many children at once and cannot be held responsible for every single thing that goes on in their purview. We would not even want them to teach our children everything, as we want to make sure the values that are important to *us* are transmitted to our children the way we see fit.

Those who sit back and say, "Oh, I'm sending my child to a good *cheder*, so I did my job. I don't have to worry about anything," are seriously in error. Parents have to worry about many things above and beyond the quality of the instruction and the supervision of the school.

A classroom contains children from different homes and backgrounds, many of whom have various problems, and some teachers are good, while others are weak. Schools should be seen as the biggest berachah in the world for those who lack the necessary tools to learn Torah with their children, and indeed, they help with what we cannot do alone. Nevertheless, we have to remember that our children, even when in school, are still *our* responsibility.

You have to know what is going on in the classroom: whether your children are doing well or not, whether help is needed, if they are getting on with friends and classmates. Since the ultimate responsibility for your child is in your hands, a school must be chosen that fits your lifestyle. Choosing the wrong place is one of the most common mistakes parents make.

---

4   *Devarim* 6:7, in the *Shema*.

Very often, parents who come from the weakest backgrounds send their children to the strongest schools, regardless of their own lifestyle or the children's inclinations. They want their children to grow up with everything they never had. If they send their children to a school where the language of instruction is Yiddish when they do not speak that language, they will be unable to help with homework, and will not even know whether or not the subject matter being taught is understood. The lifestyle of the other children in that school may not really fit in with theirs. Since they cannot speak the language, they cannot communicate effectively with the *rebbeim* or principal.

Schools must be chosen not on the basis of "My child will have the education that I never received," but "My child will absorb ideals that I know are true and I can back them up."

There is an interesting phenomenon facing many newly established schools in the United States. Many cities had just one religious Jewish school for a long time. As the communities grew and more teachers came to town, *kollelim* opened and a perceived need for *chadarim*, more religious schools, resulted. Most of the newly observant parents in those communities seem to prefer to send their children to these *cheder*-schools rather than the community school.

After speaking both to principals and parents in these communities, I have seen that the preponderant reasoning is, "I want the 'best' religious education for my child." Although there are exceptions, it is rare that the smaller, often poorly funded, and almost always less-experienced school, is really better. The new institutions will welcome every student who applies, and although many of the children do well, some become confused by the increased diversity of the families represented.

Once their children are enrolled in the *cheder*, the rules and ideals may seem extreme to *baalei teshuvah* parents, certainly more so than those of the community school. They are not coming from the same place as that of their children's friends, and some students are confused by the new, stricter standards that are being set for them.

Often parents who are highly educated professionals themselves do not understand that their children need to be in an accepting environment. They send their children to schools that espouse totally different practices than theirs. Here's a case in point: Some schools teach that the perfect example of an ignoble person is a doctor. "The best doctors go to Gehinnom,"[5] they will quote *out of context*. What will the doctor, who sends his child to that school because he wants the best Jewish education, say when the child comes home and asks, "Dad, do you know where you are going?"

Yes, Chazal say those words, but they need to be understood in context. There are schools teaching that those who study in a secular environment to become professionals are headed to a warm place down below. We have to be aware of that possibility. Mothers who send their children to a school where they are taught that certain types of dress are absolutely prohibited are just looking for trouble when those are exactly the styles worn in the home. Other schools teach that college studies are totally unacceptable, yet the parents either have degrees or are studying for them. What is the child to think?

Parents have to come to terms with the kind of life they are leading and with the standards they bring into their home. They must send their children to a school whose teachings are in consonance with theirs.

If you decide that you want to send your children to a school with the highest spiritual values, you have to be committed to growing along with them. When you decided to be a religious Jew, you did so with a certain excitement, and you intended to pass on that feeling to your children. Since you want them to be happy with the way you are living, you have to send them to a school that will be pleased with you as well.

There are schools where everything is black and white, and there are others with a bit more gray in their approach. There are also schools that are very happy to have people from all walks of life, where you and your children can be comfortable.

"Yes," you will say, "but the children will be exposed to many different things."

---

5   *Kiddushin* 82a.

I am going to tell you a secret. The first priority for your children is that they be well-adjusted and happy, with healthy self-esteem and a home that teaches *emes*. This is more important, obviously within reasonable bounds, than who their fellow students are or to whom they are going to be exposed.

> *A student of mine, who had attended the special high school mentioned earlier, recently came to see me. He is an upstanding, sincere young man who never found his place in a regular yeshiva with the requisite heavy learning curriculum but was highly successful in the work/study program we offered him. He went to work at a young age and married a very personable girl who hadn't found her place in the system either. When they first sent their children to a religious day school, they sent them to an average Talmud Torah.*
>
> *This average Talmud Torah, however, decided two years ago that it was going to become a school for the "elite" of the community it is serving. The teachers became nervous every time his wife walked into the school, as she did not dress in the same way as the other women in the community. She was not meant to be a parent in a school where the rebbeim would look down on her as someone very much less than the other mothers.*
>
> *Being somewhat of a surrogate father to this former student, I invited myself to a meeting with the parents and principal. Their child had been sent home because he'd been fighting. After speaking to the principal, the rebbi, my talmid, and then to the child himself, I finally understood what had happened. Although other kids also fight, the consensus of the administration was that "this family does not belong in our school anyway, so..."*
>
> *There was no trust between the school and the family. If there is no trust, there can be no dialogue. The staff wondered why the parents wanted their children to attend this school in the*

first place. If there is no dialogue and a child makes trouble, they send him home and don't want him back.

Prior to the meeting in the school, I invited my talmid and his wife to my office and had a difficult heart-to-heart talk with them.

"The school where I originally sent my son was not the place that they are now presenting," said my talmid. "I don't wear the prescribed white shirt, I work all day, and I know that this does not fit the school's present image. What am I supposed to do if the school has suddenly changed?"

"You have a choice," I answered. "Either be willing to change and 'upgrade' your outlook along with that of the school, or remove your child, because if you do not, he is going to be at odds with the other students, his teachers, and the principal. They are going to regard him as an outcast and a misfit. As long as he is doing well, nobody will say anything, but the minute he gets into trouble, you will have no standing with them because they think you don't belong."

Then I addressed his wife candidly. "You must get your act together. The way you dress makes you look like an eighteen-year-old rebel. I know how much you want your children to be filled with a love for Torah. You put so much into protecting them from the ravages of the street and other bad influences. From your questions, I also know that you want your son to grow in Torah and mitzvos on a very high standard. You, therefore, have to make a decision. If you want all this and you want to send him to that school, you are just going to have to conform."

"I will try," she said halfheartedly.

I looked at her skeptically.

"What am I going to do? Dress up? Make believe?" she asked.

"Out of respect, you could do that," I replied, "at least when you go to the school."

"But I am not a faker," she said.

"You are misrepresenting yourself," I said. "By dressing this way, you are making a statement that says you are someone you are not. You are a faker now because you allow everyone to think less of you. You really do want this kind of chinuch, and therefore, you do want this kind of school for your children. Let's just put everything in sync."

At the meeting the next day, she tried very hard, and was almost completely successful in presenting herself appropriately. My presence gave them a chance to have a lengthy discussion about chinuch, and the administration heard what was really important to the parents. They were pleasantly surprised to hear how this couple's home is run. Baruch Hashem, their child went back to school, and I can say now years later that they were highly successful.

If we create a happy home that is in harmony with what the school teaches, even though some of the children seem as if they come from families that do not share your adherence to the Torah to the same degree, your children can do well. They will have to choose their friends, but that will be necessary anywhere. It is wonderful if you choose the "better school," even if it may challenge your children to surpass you in the spiritual sense, but not if the school is going to consider you persona non grata.

There is another facet of this issue that needs to be considered when we send our children to the wrong schools. Almost inevitably, there will be conflict between what they are learning there and what they see at home. The children will be very uncomfortable around their classmates. They will not feel that they can discuss things that go on in their home, nor will they understand when their friends speak about unfamiliar topics. Children need to be in their own element. If they themselves demand a school environment whose spiritual level is higher than ours at the moment, and we are willing to let them grow beyond us, this should be our hope and our dream, and we can send them to whatever schools they choose.

"Yeshivish"

Please forgive this seeming digression, but there is a major social, anthropological development in the Torah society that needs to be addressed. The turn of this century has seen a technological revolution that is no less earth-shattering and significant than the industrial revolution. The spread of the internet and then smartphone technology has transformed the world we live in. The Torah world has always looked for ways to protect our homes and children from the great challenges of the "outside world."

The following is not a judgment but an observation. What began as an attempt to insulate the home became a full-fledged war on technology. That "insulation" developed into "separatism." We will not be part of a society that does not protect their children. Schools opened and communities consolidated. Shuls did the same and there is almost a line that has been drawn where the "Yeshivish" community wants to be isolated from the general population. As standards were created regarding dress codes and language, expectations with demands of fulfillment became necessary.

While not too many years ago—maybe even when you began your journey—this separatism had not yet taken place, today it is becoming a stronger and stronger movement, possibly forcing people to align with a community based on this delineation.

School Location

A common difficulty regarding choosing a school is its location. The most common reason to send a child outside the neighborhood would be that we require a school that shares the particular values we treasure. Is convenience an acceptable value? I believe that this is something we should not discount out of hand. A neighborhood school has accessibility, both for us and for our child. There is also an advantage to having the child's school friends live nearby. An exception would be if a child has needs that cannot be met in the local school.

Children need friends. As they grow older, they need them for studying as well as spending time in healthful recreation. Boys and girls alike need study partners for homework and reviewing for tests. Girls often have group activities to attend on Shabbos, Rosh Chodesh, and after school. Children who learn in the community in which they live have greater access to all school functions as well as the social life centered on the school, both important factors in helping them feel comfortable in their daily environment. Convenience is, therefore, not just a matter of physical proximity.

Another valuable aspect of balancing the choice of a school in the community against one at a distance is transportation. It is interesting to note that the *Shulchan Aruch* says, "One may send his child to a better teacher or school outside the community on the condition that the child will not have to encounter a dangerous situation."[6]

Just in terms of safety and avoiding danger, the child should not have to "cross over a river," i.e., a major intersection, to reach school. Thus the halachah rules here that if a child is placed in danger in order to get to the school, it is better to send him to one that is closer to home.

Today, unfortunately, we must be aware of dangers other than traffic. Sending children out of our community very often involves carpooling with people we do not know very well. Do we know what sort of conversation they might be hearing in the car? What are they absorbing during the rides there and back? Who is at the wheel, and who else is in the car? If they use a bus, we have to know the safety record of the driver and the security precautions in effect during traveling. I am not saying that we cannot allow our children to use some form of transportation, just that we have to be very careful.

If we send our children on a 45-minute or hour trek every day, we need to know that they are safe. We want a better school environment,

---

6   *Yoreh Deah* 245:19.

but what about getting there and back? How many parents ever rode in the carpool car or on the bus even once to see what it is like? I think that when we make a decision to send a child out of our community—and there *are* values for which we are justified in doing that—we need to do some serious research first.

It is also necessary to consider accessibility to friends for homework and projects, limited leisure time at home, and the effect of traveling on alertness in the classroom.

Dealing with School Admission

Many of us have gone through those self-righteous moments of thinking, *Well, if they don't want me, I don't want them either*, when we've been dealt a harsh blow by the person or committee responsible for admissions. This reaction is not always the most sensible one.

Swallow your pride and evaluate. Sometimes, they don't want you because they think that your being a *baal teshuvah* means X, Y, and Z. This is of course a reflexive response, and most often does *not* mean X, Y, and Z. We know that once your children are accepted into the school, everyone will see that they have nothing at all to do with any of those Xs, Ys, and Zs. They will see that your children fit in perfectly, are well-adjusted, loved, and successful, but they have to be accepted for that to happen. If you have a way of doing that, fine, but you must be confident that you are not sending your children to a school in which they are going to be the oddballs.

The need to address the following possibility disturbs me greatly, despite its rare and limited manifestation. Ignoring the issue, however, would be a gross omission of important realities in some communities.

If your children are indeed not accepted on the grounds that they come from a different background, you may or may not have recourse to a few possibilities. Who in the community can vouch for your mainstream approach to education? Which of the teachers or *rabbanim* who know you would be willing to put in a good word? Is there a way that you can contribute to the school in such a manner that they will feel your presence is a blessing?

I am embarrassed to say that there are even some school entrance questionnaires or applications that are slanted so the information requested can and will be used against you. "Do you have a computer with internet?" "Where did you go to yeshiva?" "What are the grandparents' names?"

Ask your rabbi if you need to be totally forthcoming regarding information that has no relevance except the intentional stigma. This is especially relevant if yours is a well-adjusted, smooth-functioning family and your children have done well in elementary school, making such irrational fears immaterial.

Growing with Our Children

We want our children to be in an environment of *chinuch* with which we can live, because conflict between the education they receive in school and that which they receive at home *will* cause distress and dysfunction. I see children all the time from American homes that could be considered "modern," but on making aliyah the parents placed them in a more religious environment, resulting in much discord in the family.

Do we really want to do that to our children?

If what we desire, however, is to raise the standard of *chinuch* at home, too, it means that we are willing to grow along with them. It is not inconsistent to send our children to a school whose standards are higher than ours if we intend it to be part of our own growth process.

We do not have to be on the same level as the school if we are willing to join in our children's learning process by making the necessary personal changes. These children are less likely to have issues. When the children tell over what they learned, the parents are interested to learn all about new halachos.

"Really? We'll speak to our rabbi. Maybe we should also begin to do that." When children see that attitude, they do well.

You can't compensate for your lack of background by forcing your children into a mold in which they don't belong. *We cannot attempt to live vicariously through our children.* We have to be clear on this when we choose a school, as we have to be at ease with its standards.

How can we become valued members of a school's parent body? The first rule is, as we have said, to try to find a school where you are comfortable and accepted. Second, instead of always coming to the school with complaints, be a parent that comes first of all to say a good word, and says thank you when a child comes home after a good day.

When you meet the *rebbi* or principal, thank them. Call the *rebbi* or principal on occasion just to say something nice, or offer to be helpful once in a while.

"Is there anything I can do?"

Usually there *is* something to do because there is a *siyum* that somebody has to organize, there are cakes to be made for a party, or money needs to be collected for a teacher's gift before Chanukah or Purim or at the end of the year. There is almost always something in which to be involved.

It is parents who are involved and committed, who are not there only to complain, who the principals are happy to have in the school. When a child from this family has a bit of a concern, they are happy to deal with it. The issue will be discussed because you are both looking to resolve it, not because they are looking for an excuse to get rid of the student.

You must choose a school where you can communicate with the administration. If you feel limited in this regard, try to bring somebody with you who has better communication skills. It can be a friend or rabbi, but make sure that you get your message across. If you are the kind of helpful parent we have discussed, the school will work with you.

Helping Your Child in School

Children often need to learn with others after hours, especially when their schools have a high academic level and cover a lot of ground in a short time. Some of the families with children in my son's *Talmud Torah*, where they are rapidly finishing *masechta* after *masechta*, tractate after tractate, have never learned that much, and find it impossible to help their children keep up.

I would like to offer a number of ideas to consider if you find yourself in this position. You might know an older boy who can be asked to learn with your son. You can also ask a *rebbi* to learn privately with him. It is worth paying for private lessons early on because you will pay much more when your child is older and so far behind that he is falling out of school. I am not going to tell you how much it costs to try to get a child back into school after he has fallen out of the system, but I can tell you that it is much less expensive to deal with it when he or she is younger.

Another possibility is encouraging your child to have a *chavrusa*, a learning partner/mentor. This can be either an older boy who is already twenty years old—mature, dynamic, and personable—or a positive and well-learned *kollel* fellow. Try to set it up anywhere from once a week to prepare for the weekly test, to three times to keep your son involved and trained for the coming learning. Before he enters sixth or seventh grade, a boy who teams up with a *chavrusa* will find his learning strengthened. This goes for any father who cannot learn with his son, whether because he is too busy, doesn't know enough, or just does not have the patience.

If you can't learn with your child without becoming angry and frustrated with him, don't even *try* to do it. Not everyone is a great tutor for his own children. Even those who can teach the children of others often have a hard time teaching their own because they are too emotionally involved.

Whatever the reason, if you can't learn with your children, find someone else. Please make sure that the learning is a good experience for them. Look for someone who is fun and interesting and excited about learning—someone who is articulate and can do the job right. It is up to you to make sure that this happens.

It is a good idea to arrange for a boy to learn with his own *rebbi*. You can call the *rebbi* and ask, "Do you have twenty minutes at the end of every day? I will be happy to pay you privately if you can learn with my son after school." This develops the relationship between you and the *rebbi*, and between the *rebbi* and the child. It is not always possible, but it is worth a try. Make sure that you know that the *rebbi* is well-liked, respected and caring to all the children before taking this step. Only when a *rebbi* knows how to do this properly will there be no fallout with the other boys.

In my son's school they used to give out twenty-five to thirty questions on topics the children had learned in class during the week. You needed to be a *talmid chacham* to know the answers. I am not a *talmid chacham*, but I had learned the topics in school as a child myself. I grew up studying them, and even taught those subjects, so I more or less had most of the information at my fingertips. And if not, I opened up the *Rashi* and figured it out.

Nevertheless, I felt it necessary to call the principal and say something about this.

Now, ordinarily, when you have an issue to discuss with the teacher, you should call him, not the principal. In this case it was a matter of school policy, not the actions of one particular teacher.

I began by thanking the principal for his hard work and concern for the students and my children in particular.

"Do you know," I then asked, "that there are at least twenty-five children in your school whose fathers cannot find answers to the questions sent home each week? The school needs to be aware of this!"

"I never thought about it, and no one ever said anything," replied the principal.

"Well, I am calling because someone must. The *rebbi* needs to send the answers with the questions. How is the father supposed to know which explanation the *rebbi* gave? Was it *Rashi* or *Ramban*? Is every father a *talmid chacham*? You have an elite school, and all the parents are wonderful, but the thought behind the question might be from a somewhat obscure *Sefas Emes*.[7] In order for the children and their fathers to feel successful, the answers must be sent with the questions."

It is unfair for children to come home with expectations that their parents cannot fulfill, and if no one else says anything, you can be the one to do so. If the *rebbi* and school understand the situation, send home the answers, and try to be accommodating but this is still not enough to help you, someone else must be found to learn with your child.

---

7   Rabbi Yehuda Aryeh Leib Alter (1847–1905), known by the title of his main work, *Sefas Emes*. He was a Chassidic Rebbe, the second in the dynasty known as Ger.

Most of the time the *rebbi* sends home information sheets or news-letters informing you of the material covered in class. Don't worry that your child is going to read it on the way home and learn all the answers; on his way home, he is playing with his marbles or Gedolim cards or whatever else has triggered the collecting instinct in your corner of the world. He gives the newsletter to you if he remembers to take it out of his back pocket, folded over sixteen times, or out of his lunch bag with his crushed banana.

If you can salvage it, you can look it over and ask him the questions. It is good for your child to know that you will be aware of some of the material he is learning, as this may motivate him to pay closer attention to what is being taught in class. Often the teacher sends along a report section asking if you learned with the child, if he knew the information, and any other questions that he might ask; it is important for you to fill out the form together with your child. It is improper to share any information that will embarrass your child.

Dormitories

The value of sending a child to a high school dormitory is debatable. On the one hand, high school dormitories are notorious for their lack of high levels of wholesomeness. Young, physically developing teenagers talking until all hours of the night about whatever interests them may not be the healthiest influence for all children. On the other hand, if your child needs a certain kind of school and it has a dormitory, you have to consider allowing him to live there. Before he leaves home, you will have to coach and prepare him as best you can for dormitory life, hoping that he will benefit from all the wonderful aspects of the school for which you are sending him there.

In American yeshivos, dormitories are more prevalent and accepted, partially because most high schools are connected to post–high school *beis midrash* programs. This assures the presence of older boys and exposes the younger boys to positive role models. There are usually better conditions and more supervision than in yeshivos in Eretz Yisrael, where most *yeshivos ketanos* do not have dormitories.

Many years ago, Rav Shach strongly discouraged building dormitories for *yeshiva ketanah* boys aged thirteen to sixteen, and this reduced the numbers significantly. Those yeshiva high schools that do have them usually cater to children in a specific situation and draw boys from all over the country. The parents of a child who cannot function well in the local yeshiva and needs the special attention of a smaller classroom, the special warmth, or the professionalism of the *rebbeim*, should definitely consider sending such a child away to learn.

It is rare to find a high school dormitory that is better than a home with a warm, supportive, and positive environment in which the parents get along well with the children. When we do send a child to live in a dormitory, it has to be because the school itself is a place where he can learn and grow, where the staff, with whom he can communicate easily, will understand and work with him.

Hopefully, these assets of the school will compensate for any negative aspects of dormitory life. The newfound independence, in combination with the positive atmosphere of the school and the individual attention of the faculty, will give a boy confidence, and help him grow both in character and in learning.

Be sure to clarify that the dormitory does not take the place of the home. Children belong at home unless their particular environment or local school cannot provide what they need. At times, a child cannot live with his family because his needs exceed what his home environment or local school can provide. If we do decide to send a child away, we must remember that we are entrusting him to the people who will take care of him in the dormitory and in the school, and not to a dormitory per se.

School and the Self-Esteem Factor

Rav Shlomo Zalman Auerbach[8] gave a very clear directive regarding the choosing of a child's school. The Mishnah in *Avos* says, "It is better

---

8   (1910–1995) A beloved contemporary leader and *posek*, and Rosh Yeshiva of Kol Torah Yeshiva in Jerusalem.

to be the tail of a lion than the head of a fox,"[9] meaning that one should choose to be among people who will challenge one's growth rather than among those above whom he will tower. Rav Shlomo Zalman pointed out, however, that this advice does not refer to thirteen-year-old children. In this case, he said, "Let them be the head, not the tail. Let them feel strong and good about themselves in the classroom, building their self-esteem by being among the better children in the group."

As an adult deciding where you want to live, you should choose a community in which you will be able to grow and develop, where you will be able to learn from the people around you. It is better for *you* to be the tail of a lion, but don't throw your children into the lion's den thinking that they need to look up to all the others, or they may end up looking down at their battered selves.

Sometimes, parents think that a different school might help their child become the best he can be. You may be considering a school that is more demanding due to the higher academic level. If he is motivated to go there and be challenged, fine. Ascertain, however, that he is really ready to work very hard, and is not merely seeking to please you. If he prefers to go with his friends and wants to be in a place where he knows he is going to be comfortable and is confident that he will do well, do not take that valuable asset away from him.

If your child leaves the decision up to you, then you must seriously consider whether or not he will still be counted among the good, strong students. Do not send your child to a place where he will be among the weaker students even if the school is on a higher academic level than the one he currently attends.

I would advise you not to make the decision based on where his friends are going. That may seem urgent to him at the moment, but he will make new friends. I cannot sufficiently emphasize the need for your child to remain one of the stronger students wherever you send him. Being one of the weaker students will result in lowering his self-esteem and raise the likelihood of making unsuitable friends.

---

9   *Pirkei Avos* 4:15.

Idealism

One of the questions that deeply concerns many people who have made these great changes in their lives is, "Why are my children not idealistic?"

You made this really huge odyssey, a long and difficult journey, to arrive where you are now, and your children are growing up regular FFBs! Why should this bother you? Ask yourself a couple of hard questions regarding this pattern—and pattern it is—in order to understand.

How old were you when you made your original decisions? What caused you to make them? If you were still young, there were various factors involved: disillusionment and inspiration, tragedy and reassessment, intellectual stimulation and education. If you made them when you were older, there may have been any of those reasons coupled with the alternatives with which you had already lived so much of your life. All of these brought you to a place of renewal, *teshuvah*, excitement, and idealistic change.

Your children, on the other hand, are growing up in a world of givens. Even more challenging, they are born into a world of expectations. They are going to accept life as they find it unless we somehow find a way to transfer our own idealism and inspiration to them. Anyone who ever experienced inspiration knows that you cannot force it on someone else. Inspiration needs to be, well...inspired.

We want our children to be inspired as we were because of the revelation, the excitement, and the good feelings we experienced. We forget that there were many planned, well-thought-out steps that we took or still must take in order to bring our own hopes to fruition.[10] If we do not know what we need to do to continue to be developing, inspired people, then our children are going to grow up not only uninspired, but with a need to survive the manifestations of our deep frustrations.

A number of years ago, I sat with the parents of a young woman who was very inspired and excited about the kind of life she wanted to live.

---

10   As outlined in chapters 10, 15, and 16.

She was worried, however, about her parents holding her back, and even more worried about them not letting her marry the type of young man she needed. Her parents came to my office, and we chatted for a few minutes.

"Rabbi, so what do you think?" the father asked me.

"Do you want to know what I think?" I answered. "Only one thing: You should let your child fly. Just let her fly."

Perhaps, he regretted having asked, I don't know. But he looked at me and said, "I guess you are right, Rabbi."

"You know, you are fortunate," I responded. "Everyone wants children who will fly, who will soar to greater heights."

The truth is that his daughter was fortunate, as well, because there are too many parents who are afraid to let their children soar.

If we inspire our children, they can go beyond us. That they can go further and higher than us is never going to be a problem unless we either hold them back or push them instead of inspiring them. Perhaps, if we are very fortunate, they will re-inspire us in the process!

Chapter 28

Our Tablet Children

We are the parents of a generation who have replaced the Two Tablets with a new kind of tablet.

Many of us will not understand the depth, meaning, and consequences of that statement until our children attempt to build serious relationships.

If someone had told you twenty years ago that you could have two hundred young people in a room for three hours and not one of them would find it necessary to nod, say a word, express an emotion, a thought, or an opinion to anyone else, you would not have believed him. Would it be possible for each person to be completely and totally preoccupied and self-absorbed to the point of not having any sense of comradeship or connection with anyone else in the room? You would have assumed that he either was referring to a room full of autistic individuals or those coming from another planet.

Such a scene is not unlikely or unusual today: two hundred young people may well be in the same room, communing with their own smartphones, tablets, smart watches, etc., and unless they have to leave and need to ask someone to let them by, they feel no impetus to communicate with, acknowledge, or even notice that there are 199 others present.

The danger and damage to the humanity of these young people is something we will only recognize when they will one day need to connect with another human being in marriage, the deepest and most intimate and powerful level of connection. Tragically, for the generation now growing up, other human beings don't really exist anymore. They suffer from disconnection. Should you think that this sounds a little extreme, I'd like to share some observations with you to demonstrate that it is fairly common.

When children create an isolated world of their own, thanks to the advanced technology and instantaneous communications that have developed in the past two decades, they feel as if they don't need the people around them. Even the least technologically savvy parent owns a few gadgets that, if he or she learns which buttons to push, can connect them to anyone, anywhere in the world, at any given time. Many parents, nevertheless, have to ask their eight-year-old to show them how to use the devices.

I thought I was technologically challenged because I did not own a smartphone until I was forty. Even then, I did not know how to download or send an email from it. At some point, I was practically forced to install email, a tool that allowed me to communicate with close to two thousand students over the past twenty-four years.

I realized some time ago that I was now challenged in that I didn't know how to *disconnect* myself from technology. It followed me wherever I went. There was no time or place where I could be unavailable, where I did not need to be on call, because people had come to depend on my being there for them, and I had become inured to it.

I, therefore, had to create my own form of being "offline."

This was done by leaving the phone on my desk or at home for a few hours a day, for example, or deciding not to look at my emails until the evening. Every person has to find ways to make sure that technology becomes a tool in his life as opposed to him becoming a tool of technology.

Even if we, as parents, are not detached, as soon as we and our homes are connected to the internet, we open up our children to a world where *they* need to be "connected," which, in time, leads to their *dis*connection.

"Connected" today means…to the internet—smart cars, smart appliances, smartphones, tablets, laptops—but it also means being disconnected from the rest of humanity.

When our children are connected to an outside and virtual world, within a short time the connectivity controls them. They become disconnected from others, from God, and from their deeper, inner selves. We live in a society of alienated, self-absorbed, self-contained individuals who do not know how to communicate on an emotional level, share their feelings or thoughts, or convey messages.

People once knew how to write. Most of today's children do not know how to do that, as text messaging, with its incessant abbreviations and emojis, eliminates the need to spell correctly or even at all. Messages are hurriedly sent back and forth with no content or meaning, but the correspondents feel as if they are connecting.

Worse still, children are rarely talking to their parents because they are totally self-absorbed. Face-to-face conversation involves body language, facial expression, and emotion. WhatsApp, texting, telegram emailing, and IM (instant messaging) are sterile, allowing for interaction without any of those elements. These methods of pseudo-communication are considered nonthreatening because they require so much less emotional involvement. The whole world of social media has taken over the lives of so many individuals that it has become a necessity in the minds of those who live in the society of those who are users. (It is interesting to note the parallel use of words "user" and "addiction.") The effects are well known and documented.[1] People who become serious "users" often suffer from, depression, anxiety, and ADD, and further data indicate a link with social isolation, loneliness and OCD.

Easy Access

If your children have access to the internet in your home, and you don't know far more about computers than they do, you have to assume that your child will be connected to things that would horrify you. Some people think that their children are safe because they, the parents, are involved and aware. That is a dangerous assumption.

---

1   *Public Health Implications of Excessive Use of the Internet, Computers, Smartphones and Similar Electronic Devices: Meeting Report,* World Health Organization, 2014.

There are professionals today who visit many schools. One of them challenges principals and teachers to tell him how many of their students are involved in social networking—the likes of Facebook, Twitter, and a plethora of others. He spoke recently in a Bais Yaakov high school and had all the teachers and principals leave the room. Gaining the students' trust, he asked how many of them had a Facebook account. Over half the girls in the room raised their hands. He knows that 95 percent of the parents of those fine young women had no idea that their children had such accounts. He told me, moreover, that many of the parents would be so distraught if they knew that their daughters had these accounts that they would react in drastic, illogical ways out of sheer shock and frustration.

Often gullible, we parents and teachers don't realize that children today do not have a problem being two-faced because, although it pains me to say it, we live in a two-faced generation. I don't like to be so negative, but there's very little positive to be said when referring to the internet, or about your child having an MP3 player, tablet, iPad, or smartphone without serious controls.

Some of you may not even know exactly what your child's little technological gadgets contain. The newest models can hold about twelve or sixteen *thousand* songs. Now, I don't know that sixteen thousand appropriate songs exist. So, why in the world does your child need something that carries sixteen thousand songs? Well, actually there are many hundreds of thousands of songs out there in cyberspace. Of course, they are not all recordings of suitable songs by Jewish singers.

As of June 2023, the newest USB flash drives can hold 256 gigabytes (256,000,000,000 bytes!) of data. This translates into approximately two hundred full-length HD movies that can be plugged into any computer anywhere, with or without internet connection. Smartphones and the plethora of MP3 and MP4 players can be plugged into any computer anywhere. Internet isn't needed anymore, because on this little gizmo, where your children keep their *divrei Torah* and Jewish songs, they can watch anything. Do you really know what's on your children's little USB flash drive? Sure, you can take out whatever you want taken out, and then they can go to anyone with a computer and put it back in.

We are not allowed to be naive. If you don't have extraordinarily serious controls on your computer, you don't have a chance. And if you do have controls on your computers, let me tell you a secret (which you might not know, but too many children do). When you attach a little flash drive that contains the correct programs to that same computer, you can access a browser that bypasses your controls because they control only the programs on your computer. But if they have access to a browser, your children can go anywhere in the world on the information highway. Having one barrier on your computer does not prevent access from many other exits and entrances.

"Yes," you'll say, "but my kid's a good kid."

He is undoubtedly just that, but he's human. Sure, some kids are not really interested in exploring…until they're introduced to something dangerous or stumble onto it by mistake. How often have you done a search for some perfectly innocuous piece of information and stumbled on something embarrassing? The information highway knows no bounds. Children do need boundaries, however. When they are placed into a world without them, you cannot expect them to make good decisions, even if they are "good kids."

Rabbi Noach Orlowek, one of the great educators of our generation, author of *My Child, My Disciple; My Disciple My Child*; and *Raising Roses Among the Thorns* (Feldheim), in the 1990s, said to a group of *kollel* men that to be alone in a room with a television is *yichud*! Although this may not be a halachic ruling that has enforceable quality, it is a clear perspective of what we are facing.

I can comfortably add to this thought process that being alone in a room with a computer is *yichud* ten times over. And if you let your children, or *anyone* in the house, use a computer with the door closed, you are setting them up for a fall. When I am alone in my office at home, I tell my children to keep the door open.

"Do not close the door when I'm on the computer!"

Many people shop on their home computer via the internet. How many kids receive a really cute video from a friend on YouTube when their mom isn't home, click on it, and it opens up with all sorts of other items popping up? How many times do you yourself open what is an innocuous link to something charming, funny, or even breathtakingly inspiring, with things that are decidedly not inspiring alongside it?

You are walking on treacherous ground if you allow your children to use any computer with internet access, ever! If they need to look up something for homework, you should search for what they need and print it out.

Perhaps someone will explain to me why there are teachers today who give assignments in our yeshivos and Bais Yaakov schools that are almost impossible to carry out without looking up information on the internet, which the schools absolutely forbid on pain of being expelled. Your children's reports have to be in full color with copious illustrations and pictures. Where are the kids supposed to get those pictures?

I asked a teacher this question.

"Internet? *Chas v'shalom*," she answered. "There's the *Encyclopedia L'Beit Yisrael*."[2]

"Really?" I asked. "And how are they supposed to get pictures for their projects? And how are they supposed to put them into their reports? With Scotch tape?"

The teacher did not answer my question. She knew the answer, but she adamantly refused to admit that the true answer was, "Well, everyone has a computer."

As I said, it's a two-faced society we live in, so our kids have no problem being two-faced. "Such a beautiful *d'var Torah* I read on the internet…"

It may be that your children, at this point, are still unsullied. If that's the case, you are lucky, but that doesn't mean that they're going to remain that way. And if somehow, by some *mazal*, your house is still safe, there is no assurance that it will continue to be so. Why am I being so

---

2   A Hebrew encyclopedia printed in the 1990s produced by Rabbi Rafael Halperin, to allow religious children access to encyclopedic information without inappropriate content.

pessimistic? Because things are not getting better. The world around us is not becoming safer, holier, or purer.

Think about this; it is our homes that we are talking about. They are, or should be, fortresses that protect us from the influences of the outside world. We think that we're safe because we are in a *frum* neighborhood, we send our kids to the best schools, and we're very, very careful about their choice of friends. Can we be certain, however, that when they go to someone else's house the children have no access to "connected" computers?

What You Don't Know WILL Hurt You

One of my children recently pulled out an imaginary machine gun from behind his back and began spraying imaginary bullets all around.

Uh-oh, I thought. *He didn't see that in my house!*

"Hmm," I quietly commented, "that looks like something a Jew would never do."

"But I saw a *frum* man who saves Yidden from *goyim*," he answered.

"Really? Where did you see it?"

"By Shloimy."

Turns out it was a movie made by a *frum* movie company that does a poor job of creating "Jewish-themed" non-Jewish movies.

I ended the conversation there, but I commented to myself and later to my wife, "I didn't know that Shloimy's parents allow those things."

And I wondered what else Shloimy has access to in his house. Then I realized that, yes, Shloimy's father is a very distinguished rabbi. I know what he does all day and most of the night, and it's good, but he's not really at home too much, and the mother works.

When the kids go there to play, are they really playing, or are they inside the house watching I-don't-know-what on a computer that is not being monitored?

We are so vulnerable, and our children are even more so. Are we going to set limits now, or are we going to wait until they are fourteen when we can't set limits anymore? We must begin defining and setting those limits when they're younger and still pliable.

Are we watching what happens when our kids come into the house bringing their friends, and they run to the computer to play an innocent game? Do we know whether or not one of the friends has a little drive on his key chain that he can plug into the computer, and in between playing their game, they'll be watching a movie?

You don't know? You *have* to know. You cannot just assume these days that everything's kosher. You can't very well do a physical search on every kid who walks into the house, and these flash drives are very small, so you must keep your eyes open. Even if you don't have internet on the computer, someone can easily bring in a DVD or flash drive and watch whatever they want.

If you have an application on your computer that allows you to check everything that's there, fine. I will let you in on two secrets, however. One is that if you find something that shouldn't be there, it's already too late. Two is that they know how to erase things better than you do. Just make sure they can't turn it on without you.

A few years ago, I checked the computer that our children were permitted to use and found that one of their friends had brought in something that was not allowed. After I deleted it, the DVD insert "broke" for about three months. After that time, I told the children that the reason it broke was because someone brought in something that should not have been there. They knew just what I meant. Then we "fixed" the insert.

Control and Self-Control

It's not just a question of control. We will not be successful just by making rules. We need to help them appreciate *kedushah* and *taharah*, holiness and purity, to show them the beauty of a good, strong life of self-control and satisfaction, but we have to protect them as well. We must build them up from the inside into individuals who will be able to withstand the *yetzer hara*, yet never in the history of mankind have fourteen-year-old boys and girls faced the temptation of free access to every form of decadence imaginable. Literally everything—at the click of a mouse. I don't believe it possible to give a child of twelve the fortitude to stand up to that kind of temptation.

We are living in a dangerous world. We ourselves face challenges all the time. Do we turn it off or not? Do we read a little further or not? I know that in many *kollelim*, and in one of the largest in Yerushalayim, the husband and wife have to sign an understanding that if the wife needs the computer for *parnassah*, she puts a password on it and the husband doesn't know what it is.

The Chafetz Chaim said that every single thing that comes into this world is there so that we can do good things with it. It's true. I know that it is a good thing when I can respond instantaneously to my students' questions.

Still, I know that I have to be very, very careful while the computer is on because, sometimes, in order to answer a question, I need more information, sometimes medical, sometimes educational, and I have to search for it on the internet. Although I've learned to use the computer for good things, nonetheless, without accountability, without using controls, without *self*-control, it's just not safe.

> *I remember the first time I tried applying a control, I wanted it to really be good to protect myself, and I selected a high-security zone and entered a twenty-five-digit code, which I then wrote down on paper to put in a second time for verification and then got rid of the paper. My email at the time was on an "unknown" server so I couldn't open my email because I didn't remember the code. It was quite a saga to get access to things I needed. After that, I found a program called "Covenant Eyes." Today, there is a frum version called "Web Chaver," which sends every page you open to a friend who sees where you are in real time. It helps your self-control when you know you could be very embarrassed if you wander into something nonkosher.*

You must know how to use these things. If you don't protect yourself, who will? If you don't protect your husband, who's going to protect him? If you don't protect your children, who will?

Texting

We know that the Gedolim issue warnings instructing us to use only kosher cell phones, and some of us make fun of the "primitive" kosher phones that lack even the texting facility. Children who can SMS on their phones are much more likely to be approached by the opposite gender. It's the easiest thing in the world for a boy to text a girl, or vice versa, whereas actually making a phone call is crossing a barrier. A voice is very personal, but texting can be done under their desktops in school. It's under the radar, it's nothing, almost impersonal. Text messaging makes our children accessible 24/7.

A computer professional said that when he's told parents to check their phone bills, they often find that their kids are sending messages at two o'clock in the morning, *seven* days a week! There are just no boundaries. It may be less widespread in a close-knit religious community, but can we be sure when and what our children are texting if they have other than kosher cell phones? There are a lot of children in a *frum* community, and many, if not most of them, will face a test sooner or later. We are quite sure that they won't visibly desecrate the Shabbos, but texting is just so easy to slip into, yes, even on Shabbos.

Texting is the beginning, rendering them accessible. You can text anywhere, anytime, without being overheard. Over the past ten years alone, tens of young women from many schools have come to me for advice when they fell into troubling relationships that all began with texting.

How do the boys get the cell-phone numbers? It's a simple matter to walk over to a girl with a phone and say, "I really have an emergency. Can I please use your phone for one second?" The nice girl agrees, and hands him the phone. He then dials his own number and says, "Hello, yes, I'm coming home in twenty minutes. Okay. Thank you." He closes *her* phone, and he has her number on *his* phone.

It's so easy that it's frightening. And we *should* be frightened, because if we're not, we're clueless. In this case ignorance is not bliss, but a path to Gehinnom. Our children are standing on the brink. Every child today is a child at risk.

Setting Limits

Setting limits is not easy and not always possible, but we must do what we can.

We know that we're supposed to daven the whole *Shemoneh Esreh* with *kavanah*, intense concentration. Actually, if we can get through one whole berachah with *kavanah*, we're doing well.

Regarding *kavanah* in *tefillah*, the *Pele Yoetz* says that Hakadosh Baruch Hu knows how hard it is today. This was two hundred years ago! He brings the Gemara where Rav Yosef says that ostensibly we should be excused from *tefillah* because, like drunkards, we're *all* not focused.[3] Nevertheless, the *Pele Yoetz* concludes, "We must do our best and try our hardest." He adds in the name of the *mekubalim* that the Ribbono shel Olam collects the paragraphs, the sentences, and even the words we do pray with *kavanah*, and He builds a prayer from those fragments, which He wears as a crown.

This lesson is one that teaches us that we have to do the best we can. If we don't, then we're responsible. Even as we attempt to build our children up from the inside by instilling self-confidence, the joy of living, and satisfaction, let's not fool ourselves. Young children, and sometimes even older ones, do not have the fortitude required to resist something that is not only amazingly accessible but thrilling and exciting as well.

If you leave your computer on when you go to sleep, who is to say that your children won't use it—if she wakes up in the middle of the night and goes to get a drink of water, or even if your son comes home from yeshiva late because he's a *masmid* and sees that the computer is on?

We can't rely on an absolute, "No, you can't go (there or anywhere), and you're not allowed to do (that or anything)." Limits obviously have to be set intelligently and with love, but there's nothing wrong with finding out what your kids are doing, where they're going, and with whom. Today, we have to do that. Could it be that our kids will do something behind our backs anyway? Perhaps, but it will happen a lot less if we're smart about it.

---

3   *Pele Yoetz*, s.v. "*Kavanah*" (*Toras Chaim*), vol. 1, p. 279.

Let your child know *before* you buy the computer, or any other device; that his having it is dependent on your access to it. Every once in a while, just turn on his iPod or flash drive while he is next to you and see what's on it. Take a look, just to reassure yourself. Hopefully, you will always see good things. Hopefully, you won't find anything that doesn't belong there. If you do, and if you catch it early, you can do something about it. If you catch it after the kids are already addicted, it may be too late.

Please believe me when I assure you that these things are totally addictive because they are such an easy escape. Connecting to life, to reality, communicating directly by talking, establishing rapport with others, are much more difficult. Once that was the way life was lived. Today, living in the quasi-world of just entertainment, where nothing matters, is pleasurable, but make no mistake, such disconnection can become obsessive.

Addiction

A student came into my office crying. She told me that for a year and a half she had not watched movies.

"So, how come I still want to? For a year and a half, I stopped. But in my house, that's what we do," she sobbed.

She comes from a *frum* background, but that's the way they get together for family time. There had been many movies on her iPod, and she had erased them a year and a half ago.

"But I'm here in Eretz Yisrael, and I shouldn't want to watch them."

When we spoke about the problem at length, I found out that in ninth and tenth grades she had been watching movies for two or three hours a day...and no one knew about it! How can anyone watch two movies a day for three years?

She was addicted. Every time she felt a little bit of discomfort, her first reaction was...escape.

"But I'm happier now," she said. "I shouldn't need to escape."

"When was the last time that you watched a movie?" I asked

"Well, a few months before I came to Eretz Yisrael, I got into it again. But I stopped right before I came. Why do I even want it?"

Nevertheless, it's still out there, and she's still connected to disconnection. This is the world in which we live, and parents have to be aware of it.

What to Do?

If you're not knowledgeable, your children should not be allowed to have their own computers. If you're faced with the fact that you need to have one in the house for their homework or graphics projects, however, then you need to become knowledgeable ASAP. If you cannot control it, you cannot have it. Even if you think that you can control it, you must be aware that you cannot install Wi-Fi without an access code. If you have wireless, it will not even help to try to uninstall internet access programs because you can't remove most of them without disabling Windows. The basic Word program today connects to elements on the internet in order to download pictures and images, among other things.

Other controls you must initiate are setting limited time for its use and installing a code to get into the computer. No one can use it unless *you* open it up and *you* turn it off. And if you can't do that, you shouldn't have it. You cannot have a computer that has free access.

You have to be very careful even with permitting the children to play supposedly innocuous computer games today. The new soccer games have half-time entertainment, curse words being called out in the middle of the game, and people in the crowd doing all kinds of immoral and demoralizing things. A car-racing game that someone bought for my children is touted as "mentally challenging and fun," but when I checked it out before I allowed them to watch it, I found that some of those race-car drivers are men and women mostly immodestly dressed, not people you would want in your house. When they get into the cars and drive through the streets, they crash into people, into one another; car thieves stop a car, pull the people out, and shoot them in the head.

"But it's just a race-car game, Mommy!"

Games today are extremely graphic and sexual, exceedingly violent, bloody, and with foul language to boot.

We need the courage to tell our children, "These things are just not acceptable. They will hurt our ability to do important things. We don't have them in our house because there are many things on the internet and on many devices that are inappropriate and addictive. I'm trusting you to go to your friend's house, but you have to know that you can't use or watch those things. If it's going to be hard for you to resist, tell me, and we'll bring the friend here."

By the way, if your child always wants to go somewhere else to play, and doesn't want to bring his friends home, it's something for you to think about. You must know where your kids go and what they do, and make sure that they have enough to occupy them at home, so they are comfortable being there.

It doesn't have to be a question of denigrating their friends' families. You can liken it to *hechsherim*. Some people use one particular *hechsher* and others don't. It doesn't necessarily mean the other *hechsher* is not kosher. You want your child to know that your family doesn't eat this *hechsher* and that your family doesn't watch movies. Now, that doesn't make it easy for him not to eat that *hechsher* in his friend's house, and it doesn't make it easy for him not to do what he's not supposed to.

So, what can we do? This is where our love and confidence-building come in. If we set the limitations and the children know that they are there, we check up on the boundaries, talk to children about them, and find out what's really going on, then we're doing all we can. Most of the time, we will be doing our best to protect our children from being in a situation where they're going to make poor decisions.

In short, we live in a dangerous world in which complacency is the biggest danger. An educated parent creates a safer home. We've all learned about home safety, about not keeping open cans in the refrigerator because little hands can get cut on them. We know as well that we don't leave matches lying around, or poisonous cleaning solutions under the kitchen sink, because little children don't make good decisions.

Well, we have to know that in the case of the new technology, children are being asked to make choices that even we have difficulty making. Inasmuch as it's rare that youngsters have the fortitude to make these decisions when faced with the dilemma, we have to remove our children from danger and protect them.

They don't have to live a completely sheltered life, but if you live in a bad neighborhood, you might want to teach them karate. That doesn't mean you would let them go out alone at eleven o'clock at night. That's not sheltering, that's protecting.

We all live in a dangerous neighborhood today because the superhighway that runs through our living rooms is fraught with danger. Just as you wouldn't let your child cross a thruway by himself, you cannot let him try to cross the information superhighway by himself. If you can't stop your children from having a music player, at least limit their use and make sure that the content is wholesome. If your child walks around most of the time "connected," you know that he is *disconnected*, and disconnection is an addiction.

Don't let that happen. Push it off as long as you can. Every day that they aren't connected is a day that they're still alive, and from the day that they get hooked up to technology, every minute that they're not using it, they're more alive. Do everything you can to prevent them from reaching the place where they plug themselves in and tune you and everyone else out.

Our iPod Selves

Now for some straight talk about adult use of technology.

Perhaps, the greatest challenge to the adult world, even for those not involved in inappropriate content, is the misconception that blogs are harmless. The negativity, *lashon hora*, hate, bashing, and denigration of anyone and anything comes from individuals with free rein and license to say whatever they please. While I am sure that many of the "crusaders" believed that somehow they would make the world a better place, I have yet to meet a Jew who has been enriched by the time spent interacting with, or even observing, the world of blogs.

It is not a secret that all the secrets of internet use are not secret. There is nothing that cannot be discovered with a question to Google. You have come so incredibly far, left so much behind, and let go of such tremendous exposure to the world of immorality. You have taken so many steps to build a home so carefully removed from that with which you grew up and have done so much to be more and different than your origins, yet you are also faced with the challenges of untethered internet.

It really does not matter whether you are a *baal teshuvah* or an FFB rabbi—the internet presents the challenge of private, secret, fantasy, and escape indiscriminately. The *yetzer hara* does not falter in respect to age and position. Those who have been extremely exposed in their previous lives are sometimes very zealous and careful, yet many others have confessed to being stuck in the deep rut of old habits from which they find it very difficult to extricate themselves.

> *David, twenty-nine years old and married with a child, came to me quite broken by his ongoing interest in movies, with a strong preference for those with explicit sexual content. He is not addicted (a too common problem that is out of the scope of this work), but he has been following movies and television series as both a personal pastime and social medium since his early teenage years.*
>
> *Throughout high school and college, he and his "friends" on Facebook would discuss every new movie and television series of this particular genre. When he went to yeshiva, he changed his entire life around. He left his non-Jewish girlfriend and notified his friends of the new values that he introduced into his life along with some of the restrictions that resulted from those principles. His male friends thought he had gone mad, and his female friends thought it was the coolest thing in the world—until they understood the effects on his relationships with them as they slowly fizzled out. He changed his clothing, language, social connections, and thought processes. He developed new interests, values, standards, and goals. The one thing he did not let go of was internet movies. He was embarrassed to be in touch with his old contacts who were still posting, so he adopted a pseudonym in order to continue being part of the chats and posts.*

"Nobody knows," he said to me. "It is so private and hidden that not even my wife knows how important this is to me and how much time it takes from my life."

His wife likes to surf the news, shop online, and watch an occasional entertaining video, so she does not realize how this untethered internet is affecting him. He told his wife that he wants to wean himself off the internet, so she used it only when he wasn't home. It didn't take long before he bought an iPad, which superseded the computer. We spoke about the destructive nature of sexual content to a person's inner world and value system.

"Rabbi," he said, "I am so far gone in this area that even if I would stop now, I have enough images in my head to keep me preoccupied for the next ten years."

I explained the following:

- *Every time we contaminate our eyes, we are hurting ourselves with the contravention of "Do not follow your eyes."[4]*

- *Therefore, every day that the images are not actually in front of him, he is winning a battle.*

- *Because he will have to fill those hours a week with other content, his mind will grow to be engrossed with the new material.*

- *Although he is correct that his mind will retain those images for years to come, over time, those images will fade. When they do come, he will have alternative ways to cope with them.*

Perhaps here is the place to interject the most vital and practical lesson I ever received regarding davening. My uncle, the revered Rabbi Dr. Yaakov Greenwald, *zt"l*, brilliant *talmid chacham* and world renowned psychologist, taught me the following:

---

4   *Devarim* 15:39.

The mind is like a pipeline, with thoughts running through it every second of the day. If a leaf were to enter a water pipe, you would never put your hand into the end and try to grab it because that would only stop the flow of water and keep the leaf where it is. You would just allow new water in to flush the leaf out.

While davening, we often find ourselves thinking about inappropriate things. Many people stand there and fight those thoughts, shaking their heads and trying *not* to think about them. That is like sticking your hand into the end of the pipe and keeping the thought in place. Instead, calmly fill your mind with what you *do* want to think about. Look at the words in the siddur and just read them. The stream of new words and thoughts will flush out the images or reflections that are currently filling your mind and allow you to continue to daven.

Back to David:

> He joined Guard Your Eyes,[5] which helped him to be more careful about the movies he watched. First, he brought down the level of their sexual content, then the amount of time involved with watching them. Eventually, two years later, he was happy to report that he had not only weaned himself off the movie situation but had kept a Daf Yomi shiur consistently for over a year. He was beginning to anticipate the exhilaration of making siyum after siyum with real excitement.

---

5   Guard Your Eyes (GYE), guardyoureyes.com, provides free and anonymous help for all levels of the struggle with internet content and addiction.

Chapter 29

Secular Education, Science, and Religion

In the world in which most *baalei teshuvah* were raised, secular education is held in the highest regard. Most of your parents were convinced that you needed to attend college in order to be financially successful in life. When you were told throughout your formative years that the only way to succeed in life is by getting a university degree, the mantra became embedded in your thought processes.

Raising religious families, often with more than two children and just as often with limited financial resources for their costly private schooling is challenging for many. As a result, you may need to reconcile our values with the difficulties you can expect to encounter.

You have internalized Hashem's providence, and you understand and acknowledge the ways in which He has taken care of our nation through the centuries. You want to transmit this appreciation to your children so that they will not have to deal with many of the issues faced in your own growing process.

For those readers living in Eretz Yisrael, or who are considering a move there in the future, a discussion of what *chinuch* there involves may prove helpful. You may or may not have an alternative in regard to the community in which you will settle or have choices regarding the schools where you are going to send your children.

If you send your boys to an Israeli *cheder*, you have to accept that they will be taught that they will go on to *yeshivah ketanah*, not a yeshiva high school. This is not negotiable in the minds of the school's administration. If you know that your children look to you for advice, and you can be reasonably sure they will ask you to choose a secondary school, there will be no conflict if you advise them to go to a yeshiva high school. If they are not accustomed to relying on your decisions, they will insist on listening to their *rebbi* and succumbing to peer pressure regardless of your views.

Being secure and successful in their studies will give them tools for advancement whenever they decide to look further afield because happy, thriving, and positive children can usually accomplish whatever they want to do in their lives. Many men and women have gone far without a general high school education. In the past ten years, many alternatives have developed that allow young yeshiva men to receive an equivalent high school diploma that enables them to go on to receive professional training.

The following may sound highly irreverent to those of you who have been raised on the value of higher education and college degrees. In America, in only six months, you can study for and receive a GED, a General Educational Development certificate, equivalent to a high school diploma and recognized as such, without ever having gone to high school.

Similar programs exist in Israel and in England, Canada, Australia, and South Africa. Education is no longer a guarantee for a job.[1] Of course there are areas of professional endeavor that require a university education, but there are many fields of study available today that are provided by religious or non-mainstream colleges that prepare one for the job market in a relatively short time. The world over, governments and schools are looking to revamp an educational system that is no longer relevant and helpful in preparing people for their futures.[2]

It is not healthy for you or your children to be at odds with the educational system in which you find yourselves due to your choice of where to live. This is *your* issue; you need to resolve it before it becomes

1   Ken Robinson, *Out of our Minds* (Capstone Publishing Ltd.), pp. 5–62.
2   See https://www.wsj.com/articles/more-students-are-turning-away-from-college-and-toward-apprenticeships-15f3a05d.

an issue for your children. While you are determining the problem of where you stand on this, remember to differentiate between the things your children need and those things you feel *you* need.

For those who now live in Israel and are disturbed by the educational system, look a bit further than your fellow immigrants who are having problems. Observe the many well-adjusted Israeli families in your community. The parents went to *yeshivah ketanah*, not to high school, and then they took a course in computers, or studied for and passed the external matriculation examinations (*bagrut*) in six to nine months on their own, going on to college, work, or the army.

I know hundreds of *frum* yeshiva men who today are professionals in diverse fields. Yes, they began their career training several years later than their American counterparts, but bear in mind that the average Israeli young man or woman cannot start a college education or career until completing army service at the ages of twenty-one or two. If this is important to you, you will want to make sure your child gets very good tutoring for English, just to keep options open.

Informed Decisions

We see a lot of unhappiness as a result of parents making uninformed decisions. They might not have thought carefully enough about their children's futures before urging them in a certain direction. It is possible that they were not sufficiently aware of their own needs, those of their children, and the demands of the environment in which they placed them. With proper motivation and self-confidence, a child can do anything to which he sets his mind, but you have to be there for him when he is making his choices.

This is not to say that if you do plan carefully and weigh all the factors everything will always work out. As the saying goes; "The best laid plans of mice and men go oft awry."[3] Things happen that are outside the realm of our decision-making and beyond our power to change. We have to do the best we can.

---

3   George Burns, Scottish poet, "To a Mouse."

Nevertheless, we have to be honest and real, differentiating between the kind of life we want to lead and the type of life we are actually leading. Are we merely trying to keep up with the Cohens, or does the spiritual content of our life have meaning to us? Do we have honest communication and open discussions with our children? Do we encourage them to think independently, or do we foist our lack of confidence in what we are doing on them? If our children are confident about the "box" they are currently in, they will be able to think with confidence "out of the box" if they so wish.

We inevitably have certain plans for our children's education. If we realize that they are not working out, and in our estimation, it has become necessary to make changes, we should proceed slowly and cautiously together with them. Changing direction is never easy. In general, when we see that we are barking up the wrong tree, it is time to focus on the ground in front of us. When the program we set in motion is just not working out, we must take the time to evaluate whether or not we are going in the right direction. There *are* alternative plans; not always popular and often not as exciting as the original, but it is good to know that they exist.

Life is about dealing with things realistically. If we come up against immovable walls, then kicking, yelling, and complaining will be of no avail. There comes a moment when we have to face it: the wall is there. We can turn right, left, or go back, but we have to be realistic and deal with the facts. Everyone sooner or later comes up against challenges. We have to do the best we can, use our intelligence, and see to it that our decisions are not made blindly.

An Education in Science

It is often necessary to reconcile our own scientific education with that which our children are receiving. This discussion will be from a pedagogical/*chinuch* viewpoint, not from a theological or philosophical approach, and is not a debate between science and religion.[4]

---

4   For a cogent and coherent philosophical approach to the reconciliation of the two, I suggest

Those who have adopted a Torah life as adults were, by and large, brought up in a society that reveres science as a deity, believing in the absolute truth of scientific investigation and deductions. If you have resolved your conflicts, you should be OK with allowing your children to avoid having them. The question only becomes an issue when *you* have not yet reconciled the two outlooks, and cannot accept the mainstream Torah perspective.

Is it necessary to bring the niggling issues that you may still not have resolved into your present life? Do you need to dump this burden onto your children, or can they be allowed to live healthy, normal, even exciting and happy lives without the need to reconcile anything at all? After all, they were never introduced to the scientific story of the world. Can you accept that although you may not have found resolution, your children do not need to look for it?

Just think about it: some of our most brilliant leaders, like Rav Moshe Feinstein, the Chafetz Chaim, and the Baal Shem Tov, did not buy into the scientific faith, yet they lived exemplary lives of extraordinary productivity. Did these intellectually honest people not deal with worldly phenomena with at least as much integrity as we do?

As an amateur science buff, I know that my study of science has only enhanced my appreciation of Hashem and His creation. I also recognize that sometimes I see one resolution to seeming conflicts while others have found alternate answers. An honest scientist knows that scientific "fact" is valid only as long as the theories it is based on remain strong. I may change my mind in five or ten years from now, just as cosmologists, geologists, and physicists have changed their minds and theories several times in the past decade.

Ponder this point. Those who followed and trusted in the scientific society before Copernicus and Galileo were as clueless to the truth as those who lived after them but knew nothing of relativity. Those who

---

the following readings: *The Choice to Be* by Jeremy Kagan, *In the Beginning* and *Fossil and Faith* by Professor Nathan Aviezer, *The Universe Testifies* by Rabbi Avigdor Miller, and *Not by Chance* by Lee Spetner.

believed in a shrinking universe were far from knowing "the truth" that the universe is actually expanding at a rate that could not be possible without dark matter, which itself has yet to be explained.

The entire scientific process is man's attempt to arrive at conclusions based on observation. Relativity and quantum physics have put a serious damper on absolute and unquestionable ideas. This emphasizes the folly of assuming that an introduction to the popular theories of the cosmological "Big Bang" and Darwin's theories of evolution, many times modified, will make them better people or more aware of the truths of the universe.

You do not need to trouble your young child with this; it is your issue to resolve as best you can. When your child comes home from school and says that the presiding science of cosmology is all a bunch of lies, you can smile and say, "There are many people who agree with you, even scientists, but there are others who disagree."

When they are older and their horizons broaden, you can discuss the issue further, but remember that they have been brought up with belief in the Torah, while you may have grown up with a belief in science.

There is room for debate as to which belief requires a greater leap of faith, the one necessary to accept the scientific explanation of the age and unfolding of the universe, or the one that you took in making the great changes in your lives. When you have seen to it that your children grow up with satisfaction, *emunah*, and *simchah*, they will have the tools to resolve their questions just as you did. You understand, of course, that they will be coming from a different place, and there is nothing wrong with that. Having been given the benefit of *emunah* in Torah from birth, they will not have to battle the automatic "truth" of scientific investigation that you were born into.

If you have given your children this opportunity, your approach to science can conform to that of the *Rambam* and the many thousands who followed his teachings. Through the study of science, we can gain insight into the stunning genius of the vast galaxies and minutest creatures and all that unifies them. In this, we can find Hashem and His all-pervading intelligent design in every aspect of creation.

Chapter 30

In Conclusion:
Two Voices

As we come to the end of this attempt to keep clarity in our journey, let us try to understand the concept of our inner conflicting voices. Sometimes, the voice that speaks of our ideals and goals does not always stand up to that of the challenges we meet in life. It does not always fit in neatly with that of our desires or inclinations. Understandably, if you have made quantum changes in your life and lifestyle, you will be more prone to question yourself than someone who has always lived contentedly within the same framework. Whatever your background, it is necessary to learn to identify and isolate these voices—one that wants to pull you down and the other that will try to elevate you. It can often be confusing. I have learned from two very wise men, and have confirmed from my own experience, that there are two methods to distinguish your "good" voice from the "bad" one.

One determining factor is that the bad voice is always louder and infinitely more persistent, harassing you ceaselessly. The good voice, on the other hand, is usually soft and subtle. The second indicator is that while the first is negative, the good voice is positive. The voice inside you saying that it's a good idea to take action but then adds, "...and if you don't, you're not much good," carries a negative connotation. The good voice in your mind, the *yetzer tov*, speaks the language of the *neshamah*. Remember the *pasuk*, "*Ha'kol kol Yaakov, v'ha'yadayim yedei Eisav*—The voice is the voice of Yaakov, and the hands are the hands of

Eisav."[1] Yitzchak recognized "the voice" of Yaakov not only because of the distinct voice, but from the tone and the choice of words. The good voice wants to build you, saying, "You can!"

The voice of Yaakov is that of *emes*, truth. It usually speaks in a pleasant tone, using refined language and a positive choice of words. We must be able to identify which of the voices is speaking, as both can come across as almost equally pragmatic. While pragmatism is always necessary, we need to realize which voice is using it as an excuse, and which is truly helping us to be realistic.

To hear the difference between the two requires a clear mind. There are times that you feel torn in different directions. You then have to identify which voice is friend and which is foe, which is going to help to improve your life, and which is looking to destroy it.

How will you know which is a pretext and which is *emes*? It is all in the attitude with which the voice comes across to you.

The softer voice is more likely to be encouraging and positive, requiring more of your attention to hear it. It will require you to build your character without negativity and do that which is right for you. The louder one will be insistent and more tempting, albeit blaming and negative. It is important to identify the voice with which you wish to live.

Once you have done this, you need to learn to deal with the different strategies that they present. Discovering how to give power to the soft voice and quiet the loud one is really everyone's personal journey.

"Life and death I have placed before you, the blessing and the curse, *and you shall choose life.*"[2]

Anyone who is reading this book has already made many serious choices and has recognized that *emes* is found in subtleties and in silence, not in the loud and crude venues that abound in society today.

Now that you have gone through the suggestions and ideas put forth in this book, how do you feel about yourself? Hopefully not feeling overwhelmed by all the dos and do nots, or inadequate in trying to live

---

1   *Bereishis* 27:22.
2   *Devarim* 30:19.

up to the examples set forth, because that was not its purpose. These feelings will not help you achieve your goals. The idea is to take life in small stages, one after the other.

Most people who have made quantum changes in their lives have very often already taken serious strides in a relatively short time. As there is danger in demanding more of ourselves than we sensibly should, my *rebbi*, Rav Wolbe, taught me that Hashem would prefer that we break down the large steps into smaller ones. Now that you have accomplished so much, it is time to come to terms with those achievements and examine any existent problems that have cropped up along the way in the realistic manner I have outlined.

None of us are angels, nor were we raised by them. We have made important decisions and are living with them. We are not going to become perfect, nor will our children. I hope that the reader finds the material contained in this book to be pragmatic and helpful, which does not mean that by tomorrow you should expect to implement all of its ideas!

When people go to a class on *shemiras ha'lashon*, they may decide that from then on, they will never speak another word of *lashon hara*. It would be so nice if we could really do that. When we study the laws of honoring our parents, who are so very important and dear to us, it does not mean that because we learned those halachos, we are never going to be disrespectful to them for the rest of their lives. When we look into the concept of keeping our minds pure, it does not mean that something that we may have seen, heard, read about, or done twenty-five years ago will never sneak into our thoughts.

By being practical about expectations and understanding how life works, it will be understood that everything we have outlined here is a process.

These concepts should be seen as goals and guidelines. They are presented to help acknowledge that decisions made five, ten, and twenty years ago involve processes that sometimes carry on long afterward. It is only logical to expect that you will confront some residual effects of your upbringing; they are, after all, a part of you.

These understandings are very much the purpose of this book. Know and accept that although life-affecting decisions were made once upon a time, the task is not finished. The road of life is very long.

Remember the million-mile racetrack mentioned earlier? Every Jew, no matter who he or she is, has miles and miles to go because the way to completion is endless. We are here because we hopefully have a lot to accomplish during a long and productive life, and that process needs to be seen in a positive way.

Remember that we are not concerned so much about reaching the final destination as we are about moving forward. No matter how high we climb, there will be a new step ahead of us. To paraphrase the Vilna Gaon on *Mishlei*[3] we mentioned earlier regarding perfection syndrome: "For the reason we live another day is only to fix that which we have not fixed yesterday." This world is not for perfection, when you have achieved it, there is no longer a reason to be in this world.

I remember the first time I was in Eretz Yisrael many, many years ago. I was in the Kiryat Mattersdorf neighborhood in Yerushalayim and someone asked me if I had been to Nebi Samuel, the tomb of Shmuel Hanavi.

"No," I answered.

"It is just a half-hour walk from Mattersdorf, maybe forty minutes. You can see it from where we are standing," he said. We were standing behind 13 Panim Meiros Street, at the edge of the cliff, and we could see the distinctive silhouette of the tomb apparently just two mountains away.

I was with a friend who had a slight heart condition, but he was allowed to walk for about an hour, so forty minutes, we thought, would be fine. We did not take water with us because it wouldn't be needed to walk just a half-hour, and in any case, we figured we'd be able to buy bottled water at the tomb.

---

3   *Mishlei* 4:13, "Hold on to *mussar*, do not lose grip, watch it, for this is your life."

Well, we walked down the mountain, and then up the next mountain, assuming there was one more mountain to go. But when we reached the top of the second mountain, we saw there were two more between us and our goal. Mountains have a way of coming upon you unexpectedly. That's the way life is. You get to the top of the mountain, and you see another looming ahead of you. You reach what you thought was the horizon and behold, there is a new one beyond it.

Please do not let the fact that another few horizons have been pointed out make you feel inadequate. On the contrary, let it give you hope, an understanding that these are just new things you need to watch out for as you progress along your chosen path. You want to know and accept who you are, how to live successfully, even when some of the desired goals are still not within your grasp.

I know, for example, that yelling at a child is not effective. I know it so well. I have taught it so many times. Yelling at *anyone* is not effective. Does that mean that when I am angry and lose my temper, I do not raise my voice? I wish it were so! I raise my voice sometimes, but I realize I have done something wrong and have to find ways to fix it.

Knowing that a particular action is wrong doesn't mean I am never going to do it again. It just means I have to try harder, to try to figure out how I can work on myself to curtail it. If I speak properly 10 percent of the time because I gave a class on controlling anger, it gives me renewed strength to increase that amount. The problem is, of course, that if I give ten classes, and cut down on yelling 10 percent each time, it still doesn't add up to 100 percent. Somehow, there is always another 90 to go! I am never really finished. Otherwise, I would just give another few classes and everything would be OK.

Knowledge does not change character traits. It takes work and effort to challenge our spiritual and emotional muscles in order to grow.

The fact that you have taken the time to read this book, investing energy in seeking more direction and reflecting on these topics, means you are coping well with the challenges that are cropping up along the way. You are honest enough to look for solutions, and if you truly want them, they will be discovered.

"If a man tells you, 'I have worked and not found,' do not believe him," Chazal tell us.[4] "If he tells you, 'I did not work and I have found,' do not believe him. If he tells you, 'I worked and I have found,' believe him."

The process will take time, and that is only to be expected.

"That is all very well," you will say, "but meanwhile my children are having a hard time while I am looking for solutions to help them."

That is true. Your children may now be suffering because you have not resolved all of your conflicts, but they will also gain some very special growth as a result of that suffering. You will offer them what you know to give to the best of your ability. You will know when it is good, and when you perceive that you are doing something wrong, you will try to fix it. When they see you honestly working and actually growing, they will be inspired to work harder themselves. You are doing well. A good person is not one who never errs, but one who learns from his mistakes, tries to correct them, and continues to move forward.

The following is from a letter that I consider the most beautiful and important ever written by a contemporary *rebbi* to a *talmid*.[5] In my opinion it is worth buying the *sefer Igros U'Michtavim*, a collection of letters and essays by Rav Yitzchak Hutner, part of the *Pachad Yitzchak* series, for many reasons, but this letter alone would be sufficient. In it, he writes the following to his *talmid*:

> The pasuk says, "Ki sheva yipol tzaddik v'kam—The tzaddik falls seven times and gets up."[6] Fools think that this means [simply] that even though he fell seven times, he still gets up...What a tzaddik! Even though he fell he got up again. Wise men know, however, that it means that he becomes a tzaddik

4   *Megillah* 6b.
5   Rav Yitzchok Hutner, *Pachad Yitzchok, Igros U'Michtavim* (Gur Aryeh Press, 1998), p. 217, letter 138.
6   *Mishlei* 24:16.

because *he falls seven times. It is through the falls that a person becomes great.*

The *tzaddik* becomes who he is not because everything is easy for him, and he just sails along. He becomes a *tzaddik* through the hardships, through his travails, difficulties, and challenges.

Strengthening Our Decisions

Anyone who has made great changes in life knows that it will be a challenging ride. The illusory way is to "Row, row, row your boat gently down the stream" without rocking it. In the end, however, you are left with "but a dream." We should not get mired in the idealistic pictures we originally formulated, but deal with whom we really are and then, perhaps, we will grow into whom we want to be. Our children, seeing this, can deal with their realities and can grow and develop.

The decisions that you made to live a life of *emes*, to live with Hakadosh Baruch Hu, with Torah, to give your children a better chance for a life of quality, mean that you need to be proactive and not just drift along thinking that you already have it made. Maintaining and strengthening those decisions is no less important than having made them in the first place.

Someone once told me that Magen David Adom, the Israeli ambulance organization, has a problem. Many people want to donate ambulances, and have their names printed on the outside of the ambulance. However, the organization also needs significant donations to keep the ambulances well-supplied. It seems to me that there should be two names on every ambulance: on one side the name of the person who donated the fifty or sixty thousand dollars to pay for the ambulance, and on the other side the name of the donor who set up a fund of equal value to keep it supplied.

Maintaining life-changing decisions is no less challenging than it was to make them. It may be less exciting, less sensational, but it is certainly no less important, as we must all invest in the upkeep of our choices as determinedly as when we first started out. This process will give continuous validity to those decisions for our children, our grandchildren, and the generations to come.

It is impossible to build a tower in the clouds. Without realistic foundations, there will be nothing to sustain what we are trying to construct. In order to build towers of spirituality, we need to dig deep, building foundations that will rest on the bedrock of our beliefs. With those strong underpinnings, we can build towers that reach *higher* than the clouds.

"Building from the ground up" means being honest with ourselves as well as our children. This will provide the foundation of a strong family with healthy relationships among its members as well as others.

Simchah and real communication are the bricks and mortar that will allow us to build a lasting tower with and for our families. Seeing their parents continue to grow and develop will give our children the wings to fly and develop even beyond us to their full potential.

With much prayer, and guidance from Above, may we all ascend the mountain of Hashem and stand in His Holy place.[7]

---

7   *Tehillim* 24:3, "Who will ascend the mountain of Hashem and who will stand in His Holy place."

Glossary

adam gadol: great person.

ahavah: love.

baal teshuvah (pl. baalei teshuvah): male returnee to Judaism.

baalas teshuvah: female returnee to Judaism.

beis midrash: study hall.

bentching: Grace after Meals.

bentcher: booklet of Grace after Meals.

bitachon: trust.

chas v'shalom: Heaven forbid.

chavrusa: learning partner.

cheder (pl. chadarim): elementary school.

chessed: kindness.

chinuch: education.

chochmah: wisdom.

Chumash: Five books of Moses.

Daf Yomi: daily course of Talmud study.

derech: path.

emes: truth.

frum: Torah observant.

Gehinnom: place of punishment/purification in the next world.

Gedolei Torah: great Torah leaders.

Gedolim: great (Torah) leaders.

Goldeneh Medinah (Y.): the Land of Plenty; lit., "golden land."

Hakadosh Baruch Hu: the Holy One, blessed be He.

378

halachah: Jewish law

kedushah: holiness.

kiruv: bringing the unaffiliated Jew to his heritage.

Klal Yisrael: the Jewish People.

kollel: yeshiva of advanced learning, usually for married men.

kareis: excision.

lulav: palm branch used in the Sukkos services.

machshavah: thought.

mashgiach: spiritual guide.

mechanech: educator.

mesorah: tradition.

middos: character traits.

mitzvah (pl. mitzvos): commandment.

mekubal (pl. mekubalim): master of esoteric aspects of Judaism.

mikveh: ritual bath.

minhag: custom.

minyan: quorum of ten men.

mussar: ethical teachings.

nachas: pleasure.

nudge (Yiddish): pester.

parnassah: livelihood.

peyos: sidelocks.

posek: decider of Jewish law.

protektzia: influence through connections.

p'sak: halachic ruling.

rav: rabbi

rebbi: Torah teacher.

Ribbono shel Olam: Master of the World.

rosh yeshiva (pl. roshei yeshiva): head of a yeshiva.

ruach hakodesh: Divine inspiration.

shul: synagogue.

shalom bayis: harmony in the home.

sheker: falsehood.

shemirah: protection.

shemiras ha'lashon: being careful of proper speech.

shidduch: marriage match.

shiur: class or lesson.

shomer Shabbos (pl. shomrei Shabbos): Sabbath observant.

shtiebel: small shul, usually Chassidic.

simchah: happiness; joyous occasion.

taharah: purity.

tallis: men's prayer shawl.

talmid chacham: well-versed Talmudic scholar.

teshuvah: repentance.

tzanua: modest.

lashon hara: evil speech, gossip.

tz'nius: unpretentiousness in dress and behavior.

yetzer hara: evil inclination.

yetzer tov: good inclination.

yeshiva: institution of Torah learning.

yeshiva ketanah: yeshiva for high school–aged boys.

yichud: a man and woman alone in a closed place.

Yiddishkeit: Judaism.

Yom Tov (pl. Yamim Tovim): festival.

z'man: yeshiva semester.

About the Author

Rabbi Zecharya Greenwald, a *talmid* of the late Rav Shlomo Wolbe, *z"l*, is a world-renowned *mechanech* who founded and was *rosh yeshiva* of two groundbreaking high schools for boys needing alternatives to the classic educational system. He is the author of *Preparing Your Child for Success* (ArtScroll, 2005), and he lectures widely on education, parenting, and myriad Torah topics. His "Ask the Mechanech" column in *Hamodia* ran for ten years. Presently, he has a column in *Mishpacha* magazine called "Ask Rabbi Greenwald."

Rabbi Greenwald is the *menahel* of Me'ohr Bais Yaakov Teacher's Seminary, which he founded in 2000. He is considered one of the foremost authorities on helping parents and schools deal with challenging situations. He and his wife, Linda, live in Yerushalayim with their extended family.